"T

wh

hor

hu   he

chil   e

tru

                                                         xon

THE CHILDREN COMING ON . . .

A Retrospective of the Montgomery Bus Boycott

FRED D. GRAY WILLY S. LEVENTHAL
FRANK SIKORA J. MILLS THORNTON III

And the Oral Histories of Boycott Participants

Foreword by Fred D. Gray
Edited by Willy S. Leventhal

Randall Williams, General Editor

Black Belt Press
Montgomery

The Black Belt Press
P.O. Box 551
Montgomery, AL 36101

Library of Congress Cataloguing in Publication Data

ISBN 1-881320-83-9

Design by Randall Williams

Manufactured in the United States of America

Oral histories in the Prologue and Epilogue are from interviews by Willy Siegel
Leventhal for his forthcoming book *Drum Major For Justice . . . Drum Major For
Peace: Recitals on the Unfinished Legacy of Dr. Martin Luther King, Jr.* These oral
history interviews are part of a collection at the Boston University Afro-American
Center. Other oral histories in this book, recorded by Worth Long and Randall
Williams, are excerpted courtesy of the Southern Regional Council's Civil Rights
Radio Documentary Project. Excerpts from Mills Thornton's article in *Alabama
Review* are courtesy of the University of Alabama Press. Excerpts from *Bus Ride To
Justice* by Fred Gray and from *The Judge: The Life and Opinion's of Alabama's Frank
M. Johnson, Jr.,* by Frank Sikora are courtesy of Black Belt Press. Excerpts from *I
Was There By The Grace of God* by Solomon S. Seay, Sr., are courtesy of the S.S. Seay
Educational Foundation.

*The Black Belt, defined by its dark, rich soil, stretches across central Alabama.
It was the heart of the cotton belt. It was and is a place of great beauty, of
extreme wealth and grinding poverty, of pain and joy. Here we take our
stand, listening to the past, looking to the future.*

To the Unknown Ground Crew

Contents

"The writer is just a guide who brings his reader at last to the present edge, the advancing edge of things, and stops and whispers beside him: 'This is our inheritance.'"

H. G. Wells
The Outline of History, 1919

"Each of you, descendent of some passed on traveller, has been paid for. . . . Lift up your hearts. Each new hour holds new chances."

Maya Angelou
"On the Pulse of Morning," January 20,1993

"He calmly and bravely heard the voice of doubt and fear all around him, but he had an oath in heaven, and there was not power enough on earth to make (him) . . . evade or violate that sacred oath. . . . He knew the American people better than they knew themselves and his truth was based upon this knowledge . . . Had the solemn curtain of death come down but gradually, we should still have been smitten with a heavy grief, and treasured his name lovingly. But, dying as he did, by the red hand of violence . . . his memory will be precious forever."

Frederick Douglass
Tribute at the dedication of the statue in
Lincoln Park, Washington, D.C., April 14, 1877

". . . If we cannot now end our differences, at least we can make the world safe for diversity. For in the final analysis, our most common link is that we all inhabit the planet. We all breathe the same air. We all cherish our children's future. And we are all mortal."

John F. Kennedy
Yale University, June 10, 1963

PROLOGUE

Attorney Fred Gray says his friend and mentor E. D. Nixon "was the key to the history of the African-American struggle for first class citizenship and equal rights in Alabama. He was courageous and genuinely interested in civil rights. He was not concerned with private gain and never received anything personally as a result of his efforts to gain equal treatment for others. . . . If anybody had problems with the city police or any matter where they thought their civil rights had been denied, they would always contact E. D. Nixon. . . . and he paved the way for many of us and was a role model."

Edgar Daniel Nixon, born in 1900, was an early leader of the Montgomery NAACP and the local president of the Brotherhood of Sleeping Car Porters. He was a friend and close associate of A. Philip Randolph, founder and national president of the Brotherhood of Sleeping Car Porters. Mr. Nixon received considerable recognition from Dr. Martin Luther King, Jr., in his book about the bus boycott, *Stride Toward Freedom*. However, it wasn't until 1970 when an interview with Mr. Nixon appeared in Stud Terkel's *Hard Times* that his role began to be widely acknowledged.

Lewis V. Baldwin, in his biography of Mr. Nixon, *Freedom Is Never Free*, records Mr. Nixon's wish regarding his legacy: "I'd like to be remembered as a person who helped black and white people achieve greater freedom. What could be better than that?"[1]

In 1975, as a young man just beginning research on a book on Dr. Martin Luther King, Jr., and the Civil Rights Movement, I had the good fortune to spend some time visiting and interviewing Mr. E. D. Nixon. It is from this oral history interview that we have taken the title for this book. Mr. Nixon's unique place in the history of the civil rights struggle in Montgomery—and in America—makes him an appropriate figure with which to open this retrospective.

—WSL

Mr. E. D. Nixon

You see, I will be frank with you. [In the 1920s] when I first got started working [on the railroad] with the Pullman Company at 23, I thought that Chicago or St. Louis was just like Montgomery. I didn't know no different. There were a whole lot of other folk that didn't know! But when I started traveling, I made my first trip and got to St. Louis and saw that blacks and whites were sitting together around the counter there in the station eating together. I could hardly believe it, see? I was about 24 or 25 years old.

I met Mr. [labor organizer A. Philip] Randolph somewhere along about 1926 or '27. I didn't know him prior to this. See, he had never been a Pullman porter. Oh yeah, it was a struggle, and Randolph was a powerful man. If you heard him talk, you never heard him stumble on his words, nothing like that. He said, "so and so, and so and so" right on talking—you never heard him hollering or nothing like that either. His words were like in a book when he started talking. You got to admire a man who used that kind of perfect grammar.

Well, now, I don't know if I thought about mass action personally, but you see, during the thirties I worked with the Welfare Department to help bring changes for black people—but I don't know if I really got a whole lot done in this town that way. Now I have got a whole lot done just sitting down across the table talking with people.

Back in the thirties, though, we had to keep on at it. You see, I have been working for civil rights since way before the Second World War. I used to get into Atlanta in those days, and I'd heard of "Daddy" King, but I never really got to know him personally.

One important thing is that back in the late 1930s, Mr. Randolph had spoken to President Roosevelt about the executive order outlawing discrimination—but Roosevelt wouldn't do it. And what I understand is that there was a meeting between Randolph and Melvin C. Webster, who was first international vice-president of the Brotherhood. He and Mr. Randolph left Washington, D.C., going to Miami on the train, and Randolph said to Webster, "Well, I'm convinced that there is only one thing that is going to move the President, and that's going to be a demonstration." That is what I understand was said—"There has to be mass pressure." Then Webster said, "What kind of demonstration are you talking about?" And Randolph said, "Well, I have reached the conclusion that we are going to have to march ten thousand people over to the White House." Webster said, "Well, where are you going to get

(Reference on Previous Page)
   [1] *Freedom Is Never Free: A Biographical Portrait of E. D. Nixon, Sr.,* Lewis V. Baldwin and Aprille Woodson (project research coordinator) (1992, University of Tennessee at Nashville; Office of Minority Affairs, Tennessee General Assembly; Alabama State University, Montgomery—funded by United Parcel Service)

THE CHILDREN COMING ON . . .

them?" And Randolph said, "Well, we have got fifteen thousand porters, and if we don't get nothing but their wives, we would have enough to march!"

And, believe it or not, we started talking about it, and a letter went out on the March on Washington with ten thousand people. And in about three weeks' time, he was talking about thirty thousand people, and in about six weeks' time, he was talking about fifty thousand people, and, of course, then President Roosevelt discovered that he was really building an organization.

Then Randolph saw Mrs. Roosevelt over in Pittsburgh, and they had a meeting, and Randolph told Mrs. Roosevelt that his people needed jobs, needed bread. He said that the only thing that was going to do that is an executive order. He said, "Mrs. Roosevelt, you can't issue the executive order, only the President can. Unless the President issues the executive order, I am going to march fifty thousand people on the White House."

So, from what I understand, the next morning the President sent for Randolph to come to Washington. What he did was talk about it. The President said, "Where do you think the fifty thousand people are going to sleep?" Randolph said, "In the parks, where the other folks are sleeping at." President Roosevelt said, "Well, Mr. Randolph, we have got some bad people here in Washington," and Mr. Randolph said, "Well, Mr. President, we have got some bad black people coming from Alabama and Mississippi, too. And we are gonna' sleep them in these here parks." He said, "Be aware that unless you issue an executive order, Mr. President, I am going to march fifty thousand people on Washington."

So the President issued an [anti-discrimination] executive order, number 8802, and in that executive order it was understood that Melvin C. Webster would be on the committee.[2] And so the President flew Walter White of the NAACP and Randolph to Texas because Randolph was supposed to receive the Springarn Medal at the [NAACP] meetings down there. And when he did get there, it had the list in the paper of the people who were *on* the committee—and who was *left off,* including Mr. Webster. He sent the President a telegram and told him that the march was still on and that it was agreed that Mr. Webster would be on the committee, and he is not on it. So then the President had another executive order issued with Mr. Webster on the committee . . .

Now through all these years, I followed Randolph around and got to know [NAACP leaders] Roy Wilkins and Walter White. I worked with them, and they all knew my background, and if something came down in Montgomery, they knew that they could call on me to check it out, which I did on many occasions.

They knew I would do it. All across the country they knew what I stood for, they knew that if I said "yes," I would do that thing. I had a good reputation. I built it, and I live on it. People who know me will tell you that when I say, "I will meet you at eight in the morning"—they know that I would be standing there when they got there. I found that that is the best way to live, and I have made friends with people both black and white. I live up to my promises, and I don't have no problems.

[After Mrs. Rosa Parks was arrested on December 1, 1955, Mr. Nixon,

[2]Executive Order 8802 created the federal Fair Employment Practices Commission and also prohibited racial discrimination by federal agencies involved in the national defense industries.

minister who worked with the black community throughout the 381-day boycott as the pastor of the all-black Trinity Lutheran Church, recounts another boycott related story in which the challenge to overcome fear is prominent: "As a member of both [the black and the white] ministerial groups, I tried to bridge the two organizations and the communities they represented. At one point [in the midst of the boycott] a few of us in the white organization proposed a joint worship service. After endless debate within the white group, one of our members commented, 'I just have one more thing to add before I leave. They say silence is golden. But sometimes it is just plain yellow.'

"The conservative ministers still didn't want to take part in the joint worship, but they couldn't let others think they were cowards. The vote to proceed was nearly unanimous.

"Interestingly, on the day of the joint service, more conservative white ministers attended than liberals. The liberals already had good contacts with their Negro counterparts, and they had no need to prove they were not cowards. I had indeed served as a bridge between the liberal white pastors and the Negro leadership. We had developed an informal, ecumenical, interracial, and illegal fellowship that covered the entire state. . . . [we] violated segregation laws every time [we met]." See pages 49-50, *A White Preacher's Memoir: The Montgomery Bus Boycott*, 1997, Black Belt Press.

accompanied by Clifford Durr and his wife, Virginia Foster Durr, went down to the police station and got Mrs. Parks, and, together, they all went back to Mr. and Mrs. Parks's residence at the Cleveland Court apartments and discussed what had happened. Mr. Nixon then phoned many leaders in Montgomery's African-American community, and a meeting was scheduled at the Dexter Avenue Baptist Church, pastored by the Rev. Dr. Martin Luther King, Jr., to plan a strategy. By that time the plans for a boycott were taking shape. On the following Monday, December 5, Mrs. Parks was tried in city court, found guilty, and fined ten dollars. At the next meeting of the leaders, Mr. Nixon became angry when some of the ministers suggested that they pass out boycott leaflets without the white community knowing.]

As Mr. Nixon later told journalist-author Howell Raines,

. . . and one of 'em said, ". . . Well, we'll mimeograph some little pamphlets. Everybody come in the meetin' that night we'll pass 'em one, and nobody will know how it happened."

Well, I was sittin' there boiling over, so mad I didn't know what to do, so I jumped up, and I forgot about we was in the balcony of the church. I said, "What the hell you people talkin' about?" Just like that, see, and I cussed. I said, "How you gonna have a mass meeting, gonna boycott a city bus line without the white folks knowing it?"

. . . I said, "Unless'n this program is accepted and brought into the church like a decent, respectable organization . . . I'll take the microphone and tell 'em the reason we don't have a program is 'cause you all are too scared to stand on your feet and be counted. You oughta make up your mind right now that you gon' either admit you are a grown man or concede in the fact that you are a bunch of scared boys." And King hollered that he wasn't no coward, that nobody called him a coward.³

[Mr. Nixon related to me that Dr. King] was the only one who said that he wasn't a coward. And, of course, we were already proud of him and we had already agreed—me and [Ralph] Abernathy and Reverend French—had already agreed on King being president. He [King] didn't even know it. But this was around eleven o'clock at night—we had discussed it about four o'clock in the evening of the same day. But he didn't know nothing about it.

. . . Now, we had to look a long way to find a man with any more courage . . . than A. Philip Randolph. See, Randolph gave when times were hard, I mean when it was dangerous to do what he was doing. More dangerous than 1955. When Randolph started it you could get killed real easy . . . Philip Randolph was a kindly country boy, and he vowed to get an education, a decent job, and help his people, and that is more important than anything else. To be able to sit in a hotel or motel or order something at a lunch counter and don't have the money to buy or to pay for it don't mean anything. But to be able to afford it, you need to have a job or resources and then be able to do these things and then you will get somewhere with it.

I served about twelve years as president, from time to time, at different times in Montgomery, for the NAACP. I also served two years as state president at two different terms. But I served twenty-five years as local president for the Brotherhood of Sleeping Car Porters. As a matter of fact, no one ever ran against me from Montgomery in local elections for president of the Brotherhood of Sleeping Car Porters.

He [King] would have been the best person locally. Now if it had been that A. Philip Randolph and Reverend King had been here together, then I would have chosen A. Philip Randolph. I am sure A. Philip Randolph, and as a man who had years of experience with A. Philip Randolph, I can say that he was solid as the Rock of Gibraltar. He is my kind of a man, but it just so happened at this time we needed a man who could meet with different classes of people, a man who would be on the scene at any time, a man that was intelligent enough to meet with people, and we had all this in Dr. King and, of course, the time had come that I had promised myself that someday I was going to hang him to the stars, and I did that.

The Montgomery Improvement Association or the Montgomery Bus Boycott was the big thing in the history of a whole lot of peoples' lives. And it ought to be a true story about it. And that is one of the things that haven't been written about. You see, I talked to people time after time. I have told the press time after time that we were doing things for years before December 1955, but all they want to do is start at December 1 and forget about what happened. They say that Mrs. Parks is the lady that sat down on the bus and then they want to start talking about what happened December 5. But that leaves a whole lot of folks out and ignores a lot of what was done over a long period of time to set the stage.

I think Reverend King was sincere; I think that he put his heart in this thing. Whatever he did he tried to do the best thing for the community. And I have no criticism, no fight with Mrs. King.[4] But, I mean the point is, I am talking about the record for the children coming on behind us that ought to know the truth about it. And that's what's important, not to exaggerate and add things to it.

Personally, Reverend King was a young man. I think he was about 27 years old. I believe he was, he was a young man, he was well-learned, but he had no training in this field. I don't mind telling you from December 1 through March '56, I was on the road a lot, but I never came to town a single trip that the Reverend King and I didn't spend some time together. Strategy meetings and so forth, and then some nights at twelve o'clock at night he was either at my house or I was at his. And I had to work to make a living. And in that, he was able to pick up a whole lot from me and a whole lot from other people and then when he started to go around making speeches he benefited from it.

Some people think that Reverend King was the first to organize and come in here and organize the Movement. I mean, that's not true; but I am not trying to take nothing away from Reverend King. He made his mark. But the people ought to know the truth. And the truth will set you free.

. . . I might say that this may be news to you, but do you know that under the Supreme Court decision where black people had the right or they ruled that "Jim Crow" schools or against "Jim Crow" schools—the Supreme Court on May 17, 1954, I was the first person anywhere in the United States that carried any black children into a white school. Right here in Montgom-

[4]Though Mr. Nixon, in his later years, expressed to some interviewers certain frustrations he felt about inadequate respect being shown to him by some of his former associates in the MIA, he related to me his appreciation that Mrs. King had sent him a signed copy of her book, *My Life With Martin Luther King, Jr.,* and had always invited him to special events at the King Center.

ery. In September of 1954, and it was the school right here. They didn't let them stay there. They run them out, and they run me out, too.

. . . Another thing is a lot of folks don't give credit for a lot of changes and struggle to improve things. Now, you take Lowndes County, down there in 1965, they didn't have a single voter. Now the sheriff and the superintendent of education is black down there. Take down in Greene County, they didn't even have a single voter there, ten to fifteen years ago. Now the probate judge is black and the sheriff is black.

You would be surprised to know that when the white civil rights young folks came into the South they were more protected than a whole lot of black people that lived there. The white guy come here to work with us and he knows that there is a chance that something might happen to him. And that [if something did happen] more people pay attention to him in the press than the guy who lived there.

There's a lot more that they didn't write about than they did. They missed lots of history.

One time during the boycott I was going up to Philadelphia, and I sat down beside a white fellow, and me and him started talking, and after a while somebody said . . . "Montgomery." He said, "Don't tell me that you are messed up in that mess down there." And I said, "No, I am not messed up in it; it appears to me that the white people are messed up in it." He said, "Well, you can't win." I said, "Well, I don't know about that." He said, "You want to bet?" And I said, "Like what?" He said, "I'll bet you fifty dollars. If you win I will keep my part of the bargain." He said, "Now, if you lose, will you send me fifty dollars?" And I said, "Yes, if you want I will put it in writing, 'cause we are going to win." And when we won about a week or ten days after that trip, he sent me a check for fifty dollars.

. . . When the boycott started we talked about getting the news to our people. And we had porters who—we have got fifteen thousand porters who are running all over the country. The white people have newspapers on the morning train; the porters would pick them up, tie a string around them, and take them out and throw them to the folks at some little desolated place where there wasn't any paper. You throw them off to the people going along the road. You have one hundred thousand black people reading newspapers that have probably never read them before.

We got the word out. We got the job done.

That's not the problem now. Now it's economics. We are going to have to learn that we [have to] make money. Even when we are able to work and we make money, we spend it all back with the white power structure. We are going to have to learn to do something for ourselves. And don't say we can't do it. You take [insurance executive] A.G. Gaston of Birmingham, a black man with an eighth-grade education controlling $26 million; don't tell me you can't do it. What we need to do is, we are going to have to sacrifice ourselves big, we can't spend ourselves big. I preach that at the altar every day. You can't spend yourself big, you save yourself big.

I am a long way from being a professional man. But I planned to live . . . years ago, and I take care of business every morning.

Foreword

By Fred D. Gray

The publication of *The Children Coming On* . . . is an appropriate method of commemorating the Montgomery Bus Boycott. I agree wholeheartedly with E. D. Nixon, the father of the civil rights movement in Alabama, who is quoted on the opening page of this book that the Montgomery Bus Boycott was a big thing, and it involved a lot of people. He concluded by saying, "the children coming on behind us ought to know the truth about this. . . ."

As usual, Mr. Nixon spoke wisely. It is very important that the children coming on, as well as many adults who still don't understand the significance of the African American struggle for civil and human rights, need to know the history of the Montgomery Bus Boycott.

A few months before my autobiography, *Bus Ride To Justice,* was published, I was in a men's clothing store in Montgomery. During a conversation with the white manager of the store, we talked about my forthcoming book and what I hoped to accomplish with it, which included the same goal as for this book, to educate and inform. During the course of our conversation the manager pointed out a young, African American female who was a cashier at the store. He said to me, "The young lady at the cash register does not know who Rosa Parks is."

It was embarrassing to learn that any young African American in the city of Montgomery did not know of Rosa Parks. However, this incident that occurred in Montgomery could have occurred in any city, county, state in the nation. It is true whether they are African Americans, Caucasians, or of any other race. Notwithstanding all of the news coverage, media attention, and electronic communications, there are literally thousands of persons in this country who not only do not know who Rosa Parks is, but who have absolutely no knowledge of the Montgomery Bus Boycott and the significance of that event. Therefore, it is necessary and mandatory that we leave for "the children coming on" an accurate, historical account of the Montgomery Bus Boycott, its origin, its perpetuation, what it has meant to this country, and what it still means to the nation and world even as we enter into the twenty-first century.

The Children Coming On . . . excerpts from four publications and the oral history of some of the participants in the Montgomery Bus Boycott. These sources include *Bus Ride To Justice; The Judge: The Life and Opinions of Alabama's Frank M. Johnson, Jr.,* by Frank Sikora; "Challenge and Response in the Montgomery Bus Boycott of 1955–1956" by J. Mills Thornton III, from *Alabama Review*; *I Was There By The Grace Of God* by the Rev. Solomon S. Seay, Sr.; and *Drum Major For Justice . . . Drum Major for Peace: Recitals on the Unfinished Legacy of Dr. Martin Luther King, Jr.,* by Willy S. Leventhal. In addition, this volume includes the voices of many participants in the boycott, including Johnnie Carr, a member of the board of directors of the Montgomery Improvement Association since its inception and its president longer than any other person; Marie Pake; Virginia Durr; Thelma Glass; Alfreida Dean Thomas; Idessa Williams Redden; R. D. Nesbitt, Sr., and others.

The work of each author excerpted in this volume accurately describes conditions in connection with the boycott in light of the times, and taken as a whole they make it possible to receive a clear understanding of the beginning of the movement, its historical perspective, and its importance to the nation today.

Again, E. D. Nixon was right when he said, ". . . there are hundreds of people who made a contribution." So, this book seeks to carry out the wishes of E. D. Nixon to record accurately in historical perspective the events that took place in Montgomery, Alabama, from December 1, 1955, until March 1, 1957. *The Children Coming On . . .* gives to its readers a thorough background and understanding of the Montgomery Bus Boycott, its origin, its meaning, and places it as one of the greatest events in modern history.

As I write this foreword, I find it interesting to note that "the pebble cast in the segregated waters of Montgomery, Alabama . . ." has also washed upon the shores of countries around the world. On July 8, 1996, I had the honor of being the featured speaker at the University of Hull, in Hull, England, for a three-day symposium on the Montgomery Bus Boycott. Attendees were African Americans, white Americans, and Europeans, who discussed in detail the significance of the Montgomery Bus Boycott on its fortieth anniversary.

Therefore, as a tribute to E. D. Nixon, the father of the movement, I am especially pleased that "the children coming on" will be able to learn the truth about the boycott, and "by learning the truth, the truth shall make them free."

INTRODUCTION

By Willy Siegel Leventhal

The Civil Rights Movement was a theater of war, with orchestrated demonstrations and battlefields of violent confrontation. There were nonviolent protests, organizing campaigns, and other political episodes in a real-life morality play, acted out by characters competing for higher ground upon the local, national, and world stages.

The years between the Montgomery Bus Boycott, which began in 1955, and the assassination of Dr. Martin Luther King, Jr., in 1968 were not only among the most turbulent in the American journey, but their meaning and legacy continue to generate contentious interpretation. So far, "the Movement days," particularly "the sixties," have been subject to both "politically correct" renditions by sympathetic historians and hostile critiques from antagonistic politicians.

Neither view is an adequate treatment of this vital segment of American history—especially the Montgomery Bus Boycott. It takes nothing away from the significant contributions of the leaders or the masses to point out that a great gift of the Montgomery struggle to the world was the launching of the career of Martin Luther King, Jr.

By word and example, Dr. King set the goal of the Civil Rights Movement as the creation of the "beloved community"—a society of diverse persons working for the common good. Some observers may believe that Dr. King's idea of people treating each other respectfully and nonviolently—as brothers and sisters in one family of humankind—isn't relevant in the nineties. But the power of his example and commitment to nonviolence *will* resonate as a global imperative in the twenty-first century. The ethics of the "beloved community" have not only the potential to replenish humanity, but to help us move into a sustainable relationship with the fragile planet we all share.

History is a potent authority, shaping our views of the past as well as our expectations for the future. Without historical clarity about the civil rights struggle in America, acculturated black bitterness, white guilt, and negative racial stereotyping—one race by the other—foster a destructive mutual cynicism.

Virtually *all* who have written about the United States in the 1950s and '60s have ignored or glossed over the history of the hopeful humanitarian base which made real the refrain "black and white together, we shall overcome."

But deep in the roots of the struggle to overcome legalized segregation in

Montgomery, Alabama were the potent dynamics of interracial partnership. Acknowledging the positive aspects of a troubled past helps lift voices beyond the suspicious refrains of interracial discourse which often reverberate in America today.

A panoramic view of the Movement history of the fifties and sixties can help heal the doubt and pain that many black and white Americans feel today about the issue of race. Our collective memory has been shaped by a redundant media and literary obsession with the scarred past of race relations. Brutal and tragic events did occur during the fifties and sixties, but there were also individual and collective acts of compassion, courage, and triumph.

Many of us who worked in the Movement hoped that boldly seizing the opportunity for interracial cooperation would allow us—and future generations—to move beyond our troubled past. Many Americans, young and old, of all races and religions, are still working to solve social problems—but the media gives us scant attention. Instead, American culture is saturated by a distracting fascination with sexual scandal, particularly interracial sexual scandal. Such tabloid-style media coverage contrasts with the kind of positive journalism that portrayed the dramatic and uplifting battles for freedom a few decades ago.

The African American psychologist Dr. Kenneth B. Clark noted that Dr. King was, in a sense, a societal psychiatrist to America's obsession on race. This retrospective look at the Montgomery Bus Boycott can help us to understand the foundation of Dr. King's public career and can help us see how he first took on the arduous challenge of ministering to an entire community, as he was later to try to resolve conflicts within a great, but troubled, nation. Not long after the protest began, Dr. King observed that the Montgomery Bus Boycott had "catapulted" him into a position of political prominence and leadership. As we seek to come to grips with the challenge of Dr. King's unfolding legacy, we must understand the full tapestry of the times. The history of the Civil Rights era—and the story of Dr. King's role in Montgomery and eventual preeminent position in the Movement—is filled with a lasting emotive potency and a timeless relevance to our ongoing struggle to create healthy human relations. This retrospective of the Montgomery struggle takes a broad view of both the city and the times:

▼ In Part One, the distinguished attorney Fred D. Gray gives us an autobiographical account of how the social conditions he faced growing up in Montgomery led him to vow to "destroy everything segregated I could find." Mr. Gray's career as a civil rights lawyer is legendary. But his early life was not one of privilege—the odds were against him from the start. Nonetheless, the depth of his determination and perseverance made "a way out of no way"—an inspiring legacy to future generations. Mr. Gray gives a clear and concise account of the Montgomery Bus Boycott, its origin, and the role many persons played to make it succeed. This work illustrates how personal commitment, combined with the work of others, resulted in the beginning of the Civil Rights Movement. From the viewpoint of "the children coming on," one interesting aspect of *Bus Ride To Justice* is that here readers can find the names not just of the heroes like

Rosa Parks but also of the lesser-known persons who were party plaintiffs and even those who were defendants in the early cases involving the boycott. Attorney Gray also shows the role that lawyers played in the Movement. This theme is picked up again in Part IV, which deals especially with the role of the federal courts. Overall, Mr. Gray shows how a "pebble cast in the segregated waters of Montgomery, Alabama, created a human rights tidal wave that changed America and eventually washed upon the shores of such faraway places as the Bahamas, China, South Africa, and the Soviet Union. And it all started on a bus."

▼ In Part Two, historian J. Mills Thornton III, also a native of Montgomery, recounts the city's political developments—electoral and otherwise—from the turn of the century up until the day Mrs. Rosa Parks was arrested on December 1, 1955. Dr. Thornton is the foremost Alabama historian on the Civil Rights Movement. He describes the city at the time of the boycott as only a historian can do.

Professor Thornton not only describes the day of the arrest, as other writers also have, but he provides the historical context in which Rosa Parks lived in Montgomery. For example, Dr. Thornton explains how the demise of the all-white political machine in Montgomery factored into the rising expectations of the leaders as well as the masses in the African American community during the post-WW II period. He places in proper perspective the role that the white political structure played in Montgomery, prior to and during the bus boycott. He also places in proper perspective the persons who were known to be participants in the movement. He gives an overview of E. D. Nixon, who not only was one of the strongest leaders of the boycott in 1955 but had been the first black candidate since Reconstruction to run for public office in Montgomery (in 1954, when he was a candidate for the Montgomery County Democratic Executive Committee). In his conclusion, Dr. Thornton suggests that the Montgomery protest had a crucial effect on Dr. King's later career.

▼ In Part Three, we return to attorney Gray, who gives an insider's account of the heroic players and dramatic events during the 381-day boycott. He provides insight into the backgrounds of the many African American leaders in Montgomery's "Negro" community during the mid-1950s. This excerpt and that in Part One above are abridged from Gray's autobiography, *Bus Ride To Justice*, which more than most other literature about either the bus boycott or Dr. King recognizes some of the individuals heretofore left out—including his white friend, attorney Clifford Durr, who was, Mr. Gray says, "a silent partner in my law practice from day one."

Mr. Gray also shatters some of the myths that some historians and King biographers have falsely constructed. For example, Mr. Gray clearly shows that while Dr. King *was* "drafted" to be the president of the Montgomery Improvement Association, he *was not* a "reluctant leader," as the recently fashionable version circulating in literary circles asserts. Though Dr. King, a Montgomery newcomer in 1955, was selected as a compromise choice between the established E. D. Nixon and Rufus Lewis factions, he was not reluctant, on a philosophical, political, or activist level.

▼ In Part Four, Frank Sikora (co-author of *Selma, Lord, Selma*) recounts the courageous judicial leadership displayed by then-U.S. District Judge Frank M. Johnson, Jr. Mr. Sikora, a journalist with the *Birmingham News,* uses both narrative storytelling and Judge Johnson's oral history to explain how the Judge viewed the boycott case and the decision to abolish segregated seating in public transit. This was his first civil rights case, but over the next two decades, Judge Johnson would make many similar decisions declaring that segregation had no place under the laws of the United States.

The Montgomery Bus Boycott changed history because people united in a non-violent protest against injustice and discrimination. But it took a federal court decision to actually win a victory for the boycotters. That victory came about because of an opinion written by Judge Johnson, who became a United States District Court Judge in Montgomery on November 7, 1955. This was twenty-three days before Rosa Parks was arrested on December 1, 1955. Judge Johnson was joined in the historic decision by U.S. Circuit Court Judge Richard T. Rives. Unlike Johnson, Rives was a Montgomery native. In the portions excerpted here, author Frank Sikora writes about the life and opinions of Judge Johnson and also relates the role of Judge Rives.

Together, Johnson and Rives used their judicial power to overturn the segregated status quo not only in Montgomery, but throughout Alabama. However, as Sikora explains, for both Johnson and Rives there was a serious personal price to be paid. Sikora's skill as a writer makes us realize that we take for granted—as a nation and as a diverse peoples—the just decisions reached in the fifties and sixties by some decent and courageous white males serving on the federal courts, including the Supreme Court.

▼ Part Five refutes other examples of historical omission and distortion about the Civil Rights Movement during the fifties and sixties. This chapter, which draws from my forthcoming book on Dr. King, provides consequential details about the lives and roles played in the bus boycott by courageous white Southerners like Clifford Durr, Virginia Durr, and Aubrey Williams, along with others who are not as well-known, such as Juliette Morgan and Moreland Smith. It is very important that "the children coming on" realize that although in 1955 the majority of whites in Montgomery supported segregation, there were courageous white citizens who realized that segregation was wrong and who supported the Montgomery Bus Boycott. Their stories need to be told accurately, too. The depth of their belief in equality during the forties and fifties—to freedom and justice for *all*—is probed in a broad historical overview of the times.

The full story about the Durrs and Aubrey Williams—great Americans from Alabama—reveals major gaps in the culturally authoritative version of Movement history. In fact, understanding both their close association with President Roosevelt and with Supreme Court Justice Hugo Black, as well as their tumultuous relations with racist conservatives (including J. Edgar Hoover), is key to comprehending the political forces that faced off during the fifties and sixties.

▼ In the Afterword, harsh historical critiques about President Kennedy's personal support of the movement, as well as similarly negative assertions about his administration's Department of Justice led by Robert F. Kennedy, are shown to be factual distortions.

▼ In addition to the historical information included in this book, we have added several sections of "Montgomery Voices." In these, Montgomerians Johnnie Carr, Marie Pake, Virginia Foster Durr, Idessa Williams Redden, Thelma Glass, Alfreida Dean Thomas, Gwen Patton, Rev. Solomon S. Seay Sr., and Robert Nesbitt offer their very personal remembrances.

▼ Prologue and Epilogue sections provide additional oral histories from E. D. Nixon, Harris Wofford, Bayard Rustin, Harry Ashmore, Lerone Bennett, Rev. Hosea Williams, Tom Offenhauser, Jack Nelson, Willie Bolden, Daniel Ellsburg, and Roy Campanella — who were involved in or affected by the boycott.

▼ There is also an Interlude which includes a never before published interview conducted with Mrs. Rosa Parks in 1956 a few months after the boycott began, as well as copies of her arrest report, the leaflet calling for the boycott, and the lyrics to "Sister Rosa," the unique tribute to Mrs. Parks written by Cyril Neville of the Neville Brothers. (Mr. Neville wrote the song for his daughter after she saw a television program on Mrs. Parks and said, "Thank you, sister Rosa.")

Literature scholar Professor Arthur M. Eastman explained well the unique nature of oral history:*

> One of the things which modern oral history preserves for us is the element of the poetic, if we understand that term to mean, in this broad context, the sense of private vision articulated in language which points toward both the public object or occasion and the unique sensibility perceiving it. . . . All around the edges . . . and appearing dramatically in the midst of them are 'facts': public events and personalities and occasions which we know about independently. . . . Private and public, person and events are in mixture. History of a very real and useful kind is the issue . . .

The important voices in this retrospective provide a wealth of information about both Montgomery's history and social milieu, as well as profound insights about the boycott itself. As Professor Eastman has written, oral history

    . . . often rises freely, premeditated, almost unstructured except for

*The Norton Anthology of English Literature, M.H. Abrams, ed., 1968, Norton.

loose chronology and the vagaries of association. It may not be logical, depending instead on a kind of psychologic which has its own meaning, usually evident in the style, the peculiar flavor of a distinct mind and personality apparent in the language of the recital. . . . It is direct and honest, seeking usually no end except to express itself. . . . Uncensored, unrepressed, confined only by a sense of . . . [the speaker's] . . . own authority and confidence . . . history wells up and flows out spontaneously, honestly, authentically.

Previous books on Dr. King or the Movement have included only a chapter or two on the Bus Boycott. In *Parting The Waters,* author Taylor Branch added an excellent chapter on the Rev. Vernon Johns, Dr. King's predecessor in the pulpit at the Dexter Avenue Baptist Church. However, none of the histories, King biographies, nor even the excellent memoirs by Rosa Parks, Fred Gray, Jo Ann Robinson, Rev. Robert S. Graetz and the Rev. Solomon Seay, provides the wide-angle view of the city, the involved individuals, the court cases or the American political climate found in the chapters and oral histories of this retrospective.

The current depiction of race relations in America, particularly in the media, often presents a troubling picture. For example, the August 18–20, 1995, edition of *USA Weekend* magazine included the results of a survey on "Teens and Race." Though not a scientifically representative sample, the responses of 248,000 teens revealed a generation in which many, if not most, judge each other on a racial basis—rather than on the content of their character.

And, in August 1993, on the eve of a commemorative march marking the 30th anniversary of Dr. King's "I Have A Dream" speech in Washington, D.C., a CNN/*USA Today* poll gave a pessimistic forecast for a harmonious *and* racially diverse culture in America. This poll depicted more Americans of all races as being discouraged about positive interracial relations than they were three decades ago.

Against such pessimism, the Montgomery saga and the legacy of Dr. Martin Luther King, Jr., offer a societal inoculation across barriers of age, race, religion, and economic status.

Rosa Parks, E. D. Nixon, Jo Ann Robinson, Fred Gray and so many other determined "Negro" citizens, including Martin and Coretta King, together launched the masses in a protest movement that achieved the initial legal and strategic victory in Montgomery, Alabama. It was a struggle drawn out over 381 days of nonviolent protest. These tough, disciplined, determined, and resourceful African Americans knew that their triumph could benefit immeasurably from the partnership with white allies who added their support to this just cause. Recognition of real friends, who were willing, as Dr. King later noted, to give up their privilege of race, takes nothing away from the black activists who played the heroic central roles in the Movement.

As E. D. Nixon said to me in 1975 (in an interview from which this book's title is taken), "the Montgomery boycott was a big thing in a whole lot of peoples' lives and it ought to be an honest-to-goodness true report . . . there are hundreds of people who made a contribution. . . . The children coming on behind us ought to know the truth about this. The truth will set you free."

Now, and for generations to come, all peoples can benefit by knowing that there were both black and white role models willing to risk everything to live in an America where the refrain "sweet land of liberty" was more than just a lovely ideal.

As we approach the millennium, America's celebrated promise of equality remains marred by societal racism. Nonetheless, an important element in the legacy of Montgomery—and the emergence of Dr. King's leadership therefrom—is a powerful, untapped force of hope.

In 1995 and 1996, during the fortieth anniversary of the bus boycott in Montgomery, it was fitting that the citizens of Montgomery and Alabama recalled the richness of that time and that past. But this story is larger than a single community, and the entire nation—notwithstanding periodic self-doubt and pessimism about the state of race relations—can take sustenance from Montgomery's (and Dr. King's) inspiring legacy.

In recent years, that legacy is finally gaining more recognition as a number of efforts in Alabama and elsewhere memorialize Movement history. The National Civil Rights Museum and Memorial at the Lorraine Hotel in Memphis; the Birmingham, Alabama, Civil Rights Institute, and the National Voting Rights Museum in Selma, Alabama, are three examples of currently operating facilities that have active educational programs. In Montgomery, an exhibit about the 1961 riot that erupted when the Freedom Riders came to town will be built in the former Greyhound Bus Station; a Rosa Parks Museum and Library is being constructed near the spot where Mrs. Parks was arrested in 1955; the parsonage where Dr. King and his family lived will be opened to the public; a thriving archives containing the papers of E. D. Nixon and other civil rights figures is being expanded at Alabama State University; and other, similar memorials are on the drawing boards.

Yet despite all this recent activity, the history of the Montgomery Bus Boycott and the Civil Rights Movement in America is neither broadly studied nor well understood. Few have read, for example, either *Stride Toward Freedom*, Dr. King's first book, or his last, *Where Do We Go From Here: Community or Chaos?*

Recognizing the potential of Dr. King's powerful legacy can provide the global community an antidote of renewed optimism to racial, religious, and ethnic polarization. The democratic elections in South Africa in 1994 and the embracing of Dr. King's philosophy of reconciliation by President Nelson Mandela is an astounding achievement toward building community out of chaos. Other national liberation struggles, including "Solidarity" in Poland, the "People Power Movement" in the Philippines, and even the pro-democracy advocates in China have cited Dr. King, along with Mohandas Gandhi, as a source of inspiration for their actions.

It is also true that examining Dr. King's role leads to the disturbing realization that his life ended when evil exerted a cancerous force within the American body politic. While he lived, he was persecuted by some of the most powerful bureaucrats in Washington, D.C. Yet he never lost his idealism and ability to preach about getting "to the promised land." His Montgomery-to-Memphis legacy thus holds special meaning and hope for those now working the world over to resolve nonviolently ethnic, religious, and racial conflicts.

Increasing violence in America comes, paradoxically, at a time when the federal government promotes a holiday honoring Dr. King's preeminent nonviolent leadership. That violence in our society has grown over the last quarter century is a clear indication that, though the nation he served has honored his memory, it has only superficially grasped the theory and practice of the philosophy by which he lived.

From Montgomery, there is a direct historical lineage to the King legacy of nonviolence, interracial/interreligious partnership, and conflict resolution. That legacy embraces an overwhelming faith in the connectedness of the human family and in our collective ability to sustain the earth and its people. In the 1990s we are challenged to "think globally, act locally" as we carry on the legacy of Montgomery and the Movement to address problems such as violence in all its forms, drug/alcohol abuse, homelessness, environmental racism, overpopulation and sustainable development on every continent around the world.

It often takes a basic and direct connection for an individual to get involved in community service or political activity, or to simply help others. In presenting this retrospective about the historic struggle against injustice in Montgomery, we trust that it will add hope and clarity to the past work of courageous persons of good will and may inspire others to labor in the cause of dreams yet unfulfilled.

THE CHILDREN COMING ON . . .

Montgomery, Alabama

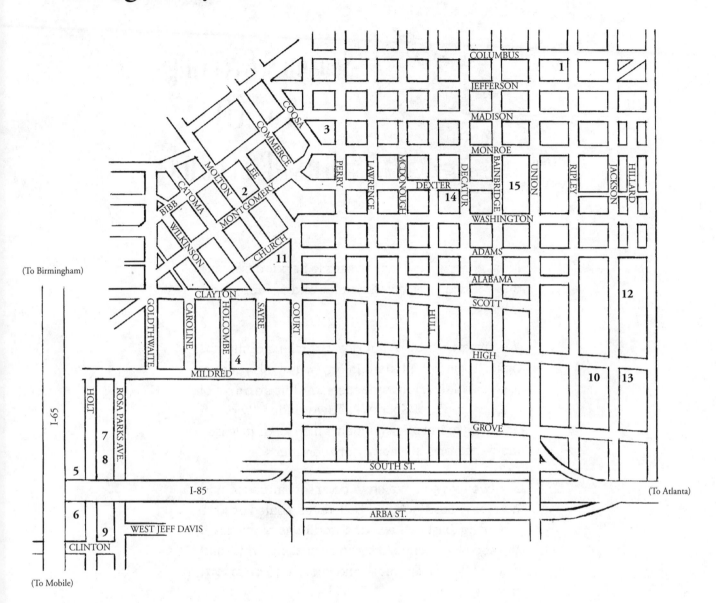

KEY

1. First Baptist Church (Abernathy)
2. Rosa Parks's Arrest Site
3. City Recorder's Court (in 1955)
4. Old Ship AME Church
5. Mt. Zion AMEZ Baptist Church
6. Holt Street Baptist Church
7. Trinity Lutheran
8. Cleveland Courts (Parks home)
9. E.D. Nixon house
10. Rufus Lewis house
11. Frank Johnson's courtroom
12. Dexter Avenue Baptist (King) parsonage
13. Ben Moore Hotel
14. Dexter Avenue King Memorial Baptist Church
15. State Capitol

The Montgomery bus company, already feeling the effects of the boycott, ran this ad in the local newspaper on Christmas Day, 1955.

PART ONE

THE LAWYER

BY FRED D. GRAY

Excerpted From

Bus Ride To Justice:
Changing the System by the System
The Life and Works of Fred Gray

The material in this section is excerpted with permission from BUS RIDE TO JUSTICE: CHANGING THE SYSTEM BY THE SYSTEM, THE LIFE AND WORKS OF FRED GRAY *(Montgomery: Black Belt Press, 1995. 400 pages, $25. ISBN 1-881320-23-5)*

1

"Mr. Chief Justice . . ."

The nine old men inside were not waiting on me as I walked up the white marble steps of the United States Supreme Court on a warm May morning in 1959. But I was waiting for them. I—and those I represented—had been waiting for several centuries.

Across the top of the building were the famous words, "Equal Justice Under Law." As I passed beneath the chiseled phrase I recalled the constitutional law teachings of Professor Oliver Schroeder and thought to myself, "We shall see."

I had my briefcase in one hand. Tucked under the other arm was a map of Tuskegee, Alabama. The map depicted one of the oddest municipal jurisdictions in recorded history, courtesy of the Alabama Legislature, which in drafting the document had exceeded even its own substantial creativity at keeping black citizens in their place.

I really wanted to use this map, but my complaint in the case at hand had been dismissed in a lower court before I got the chance. It was a fine map, made for me by Mr. William P. Mitchell, executive director of the Tuskegee Civic Association, and it cut to the heart of my case.

Mr. Mitchell's map showed the square shape of the Tuskegee city boundaries before black citizens there began a voter registration campaign in 1956. Superimposed over the original map was the twenty-five-sided shape of the boundaries after the Legislature had "improved" them. Coincidentally, the new boundaries managed to include virtually every white in the town, while excluding virtually every black.

I entered the hallway and took the map to the marshal's office for transfer to the courtroom at the proper time. I was then ready to argue *Gomillion v. Lightfoot*, challenging the Alabama Legislature's gerrymandering of Tuskegee for the purpose of denying blacks the right to vote. The case is recognized today as one of the landmarks in U.S. voting rights law. Ironically, as I write these words more than thirty years later, the gerrymandering of black voters is again an issue before the Supreme Court.

Gomillion was not my first experience with the nation's highest court. In 1956, I had won an appeal in which the Supreme Court had affirmed a lower court's ruling in my favor that segregated seating on Montgomery's city buses was unconstitutional. That was the famous Montgomery Bus Boycott case, which I had filed when I was only twenty-five years old. But this was my first time to appear in person before the Court.

I entered the courtroom as another case was being argued. As I sat and listened, I felt weak with apprehension. I remembered my childhood in Montgomery. How could I, a black man, born in an Alabama ghetto, whose father died when I was two years old and whose mother had only a sixth-grade education, argue a case before the United States Supreme Court?

When I was a boy, I never dreamed of visiting the United States Supreme Court. Now I was ready to speak before that Court. This was the opportunity of a lifetime. I sat patiently, and when the case was called, I trembled with fear.

But I stood and addressed the court, "Mr. Chief Justice, may it please the Court, I am Fred Gray from Montgomery, Alabama, and along with Robert Carter, I represent the petitioners, Dr. Gomillion and others, in this case."

Before I could get started, Justice Frankfurter, whom we feared would rule against us in this case because of one of his earlier cases, asked me to explain the map. I did.

He then asked, "Where is Tuskegee Institute?"

I replied, "Tuskegee Institute is not on the city map."

He said, "You mean to tell me that Tuskegee Institute is not located in the City of Tuskegee?"

I said, "No sir, your Honor. It was in, but they have excluded it."

"Tuskegee Institute is excluded from the City of Tuskegee?"

"Yes sir, your Honor."

I think that satisfied Mr. Justice Frankfurter. I reasoned from his questions that if Tuskegee Institute was excluded from the City of Tuskegee, then my clients were entitled to relief. It was just a question as to how the Court would write the opinion to justify its conclusion.

As you can imagine, I felt that it was a good day's work.

However, my life and work did not begin in Washington, D.C., before the United States Supreme Court, but in Montgomery, Alabama. My desire to become a lawyer did not occur in Washington, D.C., but in Montgomery, Alabama, while I was a student at Alabama State College. My secret desire "to destroy everything segregated I could find" did not originate in Washington, D.C., but on a bus in Montgomery, Alabama.

I was always on and off the buses in Montgomery. Like most African-Americans in Montgomery in the late 1940s and early 1950s, I did not have an automobile. My only means of transportation was the public buses. I was on and off the bus several times a day. I would leave home on the west side of Montgomery in the morning and catch the South Jackson Street bus which would take me through town and then to the college. In the afternoon I would use the bus a second time, catching the Washington Park bus and getting off downtown to check in for my newspaper delivery job at the Advertiser Company. My third bus ride took me from the Advertiser Company back out to my delivery district on the east side of town. A fourth ride returned me downtown to check out. Frequently a fifth ride took me from the Advertiser back to the campus to the library. Finally, the sixth bus ride, this time on the Washington Park bus, carried me back home on the west side. In short, I used the bus as often as six times a day, seven days a week.

All of the bus drivers were white. Discourteous treatment of African-American riders was more the rule than the exception. The buses were segregated. Even on the South Jackson-Washington Park bus route, which served a 90 percent African-American clientele, the bus drivers refused to allow African-Americans to sit in the first ten seats, which included the cross seats.

The bus situation, especially the discourteous treatment by the drivers, grated on African-Americans in Montgomery. Frequently, when the bus was crowded the driver would collect your money in the front and tell you to enter through the back door. Sometimes the drivers would close the door before patrons got to the back. One African-American man was killed by a bus driver. Virtually every African-American person in Montgomery had some negative experience with the buses. But, we had no choice. We had to use the buses for transportation. As Jo Ann Robinson points out in her book, *The Montgomery Bus Boycott and the Women Who Started It*, working African-American women were especially dependent on the buses. My own dissatisfaction with the bus situation grew more acute as my college years ensued.

CHAPTER

2

"To destroy everything segregated"

I was born on December 14, 1930, in Montgomery, Alabama. My mother was Nancy Jones Gray Arms (August 19, 1894–October 3, 1992) and my father was Abraham Gray (July 15, 1874–December 23, 1932). Mom worked as a domestic, particularly a cook, in several white homes in Montgomery. My father was a carpenter who received his training at Tuskegee Institute. He died when I was two.

I was born in a shotgun house at 135 Hercules Street in the Washington Park section of Montgomery. A shotgun house was one with all of the rooms built directly behind each other. It probably was so called because if a person fired a shotgun through the front door the shot would travel through each of the rooms and out the back door. In 1930, Washington Park was a typical black community in Montgomery, with no paved streets, no running water, and no inside sanitary facilities. There were no hospitals for African-American children to be born. They, like me, were delivered by a midwife.

My parents were members of the Church of Christ. My father became a member in 1925 and my mother in 1928. Religion and the church played a major role in my family life. My father was a faithful member of the Holt Street Church of Christ until his death. He helped to build the first church building. He would canvass our neighborhood and take all the children to Sunday School. After his death, Mom would take us to Sunday School and church. The church was the center of our early childhood.

Mom wanted all of her children to obtain an education, become good Christians, and make something of themselves. She taught us that we could be anything we wanted to be and then gave us the necessary shoves to fulfill that prophecy.

I was the youngest of five children and after my father's death my mother had to support us. Finding someone to keep me before I started school was a problem for her, which led to my starting school early. The usual age for beginning school then was six years, but I would not turn six until December 14. My mother and her sister, Sarah Jones McWright, a first-grade teacher at Loveless School, devised a plan where my aunt enrolled me in her class when I was five. They did this so my mother could work and because Aunt Sarah believed I was ready for first-grade work. So, my aunt and mother initiated, in 1935, a "head start" program for me. This was my first head start.

Loveless School was located on West Jeff Davis Avenue approximately two miles from home. I attended that school from the first through the seventh grades. Of course, all of the schools in Montgomery at that time were segregated.

After I finished the seventh grade, in 1943, Mom arranged to send me to the Nashville Christian Institute (NCI), an African-American boarding school in Nashville, Tennessee, operated by members of the Church of Christ. The Bible was taught daily, along with chapel programs, and emphasis was placed on teaching young men to become preachers and church leaders. From my childhood, Mom had weaned me to pursue the ministry. This school was a part of her plan.

The public schools in Montgomery opened in September, but the Nashville school did not open until October. So, when I did not enroll in Montgomery, one of my friends, Howard McCall, began to tease me, saying, "Fred is not going to school," and implied that I was a dropout.

I was not a dropout. I was a twelve-year-old on a mission for God. My mother packed me up and sent me by our minister, Brother Sutton Johnson, to Nashville. At the time, NCI was the only African-American Church of Christ-supported high school. It was a co-educational boarding school with on-campus living facilities for boys; girl students who did not live in Nashville were boarded with individual members of the church in various homes throughout the city.

NCI's principal was Professor E. Frank N. Tharpe. He was a graduate of Tennessee A&I State University with a major in history. He would brag that he taught our students at the Nashville Christian Institute history from the same book—Civilization Past and Present—that freshmen studied at Tennessee A&I.

NCI was a small high school. We had approximately three hundred students from about twenty-five states. Our facilities were meager, but we had dedicated faculty members who were genuinely interested in the growth and development of its students. They gave us a good college preparatory education, and many of the graduates of NCI are leaders across the country and preachers in the Church of Christ throughout the nation. During my stay at NCI we all developed very close ties and friendships that have lasted a lifetime.

. . . I enrolled in Alabama State College for Negroes, now Alabama State University, on December 1, 1947. All my life I had been drawn to the ministry, and when I entered Alabama State, I envisioned becoming a social science teacher and a minister, as those were the principal careers then open to college-educated African-American males. You either preached or taught school. But my studies and associations at Alabama State began to change my goals.

Professor Thelma Glass taught history, geography, and English. She impressed upon me the recipe for success in college. She advised us to learn exactly what the teacher wanted, how the teacher wanted the material pre-

> I was not a dropout. I was a twelve-year-old on a mission for God.

sented, and then to try to present it in that fashion. I have followed this advice ever since, not only in college, but in law school and law practice.

Another professor who made an indelible impression on me was J. E. Pierce, who taught political science and had done an extensive survey in the area of voter registration. Professor Pierce often talked about the importance of obtaining our civil rights. He noted my interest in civil rights and encouraged me to go to law school. The convergence of my bus riding experiences and his lectures helped me to decide, during my junior year, that I would attend law school and return to Montgomery to practice law. But I kept this goal to myself at that time.

I worked my way through Alabama State College as a district manager of the *Alabama Journal,* the afternoon paper in Montgomery. I was known on campus as the "newspaper boy." My delivery territory, District Six, encompassed the campus and all of the east side of Montgomery where African-Americans resided—African-American district managers supervised African-American areas, and white district managers supervised white areas. As a district manager, it was my responsibility to oversee the distribution of the newspaper for thirteen routes, to employ and manage newspaper carriers, and to increase circulation.

I reported to my substation before the papers and carriers arrived to make sure the carriers properly received and delivered the newspapers and that they paid their bills for them on time. In the evenings, I went back to the *Advertiser* Company in downtown Montgomery to complete my report for the number of papers we needed the next day for each route. I would submit names of any new subscribers—we used to call them starts—and discontinue persons—stops—who no longer wanted the newspaper.

Professor Thelma Glass, 1949.

Although it seems that I was always working, always getting on and off the buses, my grades never suffered. I graduated with honors in the upper 10 percent of my class.

Alabama State College was altogether different from Alabama State University as it exists in 1994. During my time there, it was entirely segregated—faculty, students and staff. However, while we had an African-American president, the policy-making body was the all-white Alabama State Board of Education, with the governor of the state of Alabama serving as ex-officio chairman. These white men all believed in the "Southern way of life" and that included segregation and second-class status for blacks in every aspect of existence. This was just the way they believed and the way it was. Alabama State College, when compared to historically white institutions in Alabama, was woefully underfunded, with inferior buildings and inadequate resources. But, we had a dedicated faculty whose members were concerned about the students. They were concerned that we receive the best education the institution could give. They taught us that we were somebody, and that with hard work and dedication we could succeed.

Social life on the campus of Alabama State College was typical of social life on historically black institutions during that period of time. There were the usual student organizations, religious organizations, sororities and fraternities. The major African-American sororities and fraternities were located on the campus. The fraternities included Omega Psi Phi, Alpha Phi Alpha, Kappa Alpha Psi, and Phi Beta Sigma. The sororities were Delta Sigma Theta, Alpha Kappa Alpha, and Zeta Phi Beta. I became a member of Omega Psi Phi, primarily because my older brother Thomas was an upperclassman at Alabama State College at the time I entered and he was a member and Basileus of Omega Psi Phi. Not only did I later become a member, but I also became its Basileus.

The Greek letter organizations were important on and off-campus. In those days, Alabama State College was the center of cultural activities for African-Americans in Montgomery. Everything in the city of Montgomery, in those days, as was the case throughout the South and in many places across the nation, was totally segregated. Churches, schools, hospitals, public accommodations—everything was segregated. Whites and blacks were segregated from the time they were born until they were buried in segregated cemeteries.

In my senior year of college, I applied to several law schools, including the University of Denver and Western Reserve University, now Case Western Reserve University in Cleveland. I selected schools in cities where job opportunities existed. As far as I could discern, Cleveland was a good place to both learn law and get a job. Another influential factor was Case Western Reserve University's schedule of classes. I could take classes from 8:30 in the morning until 12:30 in the afternoon and still have time to work a full-time job and study.

I did not apply to the University of Alabama Law School because I knew there was no chance I would be accepted. The state of Alabama, as did all of the Southern states at that time, had out-of-state-aid arrangements for African-American students who on their merits should have been admitted to white colleges, universities, and professional schools. Many Southern states inaugurated these schemes to circumvent the 1938 United States Supreme Court decision, *Gaines v. Canada, ex rel.* The Gaines case held that states that have a segregated higher education system must provide African-Americans with equal educational facilities.

If an African American student was interested in pursuing an advanced degree in a subject offered at the University of Alabama or Auburn University that was not offered at African-American institutions, including Alabama State, Tuskegee Institute, or Alabama A&M, then the student was required to file an application with the state superintendent of education for out-of-state aid. The application process included submission of proof that the student had been admitted to a school in another state. Then the Alabama superintendent of education would make available financial assistance. The state would pay the following expenses: 1) round-trip transportation once a year to the school; 2) the difference between tuition fees at the University of Alabama and the particular university chosen; and 3) the difference between room and board at the institution desired and the costs at Alabama State University. There was a specific formula to calculate expenses, but the funds were available only on a reimbursement basis. This was the catch. This policy proved especially difficult for poor African-American students to overcome because they did not

THE CHILDREN COMING ON . . .

have the money to make the initial payment. I applied for such aid and it was granted. The state superintendent at the time was Austin Meadows, a man who became a defendant in many subsequent lawsuits that I filed. After I began to practice law in Montgomery, Dr. Meadows once stated that he was proud of the fact that he, as state superintendent, had signed my papers so I could go to law school.

On one of the last few days of my employment at the *Advertiser* Company, one of the white district managers asked me what I was going to do after graduation. I told him I was going to law school. Another district manager asked me, "Well, where are you going to practice law?" I said, "Right across the street." There was a long silence. The Montgomery County Courthouse at that time was located across the street from the *Advertiser* Company.

Privately, I pledged that I would return to Montgomery and use the law to "destroy everything segregated that I could find."

I kept my plans secret. I did not want anything to interfere with my going to law school. I completed the applications without any discussion with family members.

After I was admitted to Western Reserve University Law School, I showed mother my acceptance letter. She said, "All right, Mr. Smarty, now that you have been admitted, where are you going to get the money from?" Of course I didn't have the money and she didn't have the money, but it was a rhetorical question because immediately she went to work and borrowed money to help me go to law school.

My brother, Thomas, was then in business in Montgomery. He and William Singleton operated Dozier's Radio Service, a repair shop and television and home appliances store. Thomas accompanied me to the First National Bank of Montgomery, where I applied for a loan. I told the loan officer that I had been admitted to law school. I took with me the papers indicating that I would be reimbursed for a certain portion of the money once I had paid my fees and expenses. However, I did not have sufficient security, nor did my brother. Consequently, the loan was denied. My family, a few friends, and I continued to work and raised enough money to pay the first installment on my tuition, room and board, and transportation costs.

3

Helping Hands to the Bar

. . . At long last graduation day arrived. My mother and Bernice, who by that time was my fiancée, came for the commencement ceremony, then returned to Montgomery. I remained in Cleveland to concentrate on studying. I studied day and night. This was very necessary because I was preparing myself for two bar examinations, the Ohio and Alabama. The Ohio exam was given in June and the Alabama exam in July. For the past three years I had studied and attended law school. Now I was a law graduate, and all of the hard work would be to no avail if I did not pass the bar exams. The only way I would be able to practice law in any state would be, for the most part, to pass the bar examination of that state. While I was primarily interested in becoming a lawyer in Montgomery and carrying out my secret pledge, I was realistic enough to realize it was possible that the examiners in Alabama might discriminate against me, and regardless of what I did on the exam, they could say that I did not pass. I was taking the Ohio bar exam as a precaution.

Each segment of the Ohio bar exam, which was given over a three-day period, had six questions. Examinees were expected to answer five of the six. It was suggested that we read through all of the questions first and then answer the one that appeared easiest. I tried that strategy but it didn't work for me because as I read the second or third question, my mind would flash back to the first question. So, the technique that I used was to simply read the question, and if I understood it, I would answer it. If I did not understand the question or did not know the answer, I would proceed to the next one.

I remember the last day of the exams very well. By that time I was exhausted. I passed in my paper, said goodbye to a few of my classmates, and went to the train station. The train was actually scheduled to leave at 3:45 p.m. and the exam was not scheduled to end until 4:00 p.m., but I had written all that I knew. I boarded the train to Cincinnati and transferred there to a train going to Montgomery.

The Alabama bar exam was scheduled for the fourth Tuesday in July. I arrived home in late June. From the moment I arrived in Montgomery I had very little social contact with anyone. I just studied everything I could get my hands on.

Knowing enough to pass the Alabama bar exam was not the only obstacle. There were a couple of other hurdles that I had to get over before I could take the exam. Alabama required that one register as a law student by filing an application and submitting character affidavits from five lawyers who had been practicing for at least five years. I had filed the application when I enrolled in law school, but I did not know five lawyers at the time. I completed the application, admitted that I did not know five lawyers, and informed them I would submit the affidavits as soon as possible.

At this juncture, with my dream so close to becoming a reality, all that was left for me to do was to talk to Mr. E. D. Nixon. I had known his wife for many years because she and I attended the same church. Ed Nixon had been "Mr. Civil Rights" in Montgomery and in the state for many years. By occupation, he was a Pullman car porter, so he was frequently in and out of town. If anybody ever had problems with the city police or any matter where they thought their civil rights had been denied, they would always contact E. D. Nixon. For over fifty years, E. D. Nixon advocated the cause of African-Americans in Montgomery and central Alabama. He was president of the State Conference of Branches of the NAACP and president of the Montgomery Branch of the NAACP. He was a founding member of the Montgomery Progressive Democratic Club, which later became a charter member of the Alabama Democratic Conference. Mr. Nixon believed that African-Americans should have the same rights as other Americans. He believed that segregation was wrong and he dedicated his life, efforts, and resources to eradicating those wrongs. He was also to become one of the founders and leaders of the Montgomery Bus Boycott, which ended segregation in public transportation in the city of Montgomery. He was actively involved in getting persons registered to vote

Gray, Congressman Adam Clayton Powell, E. D. Nixon, J.W. King, and P.M. Blair, on the occasion of Powell's celebrated visit to Montgomery in 1954.

and getting lawyers to defend African-Americans whose constitutional rights were violated, and he paved the way for many of us and was a role model in the field of civil rights.

So, like other African Americans in Montgomery who had problems, I talked with Mr. Nixon about my need to have lawyers sign affidavits. There were only a handful of African-American lawyers in the state. The best known African-American lawyer was Arthur Shores of Birmingham. Charles V. Henley was Grand Master of the Masons; he didn't practice law, but he had a law license. At that time, Oscar Adams, who later became the first African-American to serve as a justice on the Alabama Supreme Court, Orzell Billingsley, Peter Hall, Charles Langford, and David Hood were also practicing law, but none had yet practiced the requisite five years. I asked Mr. Nixon to help me to get the affidavits both to register as a law student and to take the Alabama bar exam. With Mr. Nixon's and Bernice's help, I soon had the necessary affidavits.

Bernice was working for the wife of Nesbitt Elmore, a white attorney. After she informed them about my predicament, a meeting was arranged. Bernice introduced me to Elmore, who, in turn, introduced me to his uncle, Clifford Durr. Mr. Nixon also introduced me to Mr. Durr. The first time I met Mr. Durr he did not sign the affidavit. This was understandable. Mr. Durr did not know me at that time. The affidavit required that you know the applicant personally, that you know his character to be good, and that you must state the facts and circumstances showing how you know the applicant. Later Nesbitt Elmore, Mrs. Elmore, and Mr. Nixon encouraged Mr. Durr to sign the affidavit. The lawyers who ultimately signed character affidavits for me included Arthur Shores, Nesbitt Elmore, Charles Henley, Clifford Durr, Woodley C. Campbell, Henry Heller, and Kenneth McGee. With the exception of Shores and Henley, the signers of my affidavits were white. Without their support I could not have taken the bar exam. I will always be grateful to them. Woodley C. Campbell still practices law in Montgomery.

(. . . Clifford J. Durr served as my advisor on a daily basis during the formative years of my career, beginning when I opened my office in 1954. He assisted and advised me generally in the development of my practice, and specifically concerning civil rights litigation. During his lifetime, there was no official recognition of his work in the city of his birth, Montgomery. However, on March 1, 1992, he was honored posthumously. On that date, Auburn University at Montgomery (AUM) inaugurated the Clifford J. Durr Lecture Series, a series of lectures in which nationally recognized speakers address issues concerning constitutional protection of civil liberties. A resolution was adopted by the City Council of the City of Montgomery recognizing his work. The speakers for that occasion were Mrs. Lyndon B. Johnson, the widow of President Lyndon B. Johnson; Tom Johnson, president of CNN; and Fred Gray. Invited to speak on "Clifford J. Durr: The Attorney," I stated among other things, "It is appropriate that this university recognize an outstanding Alabamian for the outstanding contributions which he has made in the field of civil libeties to this nation, to this state, and to this city. . . . In the real sense

THE CHILDREN COMING ON . . .

of the word Clifford Durr has been a silent law partner in my law practice from day one.")

. . . As it turned out, Dr. Solomon S. Seay, Sr., a minister and the secretary-treasurer of the Home Mission Department of the African Methodist Episcopal Zion Church [helped me find office space]. Dr. Seay occupied the upstairs offices of the building where Sears Auto Shop was located at 113 Monroe Street. He used only the front part of the building. The back part of the building was vacant. I talked with him, and he agreed to sublease that space to me. Further, he stated that if I didn't have the rent every month he would understand. The rent was fifty dollars per month. It represented a substantial amount considering I had no financial resources.

Sharing offices next to Dr. Seay proved to be a significant asset. He was a man of great knowledge and wisdom. For the next few years, he was to serve as my adviser, and, for all practical purposes, he was like a father to me. He gave sound advice and referred many clients, including my first wrongful death case. Later, I invited his son, Solomon S. Seay, Jr., to practice law with me, and we worked together for many years on many of our civil rights cases. Many years later, Dr. Seay wrote me a letter reflecting on our relationship during those early years. He said:

I WAS THERE BY THE GRACE OF GOD *(Montgomery: S.S. Seay Educational Foundation, 1990, $24.95.).*

. . . Last night during the 10:00 o'clock news I was asleep until you spoke. I heard your voice in my sleep and it awakened me. I felt proud almost to tears. Perhaps this is hard to understand on your part. I say this because so many people so often never understand the kind of person I am.

I lay in bed reminiscing first concerning you and your wife before marriage and your youthful anxieties. I thought of the factors that had to do with your determination, therefore, your goals and ultimate achievements. I remembered some things I said to you, I am sure perhaps you have forgotten.

One day I said to you: "Fred if you will continue to work hard and trust God you will make it." Those were dark days. Another time I added the following: "As you work be sure to get your fees"! I remember this one mainly because I have been such a poor example of it.

There have been three things in your favor: (1) You were born with native qualities with which to face the disadvantages confronting you. (2) You were identified with the church of your choice. (3) You married the girl that loved you and was prepared in spirit to face life with you, whatever it was like.

Well, I am Solomon S. Seay Sr. I am 72 years old. I have been preaching 51 years. I have tried to light a candle for every person traveling the dark slippery road over which I also have had to travel. I have felt the urge to put a thorn in no person's bosom even those whom I have considered unfriendly. I have tried not to be a burden to those whom I have considered friendly. In the most trying times I have never begged an enemy for mercy. I have never felt ashamed to serve in what our cultural standards would consider to be small places, for to me stations in life never make real persons. Real persons are what they are wherever they are.

. . . I shall always remember you.

Dr. Seay was a great man, and he greatly inspired me to be the best. Dr. Seay's autobiography, *I Was There By The Grace Of God,* was published in 1990.

Bernice played a major role in helping me to open my law office. I borrowed some of Nesbitt Elmore's books so that the office looked like a law office when I had open house. I invited church people, former teachers and classmates, and basically everybody that I could think of. One of my former college classmates, Mrs. Bennye Black Reasor, assisted with the selection of office stationery. She was a high school instructor, later an instructor at Trenholm State College and Alabama State University. Her daughter Joanne is now employed as a secretary in our Montgomery office. A nice group came to my open house. The next day I returned Mr. Elmore's books. I was now open and ready to do business. I was also ready to pursue my secret goal of "destroying everything segregated I could find."

CHAPTER

4

Rosa Parks

. . . Bernice recalls well the early days of my practice. "When Fred first graduated from law school, it was very difficult. He had a basic, bare-looking office, but he was very proud of it and so was I. Soon after he opened his office in 1954, he said to me, 'as soon as I make a little money we can get married,' but to me it seemed like a dream, far, far away."

Building a law practice takes time. It is slow, tedious, hard work. I had to get out among the people and make myself known to them. I had to establish contacts and earn their trust.

These were the days before advertising, but, even then, there were many ways to work oneself into a community. Since I was interested in civil rights and politics, I started attending the National Association for the Advancement of Colored People (NAACP) meetings. Rosa Parks was the secretary to the Montgomery Branch of the NAACP and also served as youth director. I worked with the youth and with Rosa Parks. In her capacity as youth director, and through my interest in the activities of the NAACP, we developed a very close relationship. Mrs. Parks was very kind, quiet, gentle, loving and would never hurt anyone. She was and is one of the kindest and loveliest persons that one would want to meet. She still maintains these qualities almost forty years later.

During the early months of my law practice, I had few clients and little to do. At lunch time Mrs. Parks often walked to my office, located one and a half blocks from the Montgomery Fair Department Store where she worked as a seamstress. We became very good friends. She would walk to my office, and we would sit down and share our lunches.

For almost a year, we met, shared our lunches, and discussed the problems in Montgomery. We had talked about the situation involving Claudette Colvin, a fifteen-year-old student at Booker Washington High School, who was arrested March 2, 1955, for refusing to get up and give her seat to a white woman on a Capital Heights bus in downtown Montgomery. We discussed the possibility of a boycott. I told Mrs. Parks, as I had told other leaders in Montgomery, that I thought the Claudette Colvin arrest was a good test case to end segregation on the buses. However, the black leadership in Montgomery at that time thought we should wait. Mrs. Parks shared my feelings that something had to be done to end segregation on the buses. There was a congruency in our thoughts and ideas that helped me understand her strong interest in me, a struggling young lawyer. She gave me the feeling that I was the Moses that God had sent to Pharaoh and commanded him to "Let My People Go." She saw that I was penniless, and she wanted to help me get on my feet. More importantly, she wanted to help our people eradicate segregation and discrimination on the Montgomery buses.

5

Jo Ann Robinson

In private moments, I often thought about the buses and about segregation. Although I personally had never had any negative experiences on the buses, I knew that many people did, especially African-American women.

While a student at Alabama State, I had become acquainted with Jo Ann Robinson, a professor of English and a leader of the Women's Political Council. Mrs. Robinson had related to me her horrendous experience on a Montgomery City bus in December of 1949. She boarded an almost empty city bus, paid her fare, and observed only two passengers on the bus—a white woman who sat in the third row from the front, and a black man in a seat near the back. She sat in a seat in the middle of the bus. The bus driver stopped, came back to where she was seated, told her she was sitting too near the front of the bus, and demanded that she move back or get off the bus. She was afraid he would hit her, so she got off the bus.

She was upset, fearful, in tears, humiliated, and embarrassed. I am confident that this was the beginning of Mrs. Robinson's determination to end racial discrimination on city buses in Montgomery. She vividly describes this incident in her book, *The Montgomery Bus Boycott And The Women Who Started It*.

Robinson was a member of the Ten Times One Is Ten Club, the oldest African-American women's federated club in Montgomery. The members of that club were the pillars of African-American society in Montgomery. There were about eight or nine of these clubs in Montgomery at that time. I spoke to the women's clubs and helped them with their legal problems or with whatever they wanted to do. Indeed, one of my earliest speeches as a young lawyer was delivered to the Ten Times One Is Ten Club on the occasion of its sixty-seventh anniversary on Sunday, October 30, 1955, in Tullibody Auditorium on the campus of Alabama State College. This was thirty-one days before Rosa Parks refused to give up her seat on December 1, 1955.

In my speech to the Ten Times One Is Ten Club, I challenged the members to bring an end to segregation in all areas of life in Montgomery. I said:

We must be alert, we must be diligent, we must not accept anything less than full integration in public schools, public transportation, and in all other public facilities.

Let us forever remember that segregated schools and segregation itself is inherently unequal; it creates an inferiority complex upon our children. We must be strong, and we must be financially able and willing to carry our cases to court if our officials will not voluntarily desegregate our schools, parks, transportation system and all other public facilities. During these crucial days, days of great decision, may the God of Heaven direct us, help us and may He through His divine guidance lead all men to realize that we were all made from one flesh, and that we are all God's children. May God bless us, assist us, and may He speed the day when all of our schools and all other public facilities will be completely integrated.

Can you imagine me, a young lawyer twenty-four years of age, telling these women, who were old enough to be my mother or grandmother, that they must do everything possible to end segregation? They were not critical of my speech. On the contrary, they accepted it and we became partners in destroying segregation in Alabama.

Jo Ann was definitely committed to ending segregation. Few realized how much Jo Ann did and the significant role she played in helping to improve conditions for African Americans in Montgomery until she published her memoirs. Little did many know that much activity that impacted on the Civil Rights Movement in Alabama occurred at Jo Ann Robinson's house.

After Claudette Colvin had been arrested and before the arrest of Mrs. Parks, Jo Ann and I had many discussions in her house and other places, with reference to what should be done in the event another incident occurred, and the bus company and the city officials did not live up to the commitments they made immediately following the Colvin incident. The night of Mrs. Parks's arrest, I went to Jo Ann's house. We discussed the strategy and what needed to be done to begin immediately a protest and make it successful.

Throughout the 381 days of the protest there was almost daily contact between the two of us, both by phone and at her residence. Jo Ann later recalled an occasion on which she had telephoned me late one evening when I was pretty tired. Jo Ann recalled that in the course of the conversation I cried, "Woman, what do you want? Go ahead and tell me what's on your mind." Those who know me will recognize that I don't usually respond like that. But, those were difficult days. In any case, the conversations and the plans made with Jo Ann helped to lay the ground work for the unfolding of the protest.

6

"The masses and the classes"

My involvement with the NAACP and the Young Alabama Democrats brought me into close contact with E. D. Nixon and Rufus Lewis, leaders in the fight for African-American voter registration. They were very different men—one a Pullman porter with limited education, the other a military veteran and college coach—but they worked for similar goals. People often said, "Mr. Nixon had the masses and Coach Lewis had the classes."

E. D. Nixon was the key to the history of the African-American struggle for first-class citizenship and equal rights in Alabama. He was courageous and genuinely interested in civil rights. He was not concerned with private gain and never received anything personally as a result of his efforts to gain equal treatment for others. Mr. Nixon wanted to get a job done, and he was one of the few African Americans in the city whose employment was such that the white power structure could not bring any type of economic reprisals against him. Mr. Nixon was also a good friend of A. Philip Randolph, the founder of the Brotherhood of Sleeping Car Porters union, and thus enjoyed an excellent relationship with organized labor. In other words, Nixon could say what he wanted to about the whites, police brutality, civil rights, and discrimination. He backed his words with actions.

E. D. Nixon not only had the ability to lead African Americans in Montgomery, but he could attract national figures to come to Montgomery and speak out in favor of voter registration. Several months before the beginning of the Montgomery Bus Boycott, New York Congressman Adam Clayton Powell came to Montgomery at Nixon's invitation to encourage African Americans to register to vote. Powell's speech was given in the gymnasium on the campus of Alabama State College, and he delivered a powerful message. Powell's visit to Montgomery was also notable because he was extended by then-Governor "Big Jim" Folsom all of the courtesies due a visiting congressman, including the lending of the governor's limousine and driver, Winston Craig. This Southern hospitality earned Folsom considerable criticism from other state officials and the media in what was becoming an increasingly polarized climate in the state. Powell was invited to the governor's mansion and had a widely publicized cocktail with Folsom. The idea of the Alabama governor drinking in the parlor of the official mansion with a black man—even if he was a U. S. Congressman—infuriated the state's rabid segregationists. The KKK even made a widely publicized demand for Folsom to fire Winston Craig, a demand ignored by the governor but which led to an incident that was typical of the racial overtones which infused every aspect of life at that time.

It seems that the KKK, failing to get Craig fired, put out the word that on a given night they were going to Craig's home in the Mobile Heights community and "get him." Several of Craig's neighbors, including my brother Tom, formed an impromptu guard committee to keep an eye out. On the early evening of the expected Klan visit, Craig passed on the news that the governor was also sending an unmarked car of highway patrolmen to watch over him. However, this turned out to be not such a blessing. Tom had the second shift on the watch committee, and he woke up not to the expected phone call to come take his turn, but to William Singleton phoning for Tom to come to the city jail to get Singleton and another watcher out of jail.

As it turned out, Singleton and his partner were patrolling the neighborhood in their car, when they pulled into Singleton's driveway to get out for a cup of coffee. The unmarked patrol car was also driving around the neighborhood and when Singleton got out, the plainclothes officer stopped and called for Singleton to approach the patrol car. Singleton was expecting some casual conversation, but as he and his partner got out of their car, the interior lights came on, and through the open car door the officers could see the shotguns the two men had with them in the car. At this point, the patrolmen drew their guns, and ordered the two African Americans to assume the position, and frisked them. In addition to the hunting weapons in the car, Singleton had a loaded .45 in his overcoat pocket. So both men were charged with possessing concealed weapons. Some thought this was an odd arrest since at the time of the arrest Singleton was in his own yard, and the hunting guns were inside the automobile, and both arrested men had valid hunting licenses. Besides which, the reason for their activity was that a KKK attack was anticipated in an African-American community. Nevertheless, they were in jail.

Brother Tom was taking all this in during the phone call from Singleton, who was basically asking him to round up bail money and come to police headquarters. Tom said over the phone, "I'm a property owner, do you think those birds will allow me to provide a personal bond for you?" At which point another voice—to the immense surprise of caller and callee—came on the line, saying, "These birds ain't going to let you do nothing." Then, when Tom got to the jail and paid the bonds, and they were all getting ready to leave, a very tall policeman came up and asked, "Which one of y'all called us birds? That's a nasty expression, don't ever call us birds, boy!" Tom says he kept quiet and expected a blow, though none came. When they were finally outside the jail, the other arrested man said to Tom, "I'll never let you get me out of jail again." They all laughed with relief, and, in retrospect it was a harmless incident. But it also shows how careful African-American men had to be about every little thing they did or said, and I think it helps explain why, forty years later, relations are still strained between the black community and law enforcement.

THE CHILDREN COMING ON . . .

Anyway, I had had the opportunity of meeting Congressman Powell at his speech, and I accompanied him in the governor's limousine, chauffeured by Winston Craig, to his next engagement in Birmingham. Craig, incidentally, was very active in the community. His work with E. D. Nixon was an example of how Nixon was able to bring together African Americans of all callings—from congressmen like Powell to chauffeurs like Craig—in support of voter registration.

Rufus Lewis was a leader of the elite African Americans in Montgomery. He was educated and lived on the east side of town where Alabama State College is located and where more of the educated African Americans lived. I lived on the west side, the less-educated side of town. Coach Lewis was primarily concerned with one aspect of the civil rights field, voter registration. He was a very good friend of Professor J. E. Pierce, my old political science instructor. I think Professor Pierce may have influenced Coach great deal. Coach Lewis had a night club called the Citizens Clul had to be a registered voter to be admitted.

Ironically, Nixon probably did more to get folks out to v(and to become involved in civil rights issues than either Lewis o Pierce. Nixon was president of the Montgomery Progressive Democratic Club, the forerunner of the Alabama Democratic Conference. The ADC today is one of the state's two major African-American political action groups, but for most of the past thirty years it was the source of black political power in Alabama. Still, in those days, there were many, including some highly educated African Americans, who thought Nixon was a little too aggressive. After all, registering to vote is one thing, but getting lawyers to defend an African-American fellow like Jeremiah Reeves, who was accused of raping a white woman, was another thing—and Nixo did this.

Rufus Lewis

I was closer to Nixon than to Lewis. The point I made clear, ever, was that I was willing to work for either and all sides. I woul(with anyone who was trying to do something positive. Mr. Nixon encouraged me to organize African-American youth into an organization known as the Young Alabama Democrats (YAD) as a part of his Montgomery Progressive Democratic Club. YAD consisted of high school students, college students, and young adults. The purpose of this group was to get young people involved in the political process.

My work with youth made it possible for me to lecture in schools, churches, and throughout the communities. The YAD deserves a great deal of credit for being one of the first organizations to promote greater youth participation in the political process.

To be sure, YAD paralleled the youth group of the NAACP; the youth of the two organizations worked together. Ms. Inez J. Baskin was an inspiration to the YAD in the same way that Rosa Parks was to the NAACP youth organization. Ms. Baskin, an employee of the *Montgomery Advertiser* and *Alabama Journal*, reported on African-American social news in Montgomery. (At that time the Montgomery newspapers each dedicated a page to report the news for the "colored" community. It had its own "colored" editor, E. P. Wallace, and Inez Baskin served as his assistant. The colored paper was identified by stars on the front. Those papers were not delivered in the white community.)

The youth divisions of the NAACP were integral parts of each branch's activities. Their purpose was to develop young people to be good students, good citizens, and good Christians. The youth were instrumental in carrying out the objects and purposes of the NAACP.

I discussed youth involvement with Mr. Nixon, and he thought it would be very important if we could get young people interested in registering to vote, to get them to encourage their parents to become registered voters, and generally to assist in taking people to the polls on election day. I was primarily interested in developing contact with these young people, because as a young lawyer in the community, there wasn't too much difference in our ages. It would serve to encourage them and, at the same time, it would give me some contact with their parents. The primary goal of the YAD was political in nature and to assist in the political process—to give these people, at an early age, an opportunity of learning and participating in political activities.

Nine months before Rosa Parks refused to give up her seat, I represented Claudette Colvin for a similar act of resistance. On March 2, 1955, Claudette, a fifteen-year-old high school student, refused to obey a bus driver's order that she relinquish her seat. She was already at the back of the bus and refused to make her seat available to a white person. When she remained seated, the bus driver called police officers who dragged her from the bus and arrested her. Claudette was a member of the NAACP Youth Council and was quite willing to follow any advice that Nixon or Robinson offered. Claudette lived in a community known as King Hill. I was fond of this community because I would visit and sometimes preach for one of our churches, known as the King Hill Church of Christ, which was located in that community. In addition, some of these young people were YAD members. One of the young ladies who was on the bus with Claudette at the time of her arrest, Annie Larkins, was crowned queen of YAD one year.

I readily agreed to represent Claudette, thinking that this well could be the chance I had been waiting on to challenge the constitutionality of Montgomery's segregation ordinances and Alabama's segregation statutes. One of the first things I did was to invite Clifford Durr to help me with the legal research. As a matter of course, I would always invite established African-American and white lawyers to join forces with me on civil rights cases. There was so much that I didn't know and the advice of my former law professor stayed in my mind. He recommended that I willingly share fees with an older lawyer who had more experience. Clifford Durr proved to be a great behind-the-scenes lawyer throughout the Montgomery Bus Protest Movement and was very important to me through the balance of his life.

Not only did Clifford Durr assist me in civil rights cases, but in any number of cases of all types he personally would help me with drafting pleadings, briefs, and other documents. He, more than any other person, taught me how to practice law. I will always be grateful to Clifford and his wife, Virginia, for assisting me in becoming a good lawyer. He provided this service without charge.

Durr, a member of a distinguished upper-middle-class white family in Montgomery, was a graduate of the University of Alabama and a Rhodes Scholar, who earned his law degree from Oxford University in 1922. His wife, Virginia Foster Durr, was the sister-in-law of Hugo L. Black, first a U.S. Senator from Alabama and later one of the nation's most distinguished justices of the Supreme Court. Clifford Durr had worked in the Roosevelt Administration and was credited with helping save the nation's banking system during the Great Depression. Then he had been appointed by Roosevelt as one of the first members of the new Federal Communications Commission, a position he resigned after Roosevelt's death when then-President Harry S Truman imposed a loyalty oath requirement on federal employees. Durr believed the oath was unconstitutional, and he refused to sign it. The Durrs then moved home to Montgomery, where he faced an unsteady future, both because he and his wife were smeared by the anti-Communist hysteria of the day and because he did not go along with the segregationists who were gaining control of every aspect of official power in Alabama at the time.

Durr made a distinction between civil rights and civil liberties. He believed that the rights of African-American people had to be preserved and protected, not because they were African-American, but because the denial of liberties to one group of Americans was an open invitation to undermine the entire body of civil law upon which this country was founded. I respected the distinction he made; however, I was more determined to remove the very real shackles that circumscribed African-American freedom. He and his wife, Virginia Foster Durr, endured public scorn and social ostracism from prominent whites in the city for their sympathetic support and involvement in these lawsuits.

Immediately after Claudette was arrested, Jo Ann Robinson and members of the Women's Political Council arranged a meeting with Mayor Tacky Gayle, the two other members of the City Commission, Montgomery City Lines Manager Clantello Bagley, and others for the purpose of discussing the case. Of course, as Claudette's lawyer, I was also invited. During the meeting, Jo Ann threatened to initiate a protest. The city officials and the bus company officials assured us they were sorry for this incident, it would not occur again, and that the bus drivers would be more courteous in the future.

As it turned out, the Colvin case proved a false start as far as giving me the opportunity to challenge Alabama's segregation laws. Even though I had developed and presented an excellent defense for Claudette, the juvenile court of Montgomery County convicted her on all charges. I appealed the decision, and ultimately the Montgomery County Juvenile Court placed her on indefinite, unsupervised probation. Although the case did not result in a challenge to the segregation laws, there were some benefits. This was the first case in which I raised the issue of the constitutionality of the Montgomery city ordinances and Alabama state statutes that provided for segregation. The case gave me courage and a faith that there would be another opportunity to challenge Alabama's segregation laws.

Montgomery Voices

I

Johnnie Carr:

My name is Johnnie Rebecca Daniels Carr. I was born in Montgomery, Alabama, on January 26, 1911. When I was a child, and you know that's been a long time, when I was a child growing up in Montgomery, Alabama, there were so many things going on around us, I think that your home life had a lot to do with how your attitude was toward it. I did have, I feel, a very good home. My mother—my father passed when I was nine, but my mother raised us, and we had a very good home life—[provided us with] a religious background because my mother was very religious and this was one of the things I felt that gave us the type of attitude that we had.

Well . . . we didn't think too much of what was going on around us as against us because we were more or less trying to achieve and make a life for ourselves, and . . . we really started to looking at how ugly segregation was and how discrimination was in the community after we got up large, but when we were small children, we didn't even think anything about it. I have some incidents that I remember very vividly from when I was a small child. My mother, in the community, was a very good cook, and people—a lot of people would come for her to make cakes for them, even white people. They would bring their kids with them, and we would play and have a good time, never think anything about I was black and they were white. But, when the cake was taken out of the pan we would all get the pan and we'd get any dough out of the pan. We never thought anything really about the color as such at that particular time.

However, as we grew older, we were in school and the things that we saw going on. We began to notice that there were differences, and of course when we would hear the stories that were happening to people in other places, then we knew that it was really bad.

Maybe I couldn't remember exactly the first time, but I know one of the first things that happened in Alabama that was really focused. That was when the "Scottsboro Boys" were arrested for, they were accused of raping two white women and this became such a world-wide thing. Course I was young at that

THE CHILDREN COMING ON . . .

particular time, but we were conscious of it, and we did what we could locally in the community to try to help the Scottsboro Boys. That was one of the first major things I know that happened, that I can remember. Of course, locally in the community there were men who were accused of raping white women and they were sentenced to the electric chair, and some were electrocuted for that. And then we began to look at the fact of what happened to black women when a white man raped her, or whatever happened. Nothing was ever done about it. Of course, that within itself began to make you really look at the picture of what was happening and know more. As we grew older then we found that these things were very prevalent in the community.

. . . Back in the late '30s and early '40s was the time when we had the Depression, and of course there were a lot of things that happened during the Depression, and before the Depression we had political things that were going on. But I can remember very vividly how the Depression came about and how people really suffered in the community because of lack of jobs, and they just didn't have anything. At that particular time, I think is when I remember most about politics is when President Roosevelt was really in his term that he served, and some of the things he did as President.

. . . Mr. E. D. Nixon and other members of the community who worked very hard to pull our people together . . . we always knew that we had terrible communities, you know places where our people were living. Very few places that we had that was very . . . places that you could look up to and feel that you had a good community and everything. Everywhere blacks were they were crowded in—and shotgun houses and alleys and that type of thing. When you looked at that and then you began to see what was happening. Because I never will forget when they built the first Project here. People were very happy that there was a place that they were building that people could have relative decency to live . . .

My early education when I first went to school, I was living out in the rural—that's where I lived—out beyond Highland Avenue. My first remembrance of going to school, it was a school called Canaan School. It was over in a community about five miles, I guess, from where we lived. We had to walk to school. But my mother was the type of mother, I think I said it a few minutes ago, that she was a religious woman, and she'd strive to do all that she could to give her children the best that she could afford at that particular time. So it was just two of us at home when I was growing up and getting in school because my older brothers and sisters were all married and out. But my younger brother and I were home, and mother put us in a private school. A Mr. Breedin who was principal of one of the city schools here, his wife ran a private school and my mother learned about that, and she put my brother and I in this private . . . and that was the first of me coming into a private school.

Alabama State at that time had a high school, junior high school, and elementary, but it was very hard for—especially people on the poor level—to get into Alabama State. Mama never was able to get us into Alabama State, but we went to this private school. After, I guess, about two years in this private school, my mother moved into the city and then she enrolled us in Booker Washington School, which was a city school. I guess not being satisfied, she learned about a school called the Montgomery Industrial School, which was Miss White's. A group of white teachers had came down from the North and ran this school for black girls. Of course, my mother got me into this school and that was where I went until I married. The school really closed in '27. The school had had many difficulties because at one time it had gotten burned because the same thing existed that these white women down here teaching black girls, and that was against the principles of the South. 'Course they had burned the school at one time, but Miss White—who was the principal of the school—began to get an age, and the teachers, you know, and they began to close the school, and the school really closed in 1927. In 1927 I married—out of junior high school. Of course, that was the extent of my education at that particular point. Of course, I've gone back to school since that time and furthered my education, but I still didn't go to college.

. . . The teachers that we had there were good teachers. What was being taught at that particular time, I think they did a good job with the students in getting it over to them. We had music—not instrumental music, but was taught music—notes and things like that. I never will forget our teacher Mrs. Lee.

. . . The Montgomery Industrial School—Miss White's—this was a school where black girls were really given an opportunity to get some of the best teaching that you could get. We had the type of instructors that, well, we used some local instructors because whenever there was a need for assistant teachers, local teachers were used. But most of the teachers who came down from Massachusetts, Boston, and up in that area of the country, they were called Quakers. They came here and set up this school to teach blacks. In this school we had some things that were given to us that I feel has helped us.

We were taught in Miss White's school that the color of your skin, the texture of your hair had nothing to do with your character. And that has stayed with me down through the years. And I firmly believe, I know now, that it really is true. That it has nothing to do with your character whatsoever. You can have lily white skin, blue eyes or green eyes or whatever kind of eyes, and if you're not right within, you're just not gon' be the right type of person. Your character doesn't deal with your skin color. They taught her those things and that we were just as good as anybody else, and we had very strict rules in this school. We wore uniforms, and we were identified because Alabama State—Normal as it was called at that time—their uniforms were blue, solid blue with white collars and cuffs. Ours was blue with white dots, white collars, and cuffs. You had to be immaculate going to school. If you came to school and you didn't look right, they would send you immediately to occupational therapy and you'd go down there and you'd get your uniform straightened out for you and then come back to class.

It was just some of the things that I feel made a lot of us have some things in us that maybe some of our other sisters didn't get. But I feel like it was really an advantage for persons who went to this school.

Some of the people who attended that school like Rosa Parks and I were classmates together in that school. Erna Allen Dungee and I were schoolmates. Her sister, Mahala, and Mahala is now an attorney recently elected as the president of the women's auxiliary to the American Bar Association. Mahala and I were classmates. Oh, there were any number of other persons—Mrs. Minnie Gaston was a student at that particular school. Several of us around the city at this particular time were students at that school, and we don't feel that we're any better than anybody else, we just felt like at that particular time in history we had an opportunity to get some of the advantages that some others maybe did not get.

If I can remember clearly, if there were vacancies and you applied, I don't think you were turned down for any reason other than you were given an opportunity if the vacancy allowed. They could only take so many girls, and of course when the role was filled they could not take any more. I don't think that there were any particular, you just had to be economically or educationally or any way, they just wanted the girls— to try to help the girls to develop.

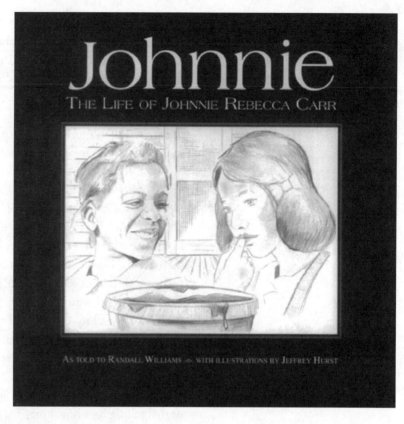

When I was out in the country, we had little country schools that we started out there because it was so far for the children to have to go, and we'd open a little country school out there. This is after I'm grown and I have a family. We had a PTA, and in our PTA meetings and getting together in the community, that was really my first kind of organizational thing other than the church. We learned then to get together meant strength. Since that time I have really learned what it means to have organizations. And that's why I fight so hard now for organizations although they may not be turning the world over, but keep organizations intact because when everything's happened, you already have your basic to work with and you don't have to go to work trying to get organized. This is something we need to do.

Well, the NAACP was really the first organization that I started working with that was on a local, state, and national level. One Sunday at church Mr. Birch, who was the manager of Atlanta Life Insurance Company, got up and said that they were having a membership drive, and he was in a contest. He wanted ten ladies in our church, which [was] Hall Street Baptist Church, to take one pack of those envelopes and solicit for him. Of course, I volunteered to solicit the ten memberships for him, but when I decided to solicit the ten memberships, I decided to go to the meeting so I could find out what the organization was all about. From that time on, I have been a part of the NAACP. I have served as the secretary of the NAACP locally. I have served as a supervisor of the youth council.

At that time, Mrs. Rosa Parks and I both were working with the organization. She wasn't working with it until she saw an article in the paper where they were having a meeting, and at this particular meeting Johnnie Carr—Johnnie Jordan I was at that time, because that was at the time of my first marriage—Johnnie Jordan was the secretary. She read it and she said, I wonder if that's the Johnnie I went to school with. She decided to go to the meeting to see if that was the Johnnie. So when she came to the meeting to find out if it was the person that she thought it was, she and I began to be together and she started working with the organization. From that time until the Movement we worked together.

. . . Mr. Nixon and I worked together on so many things. He *was* the person who we would call if we had a problem. I recall one instance when the city closed down all the stables around the city—this was long before the boycott—and they carried all the manure over to the park across the street from where I lived—they were going to make fertilizer out of it. But it caused such a smell—and flies. I didn't think it was right, but I just tried to put up with it. We had called the health department, but nothing had been done. Then one day, I was in cooking and the flies were all in the windows. And, seems like I just broke down and cried. It just didn't seem right that we should have to live with that kind of situation. So I called Mr. Nixon, and he answered the phone in that big deep voice.

"Nixon." And I said, "Mr. Nixon . . ."—and I told him what the problem was. And he thought it over for a moment and said, "Sue the city." And I started telling him how upset I was . . . and he broke in and said firmly, "File a law suit against the city." And at that time in the '40s we didn't have any black lawyers and so he told me which white lawyer to talk to. . . . And it got taken care of the day after they got the letter from the lawyer. The city came out and cleaned up all that mess.

. . . The Bus Protest grew out of what we called a swell of things that had happened, all of these things that I mentioned about—can't drink at the fountain, can't go to a restroom, can't ride this elevator, can't do this—had got through to enough people that they were really resenting things that were happening in the community. Therefore, when the time came . . . well, we had had two incidents before. Two young women had been arrested on the bus for refusing to give up their seat. One in particular was Miss Colvin. She was arrested for not giving up her seat, and she was fined. Nothing grew out of it. They had a meeting and they talked about it and raised money to help with whatever was involved. But when Mrs. Rosa Parks refused to get up off of her seat, and it was right across the street almost from where we are now, where she was riding the bus. She refused to get up off of her seat because when the busman, the driver, asked her to give this white man her seat, they arrested her. When they arrested her, someone got in touch with Mr. E. D. Nixon, and he and attorney Durr went down and got her out of jail.

When that happened, it just looked like something just broke in the community. When I say something broke in the community, it just seemed that people just said, Well this is it. We're just tired. Mr Nixon called me that night and said to me just like that, "Mrs. Carr." I said, "Yeah." "Well they put the wrong person in jail." I said, "Who they put in jail?" He said, "They arrested Rosa Parks." I said, "You don't mean to tell me that they arrested Rosa

THE CHILDREN COMING ON . . .

Parks?" He said, "Yes. They arrested Rosa Parks on the bus today. They put the wrong person in jail."

[EDITOR'S NOTE: The next day, Mrs. Parks had the following conversation, described by Rev. Bob Graetz, a white friend who lived around the corner on Cleveland Avenue in the parsonage of Trinity Lutheran Church. Rev. Graetz had heard "through the grapevine" about the proposed boycott but didn't yet know who had been arrested. "After exchanging greetings, I said, 'I just heard that someone was arrested on one of the buses Thursday.' 'That's right, Pastor Graetz.' 'And that we're supposed to boycott the buses on Monday to protest.' 'That's right, Pastor Graetz.' 'Do you know anything about it?' 'Yes, Pastor Graetz.' 'Do you know who was arrested?' 'Yes, Pastor Graetz.' 'Well, who was it?' There was a moment of silence. Then in a quiet, timid voice she replied, 'It was me, Pastor Graetz.'" (Page 54, *A White Preacher's Memoir: The Montgomery Bus Boycott*)]

From that time, he and others got together in the community, and there in the community at that time was Reverend Hubbard, Revered Wilson is still here, and Reverend Bennett at Mt. Zion, and so many of the other ministers. They came together and they started formulating, getting together to get a protest about her being arrested. But the protest that they had come up with was that they were just gonna stay off the bus one day—the day of the trial— which was December 5, 1955, and just ask everybody to stay off the bus that day in protest of Mrs. Rosa Parks being arrested.

Of course, they set the mass meeting for that night at Holt Street Baptist Church. When they had the trial, of course, they fined Mrs. Parks for refusing to give up her seat. Of course, it was appealed. But they went in the mass meeting, but leading up to that in the meetings that they had had. The first time that they wanted to notify the people to stay off the bus, they printed some little slips and asked everybody to pass them out door-to-door, because they knew everybody wasn't going to church, because the churches were the only thing that we had really to get over our message to the people. But anyway, in passing out the little slips, one person—it is said—carried one to the lady that she worked with, and said when she saw it, she said, "Oh, these niggers fixing to gon' start something," and she related it to some of the officials. I've heard a different version from that, but that is really the version that we got at the beginning that this is what happened.

Of course, when they were contacted, then there was a big spread in the paper that Sunday morning—it was blasted on the air that the blacks were fixing to boycott the buses and everything—publicity that we could never have paid for, we received. It helped, because that Monday morning when the buses started running, they were completely empty. In order to take care of the black people who would have ridden the bus that Monday, they put two policemen behind each bus as they went out on their route so they would protect the people if anybody was going to bother them about getting on the bus. And I said, well, the little slip of paper that we had, the minister in the pulpit on Sunday morning, the TV and the radio and the spread in the newspaper maybe didn't get to some people, but when they got out there and saw those two policemen behind the bus, they decided it was a no-no to ride the bus that day. We had all types of incentives to stay off the bus on Monday, December 5, 1955. What they did really played up for us what we did.

That Monday night at Holt Street Baptist Church there were so many people that they could no more get in the church than you could get out that window and walk on down to the first floor from the ninth floor where we are now. It was something else. And at that time, that's when Dr. King—in these meetings that they were having, they were trying to decide who would be the leader. Of course, there were a lot of people in the community who had been leading—Dr. Seay, Mr. Nixon and others who had been leading locally. So when they came to this particular point, Dr. King had just come into Montgomery as a new minister, and he was the person that they thought could do the leadership. He was elected to be the leader of the organization, and, of course, he *was* the person. I have said that God sent Moses to the children of Israel to get them out of Egypt. He sent Martin Luther King in this particular instance to lead our people. And he did do a magnificent job of leading our people. . . .

I did not know anything about Dr. King when he came to Montgomery. The first time that I saw him to know him, he was at the Metropolitan United Methodist Church, and he spoke there one Sunday afternoon. They brought him there as they do new ministers when they come in. There was an NAACP meeting that evening, and they presented him and he just got up and said a few words. Rosa Parks and I were sitting together in the church at the particular time and when he got up and started talking, and I told her—God, listen to that guy. I said, he's something else! Not thinking about a Movement or anything like that. But we could see something in him, the way he even delivered the few words—that he was really somebody that had something people had needed—and he gave it to them. . . .

It was just something like, you don't know what's magnetic unless you put something else to it, and it draws it. I really can't explain what it was about him. I don't, it wasn't, well he was a guy, a nice-looking guy but you wasn't looking for a person of good looks. It just seemed like the way he talked about persons and events and things that would make you know that he had something in him that could really help people—if he would just use it for that, and he did.

Timeline of the Montgomery Bus Boycott

1896—U.S. Supreme Court rules in *Plessy v. Ferguson* that "separate but equal" segregated public facilities are constitutional

1901—Alabama Constitution is rewritten to disfranchise almost all black and many poor white voters

April 15, 1945—Alabama Conference of NAACP Branches formed at Dexter Avenue Baptist Church

1945—Black World War II veterans begin to push for greater involvement in local citizenship

July 24, 1945—Attorney Arthur Madison disbarred as a result of pressure brought against him for attempting to register blacks to vote in Montgomery

December 1945—E. D. Nixon elected president of Montgomery NAACP

1948—E. D. Nixon serves as state NAACP president

1953—Women's Political Council members meet with City Commission to protest treatment of blacks on city buses

1954—E. D. Nixon becomes first black in 20th century to seek public office in Montgomery

1954—U.S. Supreme Court declares segregated education unconstitutional in *Brown v. Board of Education* decision

1954—Montgomery's first black police officers are hired

February 23, 1955—Black leaders meet at Ben Moore Hotel with white candidates for the Montgomery City Commission; the meeting sparks a white backlash

March 2, 1955 — Claudette Colvin arrested for violating segregated seating ordinance

December 1, 1955—Rosa Parks arrested for violating segregated seating ordinance

December 1, 1955—JoAnn Robinson and other members of Women's Political Council compose and mimeograph leaflet calling for boycott of city buses

December 2-3, 1955—Leaflets by the Women's Political Council distributed throughout black community.

December 2, 1955—E. D. Nixon calls black leaders to Dexter Avenue Baptist Church for a meeting to endorse bus boycott.

December 4, 1955—Sermons in black churches call for observance of the boycott.

December 5, 1955—The boycott is an almost total success.

December 5, 1955—Mrs. Parks is convicted and fined $10.

December 5, 1955—Local black leaders meet at Mount Zion A.M.E. Zion Church to form the Montgomery Improvement Association; Martin Luther King Jr. is elected president.

December 5, 1955—King leads the first weekly mass meeting; 5,000 attend at Holt Street Baptist Church.

December 1955 to January 1956—Meetings with City Commissioners to discuss black grievances over buses result in no progress; boycott continues.

January 30, 1956—Dexter Avenue Baptist Church parsonage, the home of Martin Luther King Jr., is bombed.

February 2, 1956—Attorney Fred Gray files federal lawsuit, *Browder v. Gayle,* challenging constitutionality of segregated bus seating.

March 1956—Ninety-eight black leaders indicted for violating anti-boycott statute.

May 11, 1956—*Browder v. Gayle* lawsuit is tried in Montgomery federal court.

June 1, 1956—Attorney General John Patterson enjoins NAACP from operating in Alabama.

June 5, 1956—Decision written by U.S. District Judge Frank M. Johnson Jr. finds for plaintiffs in *Browder v. Gayle* and holds segregated bus seating to be unconstitutional; city appeals.

August 25, 1956—Parsonage of Trinity Lutheran Church is bombed.

November 5, 1956—City of Montgomery sues Montgomery Improvement Association seeking to enjoin MIA's car pool.

November 13, 1956—U.S. Supreme Court upholds Judge Johnson's decision in *Browder v. Gayle;* city officials ask for rehearing, which is denied.

December 20, 1956—City officials are served copy of Supreme Court's decision and reluctantly accept it.

December 20, 1956—At mass meeting at Holt Street Baptist Church, Martin Luther King Jr. announces that boycott will end.

December 21, 1956—King, E. D. Nixon, Rosa Parks, and other boycott leaders ceremoniously board buses for first time in 381 days.

December 23, 1956—Shotgun blasts fired into Dexter Avenue parsonage.

December 28, 1956—Buses fired on by snipers.

January 10, 1957—Four churches and two homes in the black community are bombed.

January 27, 1957—Two bombs go off in the black community; a third at the Dexter parsonage fails to explode.

PART 2

THE CITY

By J. Mills Thornton III

From

*"Challenge and Response
in the Montgomery Bus Boycott
of 1955–1956"*

Thornton is author of *Power and Politics in a Slave Society* (LSU:) and *Segregation and Community: Montgomery, Birmingham, and Selma, 1945-1970*, forthcoming from University of Alabama Press.

1

Politics in Montgomery

Shortly after five o'clock on the evening of December 1, 1955, Mrs. Raymond A. Parks boarded the Cleveland Avenue bus of the Montgomery City Lines at Court Square in Montgomery, Alabama. She sat next to the window on the side opposite the driver, in the first row of seats in the black section of the bus. The bus driver, James F. Blake, wrenched the yellow bus into gear and headed it up Montgomery Street towards its stop in front of the Empire Theater—towards that moment when Mrs. Raymond A. Parks and James F. Blake would change the course of American history.[1] In order to understand how their disagreement could have had such an effect, one must understand the context of past experiences and relationships that shaped the reactions of Montgomerians to it.

At the end of 1955, municipal politics in Montgomery was in the midst of a fundamental transformation. For essentially the preceding half-century, Montgomery had been ruled by the Gunter Machine, headed for most of that time by William A. Gunter, Jr., the city's mayor from 1910 to 1915 and from 1919 to his death in 1940. Mayor Gunter had come to power after more than a dozen years of bitter factional warfare between two groups of the city's wealthy older families. Thereafter, he turned back all challenges to his rule. He could always rely upon the unwavering support of the city's morning newspaper, the *Montgomery Advertiser*, whose editor, Grover C. Hall, Sr., was one of his closest advisers, and upon the allegiance of the majority of Montgomery's older families. In the final two decades of his life, he also had the unanimous support of city employees, whom—as a result of an act which he pushed through the state legislature—he could in effect hire and fire at will.[2]

If there were no successful challenges to the Machine after 1919, however, the unsuccessful challenges were many. During the 1920s Gunter's uncompromising opposition to the Ku Klux Klan made him a special object of Klan hatred. His repeated expressions of disapproval for the prohibition experiment placed the Anti-Saloon League in the ranks of his enemies, and fundamentalists condemned him for his generally lax enforcement of public morality. During the 1930s he turned the city government into a relief operation,

[1] *Montgomery Advertiser,* December 2, 1955; Montgomery *Alabama Journal,* December 5, 1955; Trial Transcript, *Rosa Parks v. City of Montgomery* (Records of the Alabama Court of Criminal Appeals, Office of the Clerk, Supreme Court Building, Montgomery), 9. This article has greatly benefited from interviews conducted with the following people on the dates noted: Ralph D. Abernathy, February 28, 1979; Joe F. Bear, March 9, 1979; Eugene W. Carter, October 16, 1978; Jack Crenshaw, July 15, 1977; Virginia F. Durr, May 2, 1979; C.T. Fitzpatrick, January 11, 1979; Fred D. Gray, October 17, 1978; Mark W. Johnston, July 19, 1977; Walter J. Knabe, August 5, 1977; Rufus A. Lewis, July 27, 1977; William V. Lyerly, September 2, 1976; William R. Lynn, December 29, 1976; Edgar D. Nixon, August 2, 1977 Rosa L. Parks, May 22, 1978; James G. Pruett, Sr., January 2, 1977; Jo Ann Robinson, January 27, 1978; William F. Thetford, September 4, 1976. At the request of Mr. Pruett, I have regarded his interview as confidential.

[2] Thomas M. Owen, *History of Alabama and Dictionary of Alabama Biography* (4 vols., Chicago, 1921), III, 716; Montgomery *Advertiser,* April 1, 2, 1911; May 18, 20, 1919; *Acts of Alabama,* 1911, pp. 289-315, 1915, pp. 52-76, 1919, pp. 97-102; *House Journal,* 1915, pp. 1461-66; *Senate Journal,* 1915, pp. 1144-49, 1170-71, 1173-75.

putting hundreds on the public payroll and earning the bitter hostility of fiscal conservatives for unbalancing the city budgets. At the time of his death in 1940, he was admired by much of Montgomery's upper class and by large numbers of the city's unemployed. But he was also detested by many owners of small businesses and conservative citizens, strict Baptists and Methodists, and others to whom his values—rooted in the easygoing tolerance and aristocratic paternalism of his planter and Episcopalian background—were anathema.

After Gunter's death, the Machine spent the next decade searching for a leader. The mayor was immediately succeeded by Cyrus B. Brown, who had long been one of Gunter's most powerful lieutenants and was at the time president of the Montgomery County governing body, the Board of Revenue. But Brown, an elderly man, died in 1944. David Dunn, who had earlier been a political protege of former Governor Bibb Graves, obtained Machine endorsement to succeed Brown but resigned in 1946 to go into private business.

The mayoralty then passed to City Attorney John L. Goodwyn, a cousin of Gunter's wife, whom Gunter had appointed city attorney in 1930. Goodwin resigned in 1951 to accept a position in the state government; this position led eventually to his being appointed to the state Supreme Court. Goodwin was succeeded by William A. "Tacky" Gayle, a Machine stalwart who had been a member of the City Commission since 1935.[3]

During this decade of rapid changes in leadership, the Machine grew steadily weaker. The rapidity of these changes itself contributed to the process. Another factor in the Machine's decline was Gunter's penchant for surrounding himself with colorless, if often quite competent, administrators. Early in the century, the Gunter forces had secured the abolition of the mayor-council form of government for the more easily controlled three-man commission.

In addition to the mayor, there was a commissioner of public affairs, who administered the police and fire departments, and a commissioner of public works, who had charge of parks, libraries, street maintenance, and garbage collection. During the 1930s, Gunter turned to two retired military men to fill these posts. Gayle, a veteran of World War I, had subsequently served as Alabama's adjutant general and had returned to active duty in World War II. In 1943, while serving in Britain as an air force colonel, Gayle was elected to his third term on the City Commission in absentia. The other commissioner, General William P. Screws, had been the commander of the Alabama contingent in the famed Rainbow Division during World War I. This tradition continued when George L. Cleere, another former state adjutant general, was selected to succeed Gayle as commissioner of public works when Gayle became mayor in 1951. These men, for all their efficiency, were by no means Gunter's equals as politicians, and without him they had trouble in holding the voters' affection.

By far the most important reason for the Machine's decline, however, was the changing character of the city's population and residence patterns. During the first half of the twentieth century, Montgomery grew rapidly, at an average of 30 percent a decade. This steady growth concealed after 1940 an important change in the city's racial composition. In 1910, as Gunter was first

[3] *Montgomery Advertiser*, March 15, 16, 1943, August 9, 12, September 5, 6, 1944. March 8, May 5,9, 1946, March 18, 1947, March 19, 20, 1951; Montgomery *Alabama Journal*, May 9, 1946, March 18, 1947. Dunn had resigned in order to permit returning soldiers to participate in the choice of their mayor—one of his campaign pledges in 1944—but had declined himself to become a candidate in the special election "as I am entering private business here in Montgomery."

[4] The figures as to churches were developed from Montgomery city directories. After 1952, city directories ceased to designate their entries by race. Dalraida and Chisholm were not within the city limits at this period.

taking office as mayor, Montgomery's white population for the first time achieved parity in numbers with blacks. During the remainder of the Gunter years, the relative proportion of the two races remained stable at 55 percent white and 45 percent black. But after Mayor Gunter's death, the proportions began to change, under the impact both of increased black emigration to the North and of increased rural white movement into the city. In 1950, Montgomery was 60 percent white and 40 percent black; the white population grew by 47 percent during the 1940s and the black by only 23 percent. This trend continued during the 1950s. By 1955, Montgomery contained about 120,000 people, of whom some 63 percent were white and 37 percent were black.

The increasing white population meant that the number of residents in the city who could vote was growing even faster than was the population at large. The Machine had no hold upon either the gratitude or the affection of many of these new voters. Moreover, changing residence patterns reinforced this development. Resentments of Gunter's policies on the part of the lower middle class had existed in the 1920s and 1930s, but the resentment had found little institutional support. The town was small and could sustain few institutions alternative to the ones controlled by the well-to-do. During the 1940s and early 1950s, the development of housing subdivisions on the edges of the city with small homes intended for the white lower middle class effectively separated that group from the institutional control of the upper class and the upper middle class. In the eastern section of Montgomery—Capitol Heights, Dalraida, and Chisholm—there developed churches whose congregations did not contain a mix of classes and within which leadership could therefore fall to the lower middle class. In 1931, for instance, there were only seven white Baptist churches in the city, and in 1940 there were still only eleven, but by 1952 there were twenty. The number of white churches belonging to the Pentecostal sects, always a refuge for poorer elements of the population, also advanced rapidly. In 1931, white Pentecostal congregations constituted less than a fourth of the city's white churches, but by 1940 they were a third of the total, and by 1952 almost 40 percent of it.[4]

Similarly, East Montgomery developed alternative men's clubs; the Lions Club and the Exchange Club, for instance, both established separate East Montgomery units, leaving the downtown clubs in the hands of the businessmen who had dominated them. The growth to the east also demanded new schools, and with them came PTAs to be run by men and women unlikely to be leaders in a PTA in which the various classes co-mingled—as had been the case with the PTAs of the few schools in the earlier, smaller city. Power in these earlier organizations had gravitated toward social leaders. East Montgomery also developed separate shopping and entertainment areas. In these and countless other ways the simple growth of the city gave the white lower middle class a separate community life and allowed it some measure of self-consciousness as a unit.

Meanwhile, this institutional "de-intermixture" of white classes was proceeding from the other side as well when subdivisions for wealthier residents were developed in South Montgomery, particularly in the Cloverdale section.

THE CHILDREN COMING ON . . .

Between 1951 and 1954, no less than sixty new subdivisions were completed in the East and in South Montgomery, and in 1955 another thirty-three were reported to be in the planning stages.[5]

[5] *Montgomery Advertiser*, February 20, March 15, 1955.

CHAPTER

2

"Never good for a city"

The first hint of what these developments portended for the Machine came in the city elections of 1947, when General William P. Screws, a member of the City Commission since 1931, was challenged by a young East Montgomery schoolteacher and football coach, Earl D. James. James's connection with physical education at Capitol Heights Junior High School placed him in an excellent position to capitalize upon the emerging sense of community in that section of the city. Screws beat James in Cloverdale, while James swamped all of his opponents in Capitol Heights and also ran well in an older, lower middle class ward, Oak Park. James thus erected a majority upon the basis not previously seen in Montgomery politics. The division between South Montgomery and East Montgomery that was demonstrated in these returns was to become characteristic of municipal elections for the next thirty years.[6]

Nevertheless, the Machine did not yet foresee its doom. It still controlled two of the Commission's three seats. James proved an able and relatively tractable official. He was elected to a second term in 1951 but resigned in 1953 to enter business. In the special election to choose James's successor, the newly emerging shape of city politics first became completely clear. State Representative Joe M. Dawkins gathered endorsements for his candidacy from Montgomery's most prominent citizens. In the first primary, Dawkins carried every precinct in the city and missed winning without a run-off by only 523 votes. In the second primary, Dawkins faced Dave Birmingham, a man whose candidacy was regarded by the city's upper class as a bad joke. Birmingham had been an early and zealous supporter of former Governor James E. Folsom, and he shared much of Folsom's aggressive hostility to the wealthy. Birmingham was a classic demagogue. During his campaign, he suggested that the chlorination of the city's drinking water had caused the preceding summer's devastating polio epidemic. He charged—contrary to well-documented fact—that the red color that sometimes appeared in the water was not iron but mud. The burden of Birmingham's appeal was an attack on the Machine. Dawkins was, Birmingham said, "hogtied to the old ring masters . . . It is never good for a city to let one 'click' [sic] completely dominate it. Progress would stagnate." He opposed appointive municipal boards: "The ring masters through

[6] *Montgomery Alabama Journal,* March 18, 1947; *Montgomery Advertiser,* August 28, 1953, October 28, 1955.

the board masters are strangling you to death with taxes without any responsibility to you as to how they will spend this tax money." He unremittingly attacked "that cesspool of gangsters at City Hall" and particularly decried the taxes that had been levied in order to finance the extension of services to new areas of the rapidly growing city.

Birmingham beat Dawkins in the run-off by a margin of 53 percent to 47 percent. Dawkins carried the wealthier precincts; his best ward was Cloverdale. Birmingham swept the lower middle class and lower class white precincts; he ran best in Capitol Heights and did well in precincts in which a substantial minority of the voters was black. The meaning of this election for the fortunes of the disintegrating Machine was unmistakable. *Advertiser* editor Grover C. Hall, Jr., commented that, with Birmingham a member of the Commission, "The City Hall is going to be notably different for the foreseeable future." Doubtless, Hall had no real conception of just how right he was.[7]

The principal reason for the Machine's demise was the growing independence of the white lower middle class. Politicians called this phenomenon "the silent vote." In a 1955 article, the *Advertiser*'s city editor, Joe Azbell, explained the meaning of the term. In the 1920s and 1930s, in a city dominated by personal acquaintance, family alliances, and personal favors rather than issues really decided the outcome of elections. But the growth of the city had added many voters to the rolls who were not members of the family alliances. The abolition of the city spoils system in favor of appointment by civil service examination had deprived the Machine of much of its power to bind voters to it by favors. By 1955, Azbell noted, voters lacked personal knowledge of the candidates and had thus begun to make voting decisions on the basis of issues, as filtered through the mass media. Politicians therefore lacked any real sense of where the voters were moving until the election returns were counted. In 1953, 1954, and 1955, knowledgeable observers had repeatedly guessed wrong about the election outcome because the voters no longer were members of cousinries or others blocks whose behavior could be predicted. Of the 1955 municipal elections, Azbell commented, "No one seemed to care how the Hills were moving. No one seemed concerned about the political blocs. But twenty years ago a political observer would not dare comment on an election without first determining how the blocs were going. For the first time in city political history, ring politics played no important part in the local election because the old ring politics has been overshadowed by a growing city where there is no control or method of determining how the voters will cast their ballot." As a result, city administrators feared their new constituents.[8]

If the growing independence of the white lower middle class was the principal factor that had altered the structure of municipal politics, another factor of almost equal significance was the newly important black vote. The white lower middle class might be unfamiliar to the politicians, but the black community was virtual *terra incognita*. The state Democratic primary of 1946 represented the first primary in which blacks could legally vote; earlier such elections had been conducted under the white primary rule, which the Supreme Court had forbidden in 1944. Because they could now participate in the only elections that mattered in Alabama, blacks sought to register in in-

[7] *Montgomery Advertiser,* September 15, October 3, 4, 18, 24, 27, November 1, 3, 4, 1953.

[8] *Ibid.,* March 27, 1955; cf. May 12, 1954.

9 *Ibid.*, May 8, 1946, November 9, 1953, March 25, 1955; *Smith v. Allwright,* 321 U.S. 649.

creasing numbers during the late 1940s and early 1950s, particularly in the cities. The number of blacks registered in Montgomery grew slowly but steadily, and by 1955, 7.55 percent of the city's 22,210 registered voters were black. This percentage was well above the 5 percent ratio statewide. Moreover, in some wards black voters represented a substantial proportion of the total: 31 percent in Beat 7W, almost 25 percent in Beat 2, and 20 percent in Beat 6. Seven-and-a-half percent is quite a small figure, but given the near equiponderance in the rivalry between South Montgomery and East Montgomery during these years, blacks could easily represent a balance of power.[9]

THE CHILDREN COMING ON . . .

CHAPTER

3

"The first black"

The most important black spokesman in making demands upon the newly constituted City Commission was Edgar D. Nixon, a sleeping-car porter who was also president of the Montgomery local of the International Brotherhood of Sleeping Car Porters. Moving beyond his union power base, Nixon in the late 1940s and early 1950s had become more and more publicly active in demanding amelioration of conditions for members of his race. Throughout these years he was the dominant figure in the Montgomery chapter of the NAACP and was state president of that organization in 1948–49. He was also president of the Montgomery chapter of the Alabama Progressive Democratic Association, which had been organized during the 1940s as a black alternative to the regular party apparatus. In 1954, he created a great stir in Montgomery as a candidate for the County Democratic Executive Committee, the first black in living memory to seek public office. Though he lost to a white candidate, Joseph W. Carroll, he won more than 42 percent of the vote in the precinct, only a fourth of whose voters were black. In 1955, Nixon sought unsuccessfully to purchase a ticket to a Jefferson-Jackson Day dinner in Birmingham; the evening's principal speaker, Governor G. Mennen Williams of Michigan, abruptly canceled his appearance in protest against Nixon's exclusion. Such highly visible efforts made Nixon the best-known "activist" in Montgomery and gave him a considerable following in the black community.[10]

Equally as prominent in the dealings with the City Commission were two other blacks, Rufus A. Lewis and Mrs. Jo Ann Robinson. A former football coach at Alabama State College, Lewis was at the time a successful businessman and the chairman of the Citizens' Steering Committee, a group that had been formed in the fall of 1952 to press for better treatment for blacks. Mrs. Robinson, an English teacher at Alabama State College, was the moving spirit behind the black Women's Political Council, a group organized in 1949 to urge black women to register to vote; thereafter, the Council became the most militant and uncompromising organ of the black community. Led by Mrs. Robinson, Mrs. Mary Fair Burks, and Mrs. Thelma Glass, all of the Alabama State College faculty, and Mrs. A. Wayman West, Jr., the wife of a

[10] *Montgomery Advertiser,* February 6, March 21, April 20, May 6, 1954, September 23, 30, 1955; Montgomery *Alabama Tribune,* September 30, October 14, 1955; Montgomery *Alabama Journal,* February 2, 1956; Clifford J. Durr to Hubert T. Delaney, September 4, 1955, Durr to Herbert H. Lehman, March 25, 1957, both in Clifford J. Durr Papers, Alabama State Department of Archives and History, Montgomery; Thomas J. Gilliam, "The Montgomery Bus Boycott of 1955-1956" (M.A. thesis, Auburn University, 1968).

[11-12]Nixon today believes that he may have been counted out in the executive committee race (interview, August 2, 1977).

[11] Trial Transcript, *M. L. King, Jr. v. State of Alabama* (Records of the Alabama Court of Criminal Appeals, Office of the Clerk, Supreme Court Building, Montgomery) 256-57, 349-59; Martin Luther King, Jr., *Stride Toward Freedom: The Montgomery Story* (New York, 1958), 34, 73; *Montgomery Alabama Tribune,* December 23, 1955. Mrs. Burks and Mrs. Robinson organized the Council when they were refused membership in the League of Women Voters. Mrs. Robinson suggests that black women were able to be more aggressive in dealing with whites than were black men because in the environment created by segregation, women were under somewhat fewer strictures (interview, January 27, 1978). Lewis had been employed by the Montgomery Board of Education at the end of World War II to organize classes under the GI Bill for returning black veterans, and the veterans whom he taught became the backbone of his organization (interview, July 27, 1977).

[12] *Montgomery Advertiser,* November 7, December 17, 1953, April 15, 17, 23, June 20, 1954; Juliette Morgan to William A. Gayle, July 13, 1955, Juliette Morgan Scrapbook, Alabama State Department of Archives and History, Montgomery.

dentist, and sometimes aided by the more moderate Federation of Negro Women's Clubs, the Council repeatedly protested to the City Commission against discrimination and injustice in Montgomery. Indeed, with exceptions such as Nixon and Lewis, the blacks who addressed complaints to the City Commission in this period usually were women.[11]

The election of Dave Birmingham encouraged these groups for the first time to seek redress from the city government for longstanding grievances: the lack of black policemen, the inadequacy of parks and playgrounds in black sections of the city, and the conditions on the city buses. Immediately after Birmingham's election, the Montgomery County Grand Jury and the *Montgomery Advertiser* had both urged the city to join Dothan, Anniston, and Talladega in hiring black policemen. Possibly supporters of the Machine saw this action as a way to cope with Birmingham's popularity in the black community. But the two Machine commissioners apparently remained dubious. After Birmingham's inauguration, a delegation of black leaders met with the Commission; at this meeting, Birmingham extracted from his colleagues a promise to hire black officers if funds could be found to pay their salaries. Birmingham continued to press the proposal and finally, in early May 1954, succeeded in obtaining the addition of four blacks to the force. Their hiring caused consternation among the city's extreme segregationists, whose resentment expressed itself two years later, during the boycott, when the home of one of the four, Patrolman Arthur G. Worthy, became a target for bombers. In the summer of 1955, Police Chief Goodwin J. Ruppenthal sought to placate still hostile citizens by reassuring them that the new policemen were "just niggers doing a nigger's job."[12] But the doubts of many Montgomerians were not so easily assuaged, and the controversy rendered Birmingham's two colleagues increasingly unwilling to join him in taking other similar actions. The Machine could not afford to alienate either black or white segregationist voters. This difficulty virtually immobilized the two Machine commissioners on every racial issue from late 1953 through early 1955, as the city prepared for the crucial municipal elections of late March 1955. In addition, their position was rendered even more awkward by the considerable heightening of white fears and black hopes that followed the Supreme Court's school integration decision in mid-May 1954.

Meanwhile, no such hesitation bound Birmingham or the black leadership. The question of parks in black areas escalated to a new level of public controversy in January 1955, when a delegation from the Women's Political Council appeared at a City Commission meeting to urge the appointment of a black to the city Parks and Recreation Board and to suggest Council member Mrs. A. Wayman West, Jr., for the position. Commissioner Birmingham immediately moved that the next vacancy go to a black, but Mayor Gayle persuaded him to withdraw the motion until a vacancy actually occurred. The mayor, who had actively supported a city program under which three new playgrounds for blacks had been recently built, assured the delegation that its request would be given every consideration when there was a vacancy. He continued his effort to define a medial position later in the same week when he appeared before a large group of blacks gathered to celebrate the inaugura-

THE CHILDREN COMING ON . . .

tion of Governor James E. Folsom and there praised the work of the city's black policemen. But the question of black representation on the Parks and Recreation Board could not be dismissed so easily. It was to become a principal issue in the city elections in March. In August, Commissioner Birmingham, now a lame duck, offered a motion to expand the Parks and Recreation Board from five to seven members and to designate the two places for blacks, but Gayle and Cleere voted the resolution down. However, the mayor in July and the Parks and Recreation Board in September assured angry black delegations that if the city's voters would approve the proposed issuance of a million dollars in park bonds, significant improvements in Negro parks would immediately be forthcoming.[13]

[13] *Montgomery Advertiser,* December 20, 1953, January 19, July 20, August 10, September 14, 1955; Montgomery *Alabama Tribune,* January 28, August 19, 1955. The *Advertiser* alleged editorially that Birmingham's August resolution was merely the opening gun in his rumored race for a seat on the County Board of Revenue. At the July meeting with the blacks, Cleere and Birmingham almost came to blows and had to be separated by the mayor. The land that was promised as the site of a large new Negro park at the September meeting ultimately became a parking lot for a white football stadium.

CHAPTER

4

"Dealings with the city"

While the public was concerned with the issues of black policemen and black membership on the Parks and Recreation Board, tension over racial relations on the city's buses had quietly been mounting. At the end of 1953, encouraged by Birmingham's recent election, the Women's Political Council met with the City Commission to lodge three complaints: that blacks sometimes had to stand beside empty seats, in cases where the black section was filled but the white section was not; that black passengers were compelled to get on at the front door to pay their fare and then to get off and to reboard at the back door to take a seat, rather than being permitted simply to walk down the aisle of the bus; and that buses stopped at every corner in white neighborhoods but only at every other corner in black neighborhoods. Allegations of discourtesy by drivers and of buses' passing by waiting black passengers were also made. The meeting was inconclusive, but representatives of the bus lines, who were present, evidently offered to investigate specific charges of discourtesy. Several months later, in the spring of 1954, the Women's Political Council again met with the Commission and representatives of the bus company to reiterate its three complaints and to offer a list of specific instances of abuse by bus drivers. At this meeting, the delegation from the Political Council was accompanied by Rufus Lewis representing the Citizens' Steering Committee, by a delegation from the Federation of Negro Women's Clubs, and by a large group representing black trade union locals. At this meeting, as at the earlier one, the principal spokesman for the blacks was Jo Ann Robinson of the Political Council.

As a result of this meeting, the problem of buses' stopping only at every other corner in black areas was remedied. Addressing the issue of seating, the Commission, on the advice of City Attorney Walter Knabe and bus company attorney Jack Crenshaw, informed the blacks that it was legally powerless to do anything about the problem of black passengers' being compelled to stand beside empty seats. The city ordinance and the state statute on the subject were both read aloud to the petitioners. The meeting was evidently a stormy one. Subsequently, Mayor Gayle testified that several days later, Mrs. Robinson called him angrily "and said they would just show me, they were going in the front door and sitting wherever they pleased." . . . There the matter rested until the following spring.[14]

. . . Meantime, the elections that could kill the already moribund Machine were approaching. Gayle and Cleere both sought reelection. Gayle's only opponent was Harold McGlynn, a candy wholesaler who was a political associate of Commissioner Birmingham. Cleere's principal opposition came from Frank Parks, an East Montgomery interior decorator who was a former Grand Master of Alabama's Masons. Parks set out to create an electoral coalition like that which had enabled Birmingham to upset Dawkins a year and a half earlier. Though Gayle and Cleere supported each other, and Birmingham supported McGlynn and Parks, it is unclear whether or not Gayle and Cleere supported one of the candidates opposing Birmingham; at any rate, they did not do so publicly. Birmingham drew two principal opponents. Sam B. Stearns, the owner of a downtown parking garage and a nephew of a former Montgomery County sheriff, ran a vigorous and well-financed campaign, but the returns showed him much less popular than observers had thought. The real threat to the incumbent was former State Representative Clyde C. Sellers, a resident of South Montgomery and the owner of an exterminating business. Sellers effectively emphasized his extensive experience in law enforcement; he had joined the state Highway Patrol shortly after its formation, had worked his way up through its ranks, and in 1945 had been appointed director of the department by Governor Chauncey Sparks. His four years in the state legislature also strengthened his credentials. That he had been a star football player for Auburn University in the 1920s gave him additional popularity. But the issue that was to carry him to victory was provided by the events of the canvass.

Birmingham launched a typically demogogic campaign. His two colleagues on the Commission had voted to increase the city sewerage fee in order to finance the extension of sewer mains into the Allendale-Wildwood section, a South Montgomery area. Birmingham denounced this decision as class legislation and demanded that the wealthy homeowners in the section pay for the sewers themselves. Frank Parks loudly echoed this argument. Birmingham revived his accusation that chlorination of the water supply was dangerous; he alleged as proof that city water would kill Camellia bushes. He also charged that Gayle and Cleere might have favored the construction of a city sewage treatment plant only in order to make a private profit by selling the plant's effluent for fertilizer. With such allegations Birmingham hoped to hold, and Parks to build, constituencies of whites of the lower class and the lower middle class. McGlynn refused to stoop to this level, and perhaps for that reason his campaign against Gayle never really gained momentum. McGlynn did join Birmingham and Parks in a strong effort to gain the allegiance of the black vote.[15]

As the campaign of 1955 began, black leaders hoped to use the black balance of power between South Montgomery and East Montgomery to extract real concessions from the candidates. They had just passed through a year in which the city government had shown unprecedented willingness to listen to their proposals. Birmingham, Parks, and McGlynn were eager for

[14] Trial Transcript, *King v. State*, 141, 256-57, 349-59; *Montgomery Advertiser*, April 6, 1954.

[15] *Montgomery Advertiser*, February 1, 6, 9, 13, 20, 27, 28, March 10, 13, 16, 20, 23, 24, 27, 1955.

[16] 1956 Montgomery City Directory; Montgomery Advertiser, May 9, 1954, February 1, 9, 1955. An additional highly visible alteration in race relations, though one unconnected with politics, was the hiring in the winter of 1953–54 of black players for the city's professional baseball team.

[17] Montgomery Advertiser, February 9, 16, March 16, 1955, January 13, 1956.

black support. One of Birmingham's opponents, Stearns, was equally as willing to seek black votes. Nor, indeed, were Gayle and Cleere hostile. Though more reticent than were their opponents about openly campaigning for black ballots, still both men were racial moderates. The remnants of the Machine that they represented could command a certain residue of good will in the black community. Mayor Gunter's actions in the 1920s and 1930s had endeared him to many blacks, and after World War II the Machine-dominated city government had constructed a number of low-rent public housing projects for poor blacks. By 1955, the Montgomery Housing Authority, which was headed by the late Mayor Gunter's son-in-law Charles P. Rogers, administered four such developments and had a fifth in the planning stages. Its public housing record was not an unmixed asset for the Machine, however, because many blacks resented the demolition of their homes and their removal into crowded apartments, however modern.[16]

All of these circumstances so emboldened the black leaders that they decided in February to hold a public meeting in order to question the various Commission candidates about their stands on racial issues. The candidates subsequently also appeared before organized labor and the Junior Chamber of Commerce.[17] But the spectacle of office seekers appearing before blacks to submit to interrogation was a sight for which the electorate was unprepared.

The meeting, held under the auspices of Nixon's Progressive Democratic Association, convened in the Ben Moore Hotel, the city's only black hotel, on the evening of February 23. All of the candidates were present. The session commenced with Nixon's distributing to them a questionnaire asking their position on a number of specific black grievances. The first area of complaint on the list was "the present bus situation. Negroes have to stand over empty seats of city buses, because the first ten seats are reserved for whites who sometimes never ride. We wish to fill the bus from the back toward the front until all seats are taken. This is done in Atlanta, Georgia; Mobile, Alabama; and in most of our larger southern cities." Next came requests that a black be appointed to the Parks and Recreation Board and that blacks be considered for all municipal boards. The third subject mentioned was the lack of middle-class housing subdivisions for relatively well-to-do blacks. The authors of the questionnaire had been upset by the city's decision a week earlier to forbid the development of such an area because of the protests of neighboring whites. The forth plea was that qualified black applicants be considered for civil service jobs with the city. "Everybody cannot teach," the questionnaire noted, in reference to the limited professional opportunities available to Montgomery's middle-class blacks. The document concluded with three complaints about the inadequacy of city services in black neighborhoods. It asked for the installation of more fireplugs in these sections, the extension of sewer mains to eliminate outdoor privies, and the widening and paving of streets and the addition of curbing.

In their responses, Birmingham, McGlynn, and Parks all agreed to appoint a black member of the Parks and Recreation Board. Stearns, who had adopted the strategy of attempting to defeat Birmingham by outbidding him for the allegiance of the city's various groups, also agreed, and added a pro-

THE CHILDREN COMING ON . . .

posal for a sixteen-member all-black advisory board as an adjunct of the Parks Board. The press reported that black leaders were as a result closely divided as to whether they should endorse Birmingham or Stearns. Gayle and Cleere remained noncommittal on the Parks Board issue. Sellers gave a general talk that did not speak to any of the points in the questionnaire; he said later that he did not see the document until the end of the meeting. Accounts of the session do not indicate any reply by any of the candidates to the questionnaire's proposal on bus seating.[18]

After the candidates had completed their presentations, the meeting adjourned, but its repercussions were still being felt years later. Clyde Sellers quickly saw that the black proposals and their deferential handling by his two opponents presented him with the issue that would allow him to win a majority. It appeared that Stearns and Birmingham were going to divide the black vote. Sellers, as a South Montgomerian, could count on a large vote from that section in response to Birmingham's vociferous attacks on its residents. Previously, though, there had seemed to be no way to cut into Birmingham's solid following in East Montgomery. Now, demagogic exploitation of racial tensions promised to counter Birmingham's exploitation of class tensions and thus to capture support in the eastern wards. During March, before the election on the 21st, Sellers made the most blatantly and insistently racist addresses heard in Montgomery since the days of J. Johnston Moore, the Ku Klux Klan's candidate against Mayor Gunter in the 1920s. Sellers converted the Ben Moore Hotel meeting into the principal issue of the canvass. He answered the questionnaire point-by-point in his speeches and advertisements. He asserted flatly that the blacks' bus seating proposal would violate state law—not bothering to explain how, in that case, the system could be used in Mobile. He pledged himself to oppose the appointment of blacks to city boards. To the request that qualified blacks be allowed to apply for civil service jobs, he said, "If the commission were to comply with this request, it would be only a short time before Negroes would be working along side of whites and whites along side of Negroes . . . I have always felt that if a man wanted a job bad enough, he could go where the job, for which he is qualified, is available. There are places in this nation where civil services jobs for Negroes in cities are available, but not in Montgomery. I will expend every effort to keep it that way."[19] Sellers's campaign was aided by the first of the bus incidents, the arrest on March 2 and the trial on March 18 of Claudette Colvin for violation of the segregation ordinance.

Sellers had been correct about the effect of his racial appeal upon the electorate. In the returns he took 43 percent of the poll, to 37 percent for Birmingham, 16 percent for Stearns, and 4 percent for a minor candidate, John T. Weaver. Birmingham carried the wards with substantial black registration and also took the poorest white wards. But the white lower middle class areas of East Montgomery that he had swept in 1953 now went to Sellers. Capitol Heights, which had given Birmingham 62 percent of its vote in 1953, making it his banner precinct, now gave him only 31 percent, to 44 percent for Sellers. At the same time, South Montgomery voted heavily against Birmingham; Sellers took 60 percent of the poll in Cloverdale. Despite Sellers's

[18] *Ibid.*, February 18, 24, 25, March 1, 16, 20, 1955. Abernathy gives the membership of the committee that drafted the questionnaire as including himself, Nixon, Lewis, Robinson, Mrs. A. Wayman West, and James E. Pierce, a professor of political science at Alabama State (interview, February 28, 1979). Nixon, who presided at the meeting, says that all of the candidates chose to duck the bus-seating question (interview, August 2, 1977).

[19] *Ibid.*, March 16, 20, 1955.

[20] *Ibid.,* February 9, 13, March 16, 20, 22, 24, 25, 29, 1955. Because of the presence on the ballot of a minor candidate, George J. Rivers, the race between Parks and Cleere was forced into a run-off, but the geographical distribution of the vote was identical in both elections.

solid lead over Birmingham, a run-off between the two men would have been necessary. However, two days after the election Birmingham collapsed while preparing to give a television speech; his doctor diagnosed his condition as "overexertion and exhaustion" and advised him to withdraw from the race. Birmingham did so, and Sellers was declared elected. We can never know whether Birmingham could have defeated Sellers. Birmingham had come back from an even more substantial deficit to defeat Dawkins in 1953, but Birmingham's chances of repeating this accomplishment in 1955 were poor. Sam B. Stearns, the third important candidate in the race, had made shrill personal attacks on Birmingham. It is unlikely that a white voter who had cast his ballot for Stearns in the first round would thereafter have moved to the support of Birmingham.

In the mayoral election, McGlynn had seldom indulged in the demagogic appeals of Birmingham and Parks. He may have been hurt by the fact that he was a Roman Catholic, but on that point evidence is lacking. Although McGlynn received 40 percent of the vote and carried the wards with substantial black registration and also the city's poorest white ward, West End, nevertheless Mayor Gayle won easily.

In the election for commissioner of public works, the incumbent, George Cleere, had refused to follow Sellers in exploiting the racial issue. Instead, he had attempted to answer with reason the strident class-oriented accusations of Parks, particularly with reference to the sewerage fee. The result was that Parks was elected on returns whose geographical distribution was virtually identical to the distribution of the support for Birmingham in his race against Dawkins in 1953. Cleere swept the South Montgomery wards, taking more than 75 percent of the vote in Cloverdale, but Parks carried the substantially black precincts and those of the white lower class and lower middle class.[20]

CHAPTER

5

"A modest compromise"

The election's outcome puzzled Grover C. Hall, Jr.; why should the voters have elected Parks, Birmingham's ally, over Cleere, Gayle's ally, but then have repudiated Birmingham over himself and returned Gayle?[21] The meaning of the election was probably much clearer to Gayle, now the sole Machine survivor in municipal politics, seated between an uncompromising segregationist on his right and an adversary of Montgomery's wealthy on his left. The Machine's traditional policies of moderate, paternalistic racial attitudes, and a firm alliance with the city's upper class had failed to sustain it, and they held little likelihood of endearing Gayle to the constituencies that had elevated either of his two colleagues. Clearly, Gayle needed a new strategy immediately. The lesson of Parks's victory appeared to be that, given the new social realities produced by the city's rapid postwar growth, an East Montgomerian would always defeat a South Montgomerian when the issues remained class-oriented. The lesson of Sellers's victory appeared to be that the vigorous exploitation of racial antipathies could give a South Montgomerian at least a fighting chance of defeating an East Montgomerian. Gayle was, of course, a South Montgomerian. But Gayle's dilemma was much more complicated than this analysis would imply. First, he was unlikely to abandon a set of beliefs that he had held sincerely for many decades merely because political strategy seemed to dictate this course. Second, developments within the business community rendered it less than certain that a sound strategy actually dictated this course. To understand this factor, we must briefly explore the attitude of Montgomery's businessmen towards their city government.

The business community believed that the source of all genuine social ills was the lack of industrialization. Montgomery's economy rested primarily on the presence of the state government and of two air force bases, Maxwell and Gunter. One in every seven families in the city was an air force family in 1955. Aside from income generated by federal and state governmental expenditures, Montgomery relied almost exclusively on its role as a marketing center for the surrounding agricultural area.[22] By 1955, businessmen were armed with legislation passed during the preceding decade, providing Alabama municipalities with powerful tools for attracting industry to the state, particularly

[21] *Ibid.,* March 30, 1955.
[22] *Montgomery Alabama Journal,* January 13, 1956.

[23] *Montgomery Advertiser,* October 28, 1953, January 15, 1954, February 20, 24, March 7, 10, October 19, December 11, 1955. March 4, 1956; Montgomery *Alabama Journal,* November 3, December 9, 1955, January 10, 1956.

[24] *Montgomery Advertiser,* December 11, 1955.

in the form of tax advantages and of public financing of plant construction. Business leaders therefore had high hopes of broadening Montgomery's economic base.

This zealous commitment to industrialization was the source of the tension between businessmen and the city government. Business leaders believed that the city's politicians had been inept in attracting industry. Near the end of October 1953, the *Advertiser* had broken a story that DuPont had purchased 850 acres near Montgomery "as a prospective site for an industrial plant." The article had concluded excitedly, "Announcement is expected soon on the type of plant to be constructed." Months passed, and no such announcement was forthcoming. Reportedly, four other "very large companies" that had considered building factories in Montgomery had been lost to other cities during 1954 and 1955. Worried businessmen sought to discover what they were doing wrong. The Chamber of Commerce desperately debated ways to attract favorable national publicity for the city. Chamber of Commerce President James G. Pruett ominously warned the Rotary Club that "industry will come to Montgomery and Alabama only when there is a healthy climate for it and when government on all levels is not hostile to it." In this atmosphere of frustration at the repeated recent failures in the drive for industrialization, forty of the city's most important businessmen met in mid-October 1955 to organize the Men of Montgomery. Adopting the frank motto, "We Mean Business," they chose as their first project a campaign to compel the City Commission to act on a proposal that had languished in the City Hall bureaucracy for years: to construct a new terminal for the municipal airport to give visitors to the city a more favorable first impression.[23]

Mayor Gayle had always counted on business support. The Gunter Machine had been closely allied with business interests. Gayle himself was a brother-in-law of one of the most influential businessmen in Alabama, Birmingham industrialist Donald Comer of Avondale Mills.[24] Now the mayor faced a business community organized with a new efficiency and motivated by a new hostility. By the fall of 1955, his dilemma was acute. His colleagues on the Commission each represented constituencies only recently defined, and Gayle had no real access to either. The black leadership was making militant demands upon the city for the first time and was asking for public responses. The business community was suddenly dubious of his competence and disposed to press him for positive action. If he moved towards one of the newly emerging constituencies, he risked permanently alienating the elements in the city upon which he had relied ever since he had first entered politics. Against this background the city moved towards the events of early December.

At the Ben Moore Hotel meeting on February 23 bus seating had headed the list of grievances. On the afternoon of March 2 came the arrest of Claudette Colvin, a fifteen-year-old black girl who refused to vacate her seat when ordered to do so by a bus driver, Robert W. Cleere. Miss Colvin, who was returning from school, was seated far back in the bus, just forward of the rear door, on a seat with an older black woman, a Mrs. Hamilton. The bus was entirely filled, and Cleere ordered the two blacks to stand in order to give their seats to boarding whites. Mrs. Hamilton refused, and Cleere summoned police. When the police arrived, a black man got up, gave his seat to Mrs. Hamilton, and left the bus. Miss Colvin, who apparently was led into her resistance by the actions of Mrs. Hamilton, now found herself deserted to face the music alone. She became hysterical, kicked and scratched the arresting officers, and had to be carried bodily from the bus.[25]

Because of her age, Miss Colvin was brought to trial before Juvenile Court Judge Wiley C. Hill, Jr., a first cousin of U.S. Senator J. Lister Hill. She was not the first person to be arrested for violation of the bus seating ordinance, but according to Commissioner Birmingham, she was the first person ever to enter a plea of not guilty to such a charge. Her twenty-four-year-old attorney, Fred D. Gray, one of the two black lawyers in Montgomery, interposed two defenses. The first, that segregated seating violated the U.S. Constitution, was overruled in short order by Judge Hill. The second defense was more troublesome. When the city ordinance requiring segregation on public conveyances had first been adopted in 1900, it had provoked a black boycott of the city trolley lines. This boycott had lasted throughout the summer of 1900 and had ended only when the City Council agreed to amend the new ordinance to forbid compelling anyone to vacate his seat unless there was another seat to which he could move. This proviso remained a part of the city code. *Because both sides in the Colvin case agreed that the bus had been entirely filled, the bus driver, rather than Miss Colvin, had violated the segregation ordinance.*

State laws supersede city ordinances, however. In 1945 the state legislature had enacted a statute requiring the Alabama Public Service Commission to see that all bus companies under its jurisdiction enforced racially segregated seating. This statute, unlike the city ordinance, gave bus drivers absolute power to seat passengers. It was unclear whether or not the Public Service Commission had jurisdiction over municipal bus lines. A year later the state was to contend in federal court that the state law was inapplicable in such situations in order to avoid having it at issue in the suit seeking to declare the segregation of Montgomery buses unconstitutional. Now Circuit Solicitor William F. Thetford moved to meet Gray's defense by amending the complaint so as to allege a violation of the state law rather than of the city ordinance. Judge Hill overruled Gray's objection that the state law did not apply, found Miss Colvin guilty both of violating the state bus segregation statute and of assault and battery on the arresting officer, declared her a juvenile delinquent, and ordered her placed on probation. Gray filed an appeal to Circuit Court, but on the appeal the state pressed only the charge of assault and battery, and on that ground Miss Colvin's sentence of probation was affirmed. As a result, Gray was deprived of any way to use this case as a means to contest the various questions that had been raised with regard to the segregation laws.[26]

Meanwhile, Miss Colvin's arrest had moved the city's black leaders to make one more effort to deal with the bus problem through the political mechanism. In mid-March, as the municipal election campaign climaxed, blacks arranged two meetings with white officials. At the first one, Commissioner Birmingham and the bus company's manager, James H. Bagley, met in Bagley's

[25] *Ibid,* March 6, 1955; Trial Transcript, *Aurelia S. Browder v. William A. Gayle,* Civil Action 1147-N, U.S. District Court, Middle District of Alabama (Federal Records Center, Atlanta Georgia, FRC Box Number 426114), 17-20, and Colvin arrest warrant and complaint contained in case file.

[26] *Montgomery Alabama Journal,* March 18, 19, 1955; Montgomery City Code of 1952, Chapter 6, Sections 10-11; Code of Alabama, 1940, Recompiled, Title 48, Section 301 (31a); Gilliam, "Bus Boycott," 17. Gray had only returned to Montgomery six months earlier, after attending law school in Cleveland, Ohio. The Colvin case was his first joust with the segregation laws (interview, October 17, 1978). But he quickly became a leader of the black community; that summer found him serving as a spokesman for the black delegation in the meetings with the city concerning the parks.

[27] King, *Stride,* 41–42; Trial Transcript, *King v. State*, 240, 344–46; Gilliam, "Bus Boycott," 18–19; Montgomery *Alabama Tribune*, March 16, 1956.

[28] Trial Transcript, *King v. State,* 360–486, 510–47; Trial Transcript, *Browder v. Gayle*, 58–69.

office with a delegation that included the Reverend Martin L. King, Jr., a twenty-six-year-old Baptist minister who had moved to Montgomery the preceding September to take up his first pastorate, and who in the intervening six months had become quite active in the city's NAACP chapter. It appears that, at this meeting as at earlier ones, the principal spokesman for the blacks was a conspicuous member of King's new congregation, Jo Ann Robinson.

This encounter was relatively amicable. Birmingham was eager to conciliate the blacks, and Bagley did not wish to offend his customers gratuitously. The black delegation pointed out that forcing a passenger to stand in order to seat another passenger violated both company policy and the provisions of the city code. Bagley acknowledged that the policy did forbid such action; he promised to investigate and to reprimand the bus driver in the Colvin case if it was warranted. The blacks evidently brought up the seating plan proposed in the questionnaire presented at the Ben Moore Hotel meeting; Birmingham promised to secure a formal opinion from City Attorney Walter Knabe on what seating arrangements were legally permissible. Unfortunately, nothing came of either of these promises.[27]

Birmingham's failure to act is understandable; within two weeks he was a lame duck, his influence greatly diminished and his health precarious. Bagley's inattention to the matter was simply shortsighted. A principal source of friction on the buses was the company's loosely defined seating policy. In practice, the policy varied enormously from route to route and from driver to driver. Even under the company's official policy, the middle sixteen seats of the bus had no fixed racial designation; it was the responsibility of the driver to shift the racial line forward or back in order to provide a number of seats roughly proportionate to the racial composition of the group of riders at any given moment. Under these circumstances the drivers had to reseat passengers rather frequently. The embarrassment and humiliation to blacks of being thus publicly forced to acknowledge and accept legal discrimination was exacerbated by the fact that the harried drivers usually adjusted the seating simply by shouting peremptory commands over their shoulders. If Bagley had attempted to specify the seating policy more fully and had sought more vigorously to enforce company rules requiring courtesy from drivers, he could have eliminated much of the ill will between the bus line and the black community. If he had emphasized to the drivers the company policy against unseating passengers when other seats were unavailable, he would have forestalled both the Claudette Colvin and the Rosa Parks incidents.[28]

The second meeting in response to Miss Colvin's arrest appears to have been much stormier than that with Bagley and Birmingham. Bagley arranged this meeting for the blacks. The black delegation included, as usual, members of the black Women's Political Council and the Federation of Negro Women's Clubs. It also included Rufus A. Lewis of the Citizens' Steering Committee and attorney Fred Gray. Mayor Gayle and City Attorney Knabe represented the city. The bus company was represented by its attorney, Jack Crenshaw. The blacks apparently pressed the seating proposal contained in the questionnaire distributed at the Ben Moore Hotel meeting. Gray believed that the proposal violated no existing law. Crenshaw adamantly maintained that the

THE CHILDREN COMING ON . . .

proposal flouted both the city ordinance and the state statute, an opinion in which Knabe concurred.

The importance of Crenshaw's intransigence both in producing and in sustaining the bus boycott can hardly be overstated. He was an excellent lawyer, educated at Harvard. He was a political ally of the racially moderate Governor Folsom. Despite this background, however, he proved incapable of understanding the strategic advantage of accepting a modest compromise in order to forestall a full-scale assault on segregation. He dismissed Gray's arguments out of hand and informed his client Bagley that the law left the bus company absolutely no room for compromise. The meeting adjourned with the complaints of the blacks still unanswered.[29]

Through the summer and fall of 1955, a series of events kept the bus question before the public. Early in the year, a black woman, Sarah Mae Flemming, had sued the city bus line of Columbia, South Carolina, for damages for its having enforced the segregation laws against her. In mid-July the U.S. Court of Appeals for the Fourth Circuit ruled in this case that segregated seating on buses was unconstitutional—a decision that received headline treatment in the *Montgomery Advertiser*. Later in July a young black, James M. Ritter, had defied the order of a bus driver in Richmond, Virginia, to move to the rear and had been fined ten dollars for his action. In Montgomery itself another black teenager, Mary Louise Smith, was arrested on October 21 for refusing to yield her seat to a white woman. This case did not create the furor which the Colvin incident had, however, because Miss Smith chose to plead guilty; she was fined five dollars.[30]

Equally important in focusing attention on the bus company was the fact that its franchise was about to expire. National City Lines, Inc., of Chicago, owned the Montgomery bus company. That firm had been granted a twenty-year city franchise in 1936; the franchise would come up for renewal in March of 1956. In late October an official of the company came to Montgomery to open negotiations. He and the city commissioners surveyed the city from the air in order to plan revisions in the bus routes, and delegations from a number of the new subdivisions on the city's outskirts appeared before the Commission to seek the extension of bus service to their areas. At the same time, the bus company was bargaining with the bus drivers' union for a new two-year contract. Montgomerians who recalled that all bus service had been suspended during a brief strike in December 1953 watched the progress of the negotiations apprehensively.[31]

[29] Trial Transcript, *King v. State*, 256-57, 344-46, 357–59, 539-40. On Crenshaw's and Knabe's opinions of the legality of the Negro proposal, see below, notes 43, 47. Crenshaw and his brother had handled Governor Folsom's suit to compel the Dixiecrat presidential electors to vote for Harry Truman: *Folsom v. Albritton*, 335 U.S. 882; *State v. Albritton*, 251 Ala. 422.

[30] *Flemming v. South Carolina Electric and Gas Co.*, 128 F. Supp. 469, 224 F. 2d 752; Montgomery *Advertiser*, July 15, 1955; Montgomery *Alabama Tribune*, July 22, 29, 1955; Trial Transcript, *Browder v. Gayle*, 10-12.

[31] *Montgomery Advertiser,* December 12-16, 1953, October 25, 27, December 7, 20, 1955, January 25, February 16, 1956.

6

"A spark to this tinder"

In the fall of 1955 the press was filled with accounts of events in Selma. There a group of twenty-nine blacks in September petitioned the city board of education, urging the integration of schools. In mid-September the head of the recently organized Dallas County White Citizens Council, attorney M. Alston Keith, reported that the efforts of the Council had resulted in the firing of sixteen of the twenty-nine petitioners from their jobs. Blacks retaliated by refusing to buy the milk of a dairy that had agreed to discharge a petitioner. Next came incidents of arson and kidnapping, both directed against a black grocer who had been a participant in the boycott of the dairy. Finally, in late October, six young white men, two of them members of the Selma police force, were arrested and indicted for the actions directed at the grocer, and one of the accused policemen thereupon committed suicide.[32]

In early November black Congressman Adam Clayton Powell visited Montgomery to speak to the Progressive Democratic Association. Congressman Powell spent the night at the home of Edgar D. Nixon. In his speech, Powell warned the Citizens Councils that their economic pressure "can be counter met with our own [black] economic pressure." The example of the events in Selma and the force of Powell's remark doubtless made an impact upon Nixon, who because of his background in the labor movement and because of his long association with and intense admiration for his union's president, A. Philip Randolph, was predisposed in any case to believe in the efficacy of economic action.[33]

The arrest of Rosa Parks struck a spark to this tinder. When Mrs. Parks boarded the bus, it was divided into twenty-six seats for blacks and ten for whites. Two blocks farther on, when the bus stopped in front of the Empire Theater, it was completely filled, and both whites and blacks were standing; all white standing room was taken. Driver James F. Blake undertook to readjust the seating to a more equitable ratio by clearing one row of seats, altering the racial division to fourteen white and twenty-two black. Since the four unseated blacks would have to stand, Blake's action violated both company policy and the city code. At the same time, inasmuch as company policy forbade allowing whites to stand in the black section, if Blake had not taken his

[32] *Ibid.*, September 8, October 22, 23, 26, 1955; Montgomery *Alabama Tribune*, September 16, October 28, 1955. A petition seeking the integration of Montgomery's schools was also presented to the local board of education in August, and similar petitions were submitted throughout Alabama, evidently at the instance of the national NAACP. These petitions appear to have been the trigger for the establishment of a great many of the Alabama chapters of the White Citizens Council.

[33] *Montgomery Advertiser*, November 6, 1955; interview with Nixon, August 27, 1977. In the 1930s both Powell and Randolph had organized black boycotts of Northern merchants who refused to hire blacks.

action, none of the whites waiting to board could have been accommodated, although standing room was available in the rear of the bus.

Rosa Parks had been for most of the preceding decade the secretary of the Montgomery chapter of the NAACP. She had grown up on a farm in southern Montgomery County. Against great odds, she obtained a high school diploma in 1933. Montgomery then provided no public high school for blacks. But Mrs. Parks's family, ambitious for her advancement, had arranged to send her to the laboratory school of Alabama State College. Although she thus became one of a very small number of black high school graduates in the city, she found herself unable to obtain employment commensurate with her educational level. She worked at a number of relatively menial jobs; in 1955 she was a seamstress altering ready-to-wear clothes in the city's principal department store, the Montgomery Fair. This situation very probably produced a certain bitterness in her and contributed to her decision during World War II to become an active member of the NAACP. She was elected the chapter secretary in 1943 and later also became the adviser to the chapter's youth auxiliary. She had therefore been particularly concerned with the arrest of Claudette Colvin. In the summer of 1955 she had attended an integrated seminar on race relations at the Highlander Folk School, an invitation she had received at the suggestion of Mrs. Clifford Durr, the wife of a liberal white attorney. Mrs. Parks worked for Mrs. Durr on a part-time basis as a seamstress. All of these circumstances had made Mrs. Parks peculiarly sensitive to the importance of the series of meetings, petitions, and remonstrances in relation to the bus situation during the years before 1955. We may well suppose that, had she not been so intimately connected with the controversy, she might have been inclined to join the other three blacks on the row of seats in obeying Blake's instruction. But she, alone of the four, did not move. Blake summoned the police, who took her to the city jail. From the jail, she contacted her colleague in the NAACP chapter, Edgar D. Nixon. Nixon made bond for her.[34]

If Mrs. Parks had not been a close friend of Nixon's and a prominent figure in the black community, Nixon might not have been moved to such decisive action, and the people whom he contacted might not have responded so readily. But Mrs. Parks and her husband, a barber at Maxwell Air Force Base who had resided in the city for more than a quarter of a century, were distinctly civic leaders and, at least socially, members of the middle class. Nixon returned from the jail and began calling the city's most prominent blacks to suggest that blacks stage a strike of the buses.

[34] Interview with Rosa L. Parks, May 22, 1978; interview with Virginia F. Durr, May 2, 1979; Trial Transcript, *Parks v. City of Montgomery*, 7-9; *Montgomery Advertiser*, December 2, 6, 1955; *Montgomery Alabama Journal*, December 5, 1955. From the jail Mrs. parks telephoned her mother, who located Nixon. Nixon called his close friend Durr, a former member of the Federal Communications Commission during World War II, and together they arranged the bond.

CHAPTER

7

"King's greatness"

. . . At the outset of the boycott, the *Montgomery Advertiser* had stated editorially, "The boycott makes an innocent sufferer of the bus company. Had the company defied city and state laws, its franchise would have been canceled. The quarrel of the Negroes is with the *law*. It is wrong to hold the company a hostage."[35] The blacks replied over and over again—though the whites never seemed to listen—that their quarrel was not at all with the law, that they had no intention of asking the company to abandon segregation, that they merely wished to have the company apply the law in Montgomery as it did in Mobile. In a peculiar sense, the *Advertiser* was right, and the blacks were wrong. What the boycott taught the city's black leaders as it dragged on was that their quarrel was—had to be—with the law. Compromise with segregation was impossible because segregation so forged and underlay social relationships that even the most modest reform of its requirements threatened—just as the white politicians claimed—the entire social fabric. In such a situation, reform was impossible; only "revolution" would do. The white response to the boycott revealed this truth forcefully to the blacks; that revelation is the boycott's supreme achievement, and it is something which no court suit could ever have accomplished.

Perhaps the most interesting single aspect of the boycott is that the inflexibility of segregation was something which black leaders had to learn. It was so much the fundamental presumption of the Civil Rights Movement in later years that we find it difficult to believe that there could have been a time when a black—when anyone—was unaware of this characteristic of the system. Indeed, it is this difficulty that makes the MIA's position in the initial stages of the boycott seem so peculiar. But segregation revealed the true extent of its inflexibility only under the pressure of the Civil Rights Movement itself. For those who had lived inside the segregation system, black and white, the pervasiveness of its impact was not so readily apparent. It is not the author's intention to maintain that blacks were not acutely aware of the constant humiliation that segregation entailed. Yet, the enormous variety of interracial associations even under segregation made the institution seem less fundamental to the shaping of attitudes than in fact it was. Particularly in a city like

[35] Montgomery *Advertiser*, December 8, 1955.

THE CHILDREN COMING ON . . .

Montgomery, in which the Gunter Machine had defeated the Ku Klux Klan and ruled with relative benevolence, it was easy not to know how exceedingly far, into how many unrelated organs, the infection had spread. Black leaders had been too ready to believe that the brief thaw that Dave Birmingham's tenure had represented for them marked the beginning of spring. The writer believes that they made this mistake because they, in common with most white Southerners, had conceived of their world, though suffused with segregation, as fictile. Only after segregation came under assault and its supporters roused themselves to fight back were blacks, and later whites, able to discover the omnipresence and the rigidity of the system.

In a sense Martin King, having learned these lessons during the bus boycott, spent the rest of his career arranging demonstrations of them for others. Blacks, especially older blacks, in other Southern cities had to be shown that they were more fully imprisoned than they had believed. Moderate whites had to be shown that, whatever the extent of their good will, segregation had the power to render their best efforts vain. In these demonstrations the medium was the message; the immediate goals in a given city were less important than the process of placing segregation under stress in order to reveal the nature of its hold upon society. Iconoclasts sometimes note that King did not create the boycott, as a way of questioning his greatness. But King's greatness actually lies in the fact that during the boycott, by observing what was happening, he grew. He, far more than any of his contemporaries, white or black, learned the truths which the events of the boycott contained about the nature of the Southern dilemma.

In the end, the bus boycott teaches that segregation could have been disestablished only in the way in which it was disestablished: by internal pressure sufficient to compel intervention from outside the South. For all its diversity and complexity—in large part because of its diversity and complexity, since any fundamental reform would affect an infinite variety of interests— the South did not possess within itself the capacity to save itself. The strength of segregation was bound up with the pluralism of Southern society. As no man could untie the Gordian knot, so segregation would not—could not— yield to negotiation. Thus the boycott, because it failed to achieve its initial goals, succeeded for that reason in changing the course of American history.

MONTGOMERY VOICES

II

Marie Pake:

The contradictions began to appear when I went to New York, after I was in my twenties, and did newspaper work there and met other people and talked to them, who were appalled at some of my views. Then I found that my whole idea of the South, a gracious and beautiful life, my whole idea was wrong. I never thought of it being, depending on not exact—certainly not slavery—but on the roots of, I'm trying to think of the right words for it, help me if you can. Anyway, life was made possible because we had people working for us in various and small ways, who were discriminated against. I accepted that kind of life. Well, I found out that there were other view points and I began to read all the periodicals—I had a friend who was working for *The Nation.* I remember there was a nice young man that I was going with and he was appalled at all of my views, which seemed to me perfectly legitimate. I remember the first time I began to do a quick change in my thinking, there were two things that made me think differently when I was in New York: one of them, I was on the elevated train and there were not many vacant seats, and one of them was next to a black woman—well, I walked around until I found one that had a white woman there. So finally I found a seat, and I sat down and it came time for my station. I got up. The "el" was crowded and a black woman back of me took hold of me, took hold of my arm—she had an umbrella—"Get out of the way, let this lady pass, y'all are making it hard for her." And she saw to it that I got off at the platform. Well, I think when I went home that night, I thought, well I've always been, I'm sure I didn't say prejudiced, but I never thought of the blacks in that light. I had thought of them as my friends, but necessary to serve me, but not coming to my help in a case like that.

. . . The average (white) Southerner is generous—and sweet and kind in my family, which is wonderful. My relations with the black people, always, looking back, seem to me quite wonderful, because I, we, really loved the black people—that is true. That is one of the contradictions that has been at the heart of change. People themselves are torn both ways. People will tell you when you try to talk to them, "Yes, we were always good to them, we never abused . . ."—things just flowed into my consciousness and became part of my way of looking at life.

When I came back from New York, I fled the South because finally it became intolerable to me, but when I came back years later and thought and decided, tried living here, I came across an article that said: "You never escape the spell of the South"—and I found I loved the South. There was so much that was beautiful and much creativity of thoughts and much generosity of spirit, much physical loveliness and all those things, I became very much in love with my own birth place, enabled to accept it and the contradictions along with it.

Virginia Durr:

I was born in Birmingham on August 16, 1903 . . . I always thought in political terms . . . I was brought up in a political family. On my Mother's side, my grandfather was a Congressman from Memphis and my uncle was Governor of Tennessee and so on my Mother's side, politics was in the family.

My father was raised in Union Springs, Alabama, and I was raised there too, as a typical Southerner, benevolent, paternalistic. But the thing is the blacks . . . as children, you see, there was no difference. We played with the black children. They played with us and I had, of course, a black maid. All the people on the place were black, and so I grew up in a black world, in a way, and a white world too, at the same time.

. . . I must say that as a child you were not conscious of the tensions, difficulties, it just seemed like Eden. You see, everything was grown on the place. They had wonderful fruit trees and grapevines. I never was conscious of any tensions between black and white until I was seven years old and they wouldn't let me invite the black children to my birthday party. I had a big tantrum then and a temper fit because I had been playing with them for seven years. And then at seven, that was the sort of cut off point. You started going to school then and, of course, there were no black children in the schools. At that point you ceased being children together.

This idea of being raised with blacks and playing with black children and having a black nurse, it makes you unpopular these days. It sounds like you're being extremely benevolent. But the fact of the matter is that a great many poor white children were raised by black women and they loved them very dearly. We did play with black children up until a certain age. The difference, really, the change, all these ideas about black people, not being able to sit by them or eat with them, are so stupid when we slept with them and ate with them and were nursed by them. So when the time came, when we were told we couldn't do these things, it creates terrific contradictions. . . .

And the reality and the taboos totally clashed. And I didn't resolve it, really, until I went to Washington in '33 and began to work in the Women's Division of the Democratic National Committee. I worked with Ms. Bethune and Mrs. Mary Church Terrell and a number of black women who were brilliant women . . . Southern women. . . . Ms. Bethune came from South

Carolina . . . Mary Church Terrell came from Memphis and she knew my mother's family up there.

They were very kind to me, and they used to laugh at me and tease me. But they taught me a lot. So I really got my first lesson in integrated living and working with blacks on a perfectly equal basis in the Democratic Party. And it was a big change. I had to learn like a child; I had to learn over. . . .

. . . The thing was the Women's Division of the Democratic Party was not considered to be very powerful. One thing is, the Southern women didn't vote . . . the poll tax kept them from voting, as well as the blacks and the poor white men. And so the women who voted in the South were very few. So the Women's Division didn't have much money and Jim Farley didn't think much of it.

. . . Women's rights were not very strong at that time. We'd gotten the right to vote, but of course in the South here, the black women had all the restrictions the blacks had but the white women also had the restrictions of the poll tax . . . and so many people were poor, that kept them from voting.

Farley was the chairman of the Democratic National Committee. And when he found we were working against the poll tax in the Democratic Committee, he got furious because it made all the Southern senators . . . You see, by the fact that he had restricted the vote so, only about 13 percent of the voting population in Alabama ever voted and about 12 percent in Mississippi. I think it was 19 percent in Texas. Those figures are very easily found.

But the thing was . . . the blacks had been totally restricted from voting and the poor whites, by the poll tax. . . . Women and men had been restricted. So the Southern states were disenfranchised. Each Southern state was run by a small group of powerful men who stayed in office year after year, like Cotton Ed Smith of South Carolina. . . .

The first break came when Roosevelt was elected. But it really came before that, in Alabama, when Hugo Black, my brother-in-law, was elected and Bibb Graves was elected. Lister Hill was elected and John Sparkman was elected. Carl Elliott was elected and a group of liberals were elected to the Congress and to the Senate.

. . . They supported Roosevelt. Instead of fighting him all the time, they supported him. And they supported all the relief measures: the WPA and the NYA and the PWA—all the relief work. Aubrey Williams, from Alabama, was one of the moving spirits in that whole movement. He was Hopkins's assistant and he'd grown up as a very poor boy near Birmingham. His family had been so poor—but the one thing they had refused to do was to take charity . . . he had this horror of giving people charity.

Mr. Roosevelt, on the other hand, and even Hopkins, thought that the dole system at that time was the best way to relieve the people—to just give them a certain amount of money to live on. Aubrey Williams fought tooth and toenail against [it]. . . . He said give them work because to give a man a check or a woman a check just hurt their spirit and that you must give them work to do. So that's when the work program was started. . . .

. . . One of the things that my brother-in-law did, Hugo Black, was that he was a great advocate of labor. . . . He was a great advocate for the thirty cents an hour program. They had a program they introduced that you couldn't pay a man less than thirty cents an hour. . . . Particularly where they cut the wood and made the turpentine, they were paying ten cents an hour. So he introduced a bill in the Congress to make it mandatory that nobody could be paid less than thirty cents an hour.

There was a great . . . tremendous amount of fuss and yelling over that. I remember Cotton Ed Smith got up and said, "Ain't no nigger worth a dollar a day." I can remember that phrase that he used . . . in the Congress. But he (Black) won that struggle. . . . Seems like mighty little now, but those days it was a big change from ten cents an hour.

. . . Down in southern Alabama . . . so much lumber around Montgomery . . . and, of course, Hugo Black was a great advocate of the Wagner Act, too, to organize because he had been representing the unions in Birmingham; when he married my sister he represented the steel workers, he represented the coal miners, and he represented all the unions that existed.

Well . . . he was elected first in 1926, that was the year my husband and I married, and then he was elected again in '32. And then he was put on the court in '38. He was just getting ready to run for his third term when he was put on the Supreme Court . . . of course, Roosevelt put him on the Supreme Court because he had come to think, by that time, that the southern bloc in Congress was his greatest enemy because they were blocking and voting against all of his relief measures.

See . . . the Southern power structure believed that the one thing the South had was cheap labor and so they had been fighting the unions and trying to keep labor down as low as possible to attract industry. . . . You'd see advertisements all the time . . . nonunion cheap labor in North Carolina, South Carolina, Alabama, Mississippi, Georgia . . . trying to attract industry. And a great deal of it came that was attracted by the lack of unions and the lack of any . . . . We didn't have Workmen's Compensation, even.

. . . Mostly textile . . . of course, the great industry came south, like in Birmingham, the United States steel was all owned in the north. And . . . food processing. They had some food processing plants here . . . but the great, big corporations were owned in the north . . . we were more or less a colony of the north because the profits all went north. . . .

. . . In the early days it was to the advantage of these Northern corporations that came down to keep the racial issue going because they kept the wages down . . . the blacks were used as strike breakers. You see . . . it was easier for a black woman to get a job than it was for a black man . . . it was very difficult for a black man to get a job . . . if he was offered a job he'd take it. Unions didn't mean anything to him because they didn't let him in . . . it was only the mine workers that finally let the blacks in.

. . . If you read down human history, from the very beginning of mankind, if people get in power, by whatever means they may achieve power, they try to keep somebody to do the dirty work . . . that nobody wants to do . . . as cheap as possible. And I think that slavery was a result of that. That existed . . . in every country in the world, almost. And then, after slavery, the fight against the unions, trying to keep wages as low as possible. . . .

That's one of the reasons there was so much bad feeling between the poor white blue collar workman or the no collar white workman. Because he saw the black as a potential strike breaker who would get his job . . . .

. . . Mrs. Parks was a great friend of mine. She was working down at the Montgomery Fair for twenty-three dollars a week as an assistant to the . . . person that did the . . . alterations . . . so, I met her through Mr. Nixon.

I was my husband's secretary, I did do that. I learned to be a secretary and I was his secretary. . . . I had three daughters at home. . . . I asked Mr. Nixon if he knew of anybody who would help me sew because I was just always taking up hems and putting in hems and taking in and taking out dresses. He recommended Mrs. Parks.

So, I met Mrs. Parks. In those days, she was an extremely beautiful woman. She is still . . . a lovely looking person. . . . In those days I would consider her, really, a beautiful woman . . . she was a merry kind of a person. She used to laugh a lot. She was very cheerful and we'd sew together . . . she'd come over to my house and help me sew and I'd go over to her house and take the kids and we got to be great friends. Her mother I became very fond of, too. . . . Her husband was sick all the time so I never saw very much of him . . . but her mother I became very fond of, and Mrs. Parks.

But the reason we got her out of jail was because our friend Mr. Nixon . . . was president of the NAACP . . . and so, the afternoon she was arrested for refusing to move back on the bus . . . now she talked to me about it a whole lot . . . about the humiliation that you suffered by having to put your money in the front and then run around to the back and get in the back and then sometime they'd slam the door on you and leave you standing . . . .

They had had several cases that had not succeeded in court for various reasons . . . so the day that she refused to move . . . it was December, she had bursitis in her shoulder, she was just tired. . . . . See, the drivers had police powers and they didn't say, "Madam, would you kindly rise," they just yelled back, "Nigger, will you move back?" And, you're supposed to get up and give your seat to a white person.

And Mrs. Parks had really been extremely bitter about this and she had talked about it a great deal. So, that afternoon, I think she just decided this was just one time she just wasn't going to move and so they arrested her and took her to jail. . . . Fred Gray was the lawyer for the NAACP but he happened to be out of town, so when Mr. Nixon called—somebody had told him that Mrs. Parks had been arrested.

They wouldn't tell him what she was in for. . . . He called my husband . . . Clifford Durr, so Cliff called down there and they were very respectful to him and they told him that she was in for breaking the city segregation ordinance, for not moving to the back of the bus.

So Mr. Nixon came by and got Cliff and me and we went down to the jail and Mr. Nixon signed a bond for her because we didn't own any property at that time and he did, so he had to sign the bond for her. And we got [her] out of jail and then we went back to her apartment.

She said then that she wanted to make a class case and take it all the way up to the Supreme Court. And so my husband told her that she'd have to get the NAACP to back her up because it was going to cost a fortune to take a case all the way, the state courts and the federal courts and up to the Supreme Court.

. . . And so, you see, Fred Gray was the lawyer of record but my husband worked with Fred a great deal . . . they worked together.

So we won the case . . . with Judge Rives and Judge Johnson. See . . . it got into the federal court. That was my husband's suggestion to take. He felt like it would be stalled in the state courts forever. So he suggested that they remove it to the federal court and that was Judge Johnson and Judge Rives who voted that it was wrong, unconstitutional. I can't remember the name of the third man. He was from Birmingham, he voted the other way. That was the beginning of the end of segregation ordinances.

Mrs. Parks was a woman of a great deal of pride. She had been to Mrs. White's school, you see. After the Civil War was over, this group of New England spinsters . . . came down here and started a school called Mrs. White's school. Mrs. Johnnie Carr went there, too. . . . They taught their pupils, not only all the things they should teach in school, but they also taught them they were American citizens and were as good as anybody else and had all the rights and entitlements of American citizens.

So Mrs. Parks was a woman of a great deal of pride and she had been active in the NAACP ever since she was grown. And she was a . . . well-educated woman. She had read and kept up with things. She was a perfect case . . . that people could really rally around.

. . . She was arrested, I believe, on Friday, and the case was set for Monday morning . . . then Mr. Nixon . . . on Saturday devised the idea of boycotting the buses on Monday. The idea, at first, was just have a one-day boycott.

Then that Sunday morning . . . it came out in the paper, on the front page, that blacks were going to boycott the buses on Monday. So it got all over the black community and then the preachers, too, in the churches told the people not to get on the bus on Monday.

So there was only supposed to be this one-day boycott . . . but that night they had a big meeting at the Holt Street Church. I couldn't get in. I tried to go but it was such a crowd, thousands of people around the church, even . . . that night they decided to . . . keep on boycotting the buses.

So Mrs. Parks promptly lost her job, within a few weeks. Then, she had a pretty hard time for awhile because she didn't get another job. [At the] Montgomery Fair, her job had been assistant to the alterationist at the Montgomery Fair and she got fired from that. . . . They never said they fired her because of what she had done . . . what excuse I don't know, but anyway, they fired her.

Then she couldn't get another job. . . . She finally just, her brother was working for the Ford Motor Company and he was making a pretty good income, so she just moved the family up to Detroit. And then she got a job, finally, with the Congressman Conyers as his receptionist. I hear from her fairly often, talk to her over the telephone. She seems to be in pretty good spirits and she seems to be leading a pretty happy life.

INTERLUDE

ROSA PARKS: AN EARLY INTERVIEW

Conducted by Sydney Roger, 1956

(From Pacifica Radio cassette, "Rosa Parks," BB0566)

Introduction by Sydney Roger: Several months after the event in Montgomery, I had the pleasure of speaking to Rosa Parks in the small apartment in West Oakland, where she was visiting. I asked her then what actually happened to set off this train of history, and this was her answer:

Sydney Roger: Mrs. Parks, what ever made you decide to be the person who, after all these years of Jim Crow and segregation—what made you at that particular moment decide that you were going to keep that seat?

Rosa Parks: I felt that I was not being treated right, and that I had a right to retain the seat that I had taken as a passenger on the bus.

Sydney Roger: But, Mrs. Parks, uh, you had been mistreated for many, many, many years. You've lived most of your life in Montgomery, Alabama. What made you decide the first part of the month of December 1955 that you had had enough?

Rosa Parks: The time had just come when I had been pushed as far as I could stand to be pushed, I guess.

Sydney Roger: Well, Mrs. Parks, had you planned this?

Rosa Parks: No, I didn't.

Sydney Roger [skeptical]: It just happened . . .

Rosa Parks: Yes, it did.

Sydney Roger: Well, had there been many times before in your life when you thought that maybe you were going to do just that kind of thing?

Rosa Parks: I hadn't thought that I would be the person to do this. It hadn't occurred to me.

Sydney Roger: But don't you suppose you and many others also thought, one time or another, you are going to do this thing sooner or later?

Rosa Parks: Well, we didn't know what to expect. In our area, we always tried to avoid trouble and be as careful as possible to stay out of trouble along these lines. [Loudly] I want to make very certain that it is understood that I

THE CHILDREN COMING ON . . .

had not taken a seat in the white section, as has been reported in many cases. The seat where I occupied—we were in the custom of taking this seat on the way home, even though at times on this same bus route, we occupied the same seat with Whites standing if their space had been taken up. And I was very much surprised that the driver, at this point, demanded that I remove myself from the seat.

Sydney Roger: The driver asked you to get up to allow someone else to sit down.

Rosa Parks: Yes, a white person.

Sydney Roger: A person who may or may not have been as tired as you—

Rosa Parks: Well, that's true.

Sydney Roger: But who had not paid any more than you had.

Rosa Parks: No.

Sydney Roger: And then what happened?

Rosa Parks: The driver said that if I refuse to leave the seat, he would have to call the police, and I told him, "Just call the police." Which he did, and they came. They placed me under arrest.

Sydney Roger: Wasn't that a pretty frightening thing to be arrested in Montgomery, Alabama?

Rosa Parks: No, I wasn't frightened at all.

Sydney Roger: You weren't frightened? Why weren't you frightened?

Rosa Parks: I don't know why I wasn't, but I didn't feel afraid. I decided that I would have to know once and for all what rights I had as a human being and a citizen, even in Montgomery, Alabama.

"SISTER ROSA" [SONG]

Lyrics by Cyril Neville. Courtesy of Cyril Neville, NEVILLE HOUSE EN-TERPRISES and Cyril Neville, Endangered Species Records. This song was originally written as a poem for Neville's daughter.

From the concert version on the "Live On Planet Earth" album (1994) / original version on the "Yellow Moon" album (1989).

[CYRIL'S DEDICATION] "Is there a spirit in the house tonight? Come on, y'all. We're going to send this one out to one of the greatest human beings who ever walked the planet. If it wasn't for this particular person, the kind of gathering we see here, have in America today, may be impossible. I'm talking about the mother of the American human rights movement, Sister Rosa Parks . . . and to my mother, and my sister, and my wife—my queen—and my daughter, and the strong women everywhere—we can't do without them."

"SISTER ROSA"

December 1, 1955
our freedom movement came alive,
and because of Sister Rosa, you know,
nobody rides on the back of the bus no more.
Sister Rosa was tired
one day after a hard day on her job
and when all she wanted was a well-deserved rest
and not a scene from an angry mob.

The bus driver said "Hey, lady, you got to get up,
Cause a white person wants that seat."
Sister Rosa said, "No, not no more,
I'm going to sit here and rest my feet."

(refrain)

Thank you Ms. Rosa. You are the spark
that started our freedom movement.
Thank you Sister Rosa Parks.
Thank you Ms. Rosa, you are the spark
that started our freedom movement.
Thank you Sister Rosa Parks.
(Thank you Sister Rosa.)
(Hey, check it out.)

Now the police came without fail,
took Sister Rosa off to jail.
Fourteen dollars was her fine.
Brother Martin Luther King knew it was our time.

The people of Montgomery sat down to talk,
decided all God's children should walk
until segregation was brought to its knees
and we obtained freedom and equality.

(refrain)

Free at last.

[Cyril to the audience:] Everybody, everybody, throw your hands in the air and wave them like you just don't care. Everybody, say "peace." Everybody,

THE CHILDREN COMING ON . . .

say "peace." Everybody, say "peace." Everybody, say "peace."

Listen, so we dedicate this song to thee,
for being a symbol of our dignity.
Thank you Sister Rosa. Thank you Ms. Rosa. You are the spark—
started our freedom movement,
thank you Sister Rosa Parks.

(refrain)

Free at last.

Thank you Ms. Rosa.
You are the spark—
started our freedom movement,
thank you Sister Rosa Parks.

Thank you Ms. Rosa.
You are the spark—
started our freedom movement,
thank you Sister Rosa Parks.
(Free at last.)

Thank you Ms. Rosa.
You are the spark—
started our freedom movement,
thank you Sister Rosa Parks.

Thank you Ms. Rosa.
You are the spark—
started our freedom movement,
thank you Sister Rosa Parks.

a fork, then everybody would do that. And we used to have a little thing, if we were in any kind of group mass setting, and one of us stomped our foot, that meant that we were getting ready to get up and leave out of there. We had gotten to a point of non-verbal communication. The school didn't know what to do with us.

Getting back to the march. ASU students had come to join us, and the school has sanctioned—by default—so Dean Phillips who was the Dean of Students (and we love him dearly and we loved him then) was there. So now we get into all this discussion about who's gon' do the demonstration, who's gonna be on the front. And it looked like every preacher, even those who thought they would be a preacher in the future, wanted to opt for that role. I didn't even want to be bothered with the discussion. I left that discussion with George Ware, George Davis and all them SNCC folk. So they worked out something. So here we are, we're coming on around Ripley Street come on up to Dexter Avenue—big, strong . . . we were at least 2,000 folks. And we get to

PART THREE

THE BOYCOTT

By Fred D. Gray

From

Bus Ride To Justice: Changing the System by the System The Life and Works of Fred Gray

The material in this section is excerpted with permission from BUS RIDE TO JUSTICE: CHANGING THE SYSTEM BY THE SYSTEM, THE LIFE AND WORKS OF FRED GRAY *(Montgomery: Black Belt Press, 1995. 400 pages, $25. ISBN 1-881320-23-5)*

CHAPTER

1

"We waited. Finally everything fell into place."

. . . Although I was disappointed by the result of the Colvin case, I learned some important lessons. It was evident that at least a small circle of people, most notably E. D. Nixon and Jo Ann Robinson, were ready to get behind a legal challenge to the city's segregation ordinances and to mobilize support to destroy segregation on buses. We knew that there would be another opportunity and we would be ready. We waited. Finally, everything fell into place.

. . . December 1, 1955, was a typical day in Montgomery. It was late fall, it had not begun to get cold. We had lunch together that day, just as we had done many times before. When 1.00 p.m. came and the lunch hour ended, Mrs. Parks went back to her work as a seamstress. I continued my work and left the office in the early afternoon for an out-of-town engagement.

Upon my return to the city later that evening, I was shocked to learn that Mrs. Parks had been arrested in an incident involving the buses. I immediately began to return the numerous phone calls informing me of her arrest. Subsequently, I met with Rosa Parks, E. D. Nixon, and Jo Ann Robinson.

That day was, for me, the beginning point of all the monumental events that soon began to unfold. My immediate little world began to change. And so did the larger world. I had pledged to myself that I would wage war on segregation. The opening shot had now been fired. With Mrs. Parks's arrest came the beginning of the Montgomery Bus Boycott. It changed the history of civil rights in Alabama, in the nation, and in the world. And it launched my legal career.

. . . Mrs. Parks was arrested for disorderly conduct—not for violating the segregation laws. This was the first of several crucial mistakes made by the white authorities. Anyone who knew Mrs. Parks knew that she would never do anything disorderly. She was soft-spoken, trustworthy, and very reliable. Disorderly conduct was altogether inconsistent with her reputation and character. Rosa Parks had the right temperament to test the segregation laws.

It is always stated that she refused to give up her seat to a white man. Technically, what happened is that she refused a bus driver's order. She had

THE CHILDREN COMING ON . . .

boarded at one stop and sat in the first row of seats behind the white section. On Montgomery buses, this was an arbitrary line that was adjustable by the drivers to accommodate the number of white passengers on board at a given time. At the third stop after Mrs. Parks boarded, all the seats were filled and a white male passenger was left standing. The driver then ordered Mrs. Parks and the other three African-American passengers on the row with her to get up and stand in the aisle in the back. The others complied, but Mrs. Parks did not. The driver asked her again, and when she still would not move, he got off the bus and found two policemen, who came on board the bus, put Mrs. Parks under arrest, and took her off. A good description of the arrest, in Mrs. Parks's own words, is found in the book *My Soul Is Rested.*

As I related earlier, after my lunch with Mrs. Parks on December 1, I went out of town to keep an engagement. Upon my return in the early evening, I had many calls from Mrs. Parks, Mr. Nixon, Jo Ann Robinson, and just everybody, telling me that Mrs. Parks had been arrested. Of course, by the time of my return, Mr. Nixon, with the assistance of Attorney Durr, had posted her bond and she had been released. In fact, she was never actually jailed. The normal procedure of the police department in such a case at that time would be to arrest her on the bus, place her in a police car, take her to the city jail (then located on North Ripley Street), fingerprint her, "book" her, and then give her an opportunity to make a phone call so that bond could be arranged. All of this had already occurred by the time I arrived back into town that evening.

Bernice was one of the persons who had called me, and I returned her call. She explained to me what had happened, and I told her of the calls I had received and that I was going to follow through on those calls. She was very concerned about Mrs. Parks and her well-being.

Rosa and Raymond Parks lived in the Cleveland Court apartments, not far from downtown on Montgomery's west side. At Mrs. Parks's invitation, I immediately went over to her house. She told me what had happened and asked me to represent her, and I took it from there. I left her house in Cleveland Court and went a short distance to Mr. Nixon's house on Clinton Avenue, where he and I discussed the matter at length.

(Just for the record, you will notice that I was not riding the bus between these various stops. Not long after taking the Alabama Bar exam, I had bought my first car, a new tan 1954 two-door, stick shift Ford.)

Later that same evening, I went to Jo Ann Robinson's house and we discussed the incident. During the course of our discussion, we outlined a strategy for action. We concluded:

(1) If we were ever going to have a bus protest in Montgomery, Alabama, we must have it now.

(2) For the bus protest to be successful, the African-American community must support it. We must have the wholehearted support of the African-American preachers and both E. D. Nixon and Coach Lewis. We could not risk losing the support of either.

(3) A leader must be selected who would be able to organize, motivate, and keep the people together. Jo Ann believed that her pastor, a young new-

comer to Montgomery, the Rev. Martin Luther King, Jr., could be that person.

So Jo Ann and I made the necessary phone calls and divided up some specific assignments. Recommendations were also made concerning who should do what in preparation for the protest.

It was a long, adrenaline-filled night, yet I enjoyed every minute of it because things were beginning to fall into place. We designed a road map to accomplish a successful protest and to accomplish my goal of ending everything segregated I could find. The buses were just the beginning.

Over the next four days, we made numerous phone calls and had frequent conversations and meetings with Montgomery's African-American leaders. It was all happening quickly. The mood was electric. This was the beginning of the Montgomery Bus Boycott. My days of having little to do in my fledgling law practice were over.

Initially, the Women's Political Council (led by Mary Fair Burks and Jo Ann Robinson), E. D. Nixon, and Rufus Lewis were more interested in the protest than were the ministers. This soon changed as the ministers' interest caught fire. Meanwhile, as the Protest gained momentum I could see that we would need a new, legal organization. Prior to the Protest, we had only one organization that had taken the lead in civil rights cases and that was the NAACP. Some people felt that the NAACP was not a viable organization and there were too many factions in the African-American community. I believed we needed one key organization that could involve everyone. The Protest was a new movement and there was no reason to get the older organization involved in it. We would run the risk of getting bogged down legally. (As it turned out, my concerns were well-founded, because on June 1, 1956, the State of Alabama sued and enjoined the NAACP from conducting business in the state.)

Selecting a leader or spokesman for the new organization required much diplomacy. If E. D. Nixon had been made the spokesman, some of Coach Lewis's followers would have been unhappy. If Lewis had been made the spokesman, Nixon's folks would have felt left out. Martin Luther King, Jr., was fresh, a newcomer, young, articulate, knowledgeable, highly educated, and had not identified himself with any community activities other than his church. It was generally agreed to arrange it so that Dr. King would be designated the spokesman.

In fact, the first official planning meeting for what was to be named the Montgomery Improvement Association was held at Dr. King's church, Dexter Avenue Baptist, on December 3, 1955. The Reverend Roy Bennett, pastor of Mt. Zion A.M.E. Zion and president of the Ministerial Alliance, presided. Bennett also presided at a second meeting held later at his own church. At that second meeting, Reverend Ralph D. Abernathy nominated Dr. King, who was not present at the time, to lead the new organization. Abernathy was then himself nominated as vice president. My brother Thomas nominated E. D. Nixon for treasurer. These nominees were unanimously elected. Rufus Lewis was appointed chairman of the transportation committee. Jo Ann Robinson, as a professor at Alabama State College, was a state employee; for her to have any official position would have cost her job.

It was very important that two key positions be designated for Nixon and Lewis. Nixon as treasurer had the primary responsibility for raising funds to finance the boycott. Lewis as chairman of the transportation committee had the responsibility of designing and implementing an alternative transportation system for Montgomery's forty thousand African Americans. Martin King was the spokesman; Ralph Abernathy was his assistant.

I was chosen to handle the legal work. Whatever Dr. King was involved in legally, from then until he left Montgomery, was my responsibility. So, while I was to direct and coordinate the legal activities, Jo Ann Robinson performed other critical duties. Specifically, on December 4, 1955, Jo Ann went over to Alabama State College and, with the help of a couple of students, mimeographed thirty thousand leaflets calling for people to stay off the buses. The memo read:

> This is for Monday, December 5, 1955.
>
> Another Negro woman has been arrested and thrown into jail because she refused to get up out of her seat on the bus for a white person to sit down. It is the second time since Claudette Colvin (sic) Case that a Negro woman has been arrested for the same thing. Negroes have rights, too. They help to keep the buses rolling. If it were not for Negro riders the buses could not operate. So we must stop these arrests now. The next time may be you, or you, or you. The woman's case will come up Monday. We are, therefore, asking every Negro to stay off the buses Monday in protest of the arrest and trial. Don't ride the buses to work, to town, to school, or anywhere on Monday. You can afford to stay out of school for one day if you have no other way to go except by bus. You can afford to stay out of town for one day. If you work, take a cab, or walk. But please, children and grown-ups, don't ride the bus Monday. Please stay off all buses on Monday.

At that time, very few Alabama lawyers handled civil rights cases. Notable exceptions included Arthur Shores, Orzell Billingsley, Peter Hall, and David Hood, all of Birmingham.

Arthur Shores is the dean of African American lawyers in Alabama. He handled civil rights cases throughout the state, from the Gulf of Mexico to the Tennessee line and from Mississippi to Georgia. In 1952, he represented Autherine Lucy in her efforts to integrate the University of Alabama. He is my mentor and assisted me in many civil rights cases. He also assisted me in successfully integrating the University of Alabama with the admission of Vivian Malone. Mr. Shores recently retired from the practice of law; his daughter now heads his law firm in Birmingham.

Most white lawyers, except Clifford Durr and one or two others, just would not handle these types of cases. A civil rights practice was precisely what I wanted to do, and as a matter of principle I tried to involve as many of the African American lawyers as possible in my civil rights cases.

December 5, 1955, *City of Montgomery v. Rosa Parks*

The beginning of the boycott was planned to coincide with the trial of Mrs. Parks on December 5, 1955. At the time, I was living at 705 W. Jeff Davis Avenue, on the west side of the city. Mr. Nixon and Mrs. Parks also lived on the west side. Dr. King, Rev. Ralph Abernathy, and Coach Lewis lived on the east side. I got up at 5 a.m. and drove all over the city to see if our people were riding the buses. They were not. I later met with E. D. Nixon, Dr. King and Jo Ann Robinson. We were all elated that our people were staying off the buses. Then, it was on to Montgomery's municipal court.

The trial of Mrs. Rosa Parks took all of thirty minutes. The drama leading up to the trial and the trial itself was a lifetime in the making. The case was scheduled to begin at 9 a.m. in the Recorders Court of the City of Montgomery. At 8 a.m. I met with Mrs. Parks, Mr. Nixon, Rev. Abernathy, Dr. King and other leaders at my office, which was a block and a half away from the court. After deciding on the final tactics, we walked from my office down Monroe Street, turned right on Perry Street, passed by the main City Hall entrance, turned left on Madison Avenue, and entered the Recorder's Court chambers. Police officers and people were gathered everywhere. Hundreds of African Americans were outside the courtroom and could not get in.

The courtroom, of course, was segregated. I walked up the aisle, white people sitting on one side and black people sitting on the other. Mrs. Parks took a seat on the front row. This was a momentous occasion for me. It was a very emotional experience because, not only was I representing Mrs. Parks as her attorney, but we were friends. In addition, this was my first case with a large audience. And I knew this case, if not necessarily this particular hearing, would allow me an opportunity not only to represent Mrs. Rosa Parks, but to raise legal issues which ultimately would be decided by the United States Supreme Court. Was I nervous? Maybe a little. Was I determined? You bet.

When the case was called, Mrs. Parks and I approached the bench. I identified myself and indicated that I represented her. The stage was set. Attorney D. Eugene Loe prosecuted the case for the City. I raised certain constitutional issues, which were summarily denied. I knew that this was not the forum to challenge the segregation ordinances. The only victory that we could hope for with this case was to get Mrs. Parks exonerated because she was charged with disorderly conduct and not with violating the City's segregation laws. We vigorously defended Mrs. Parks; however, Judge John B. Scott found her guilty and fined her ten dollars and costs. We appealed, but ultimately lost on a technicality.

This case was important because it triggered the Montgomery bus protest. Most scholars believe that this case ignited the Civil Rights Movement of the fifties and sixties. This case and the Montgomery Bus Boycott also gave an opportunity for Dr. King to exhibit his leadership; thus, it paved the way for the development of one of the greatest leaders in modern history.

Some five hundred or more African Americans were in and around the courtroom that Monday morning. Once the trial was over, it was a sigh of relief for all. However, since this was the first day of the bus boycott, most of the five hundred people who came had to walk back to their respective homes. I walked back to my office with King, Abernathy, Nixon, and the other leaders, where we spent the day in conference and prepared for a mass meeting that had been announced for Holt Street Baptist Church that evening. Mrs. Parks went home.

According to earlier plans, I had prepared two resolutions for possible adoption at the mass meeting. Resolution One to be presented to the body acknowledged the fact that Mrs. Parks had been unfairly treated, tried, and convicted; that segregation on buses in Montgomery, Alabama, was wrong; that we have the capacity to conduct a boycott, but will not proceed at this time; and we will seek to resolve these matters with the city officials. If the first day's boycott had been unsuccessful, then we would present Resolution One and would call a protest at a later date.

Of course, the events of that day were such that Resolution One was not needed. The essence of Resolution Two was that we called upon the residents and all African Americans in the city of Montgomery to refrain from riding the buses until we could return to them in a nonsegregated manner.

I arrived at Holt Street Baptist Church about 6 p.m., an hour before time for the meeting, only to find that I could not get a parking space within three blocks of the church. People had been assembling since 3:00 that afternoon. This was to become typical of every mass meeting for the three hundred and eighty-one days that the boycott lasted. As I entered the rear entrance to the church, I immediately went to pastor A. W. Wilson's study, where the leaders were assembled to make last-minute plans for the meeting. Dr. King was set to give the first of what would become known as the pep-talk for each of the Monday night mass meetings.

These talks were for many their first glimpse of the genius that was within Martin Luther King, Jr. He was elected president of the MIA at a meeting at which he was not present, at Zion A.M.E. Church on South Holt and Stone Streets. He presided over a cross section of preachers, three college professors (including one woman), two physicians, three housewives, a Pullman porter, and most of the rest being preachers. He soon became a favorite of all of them. He rose in stature to the point that many of the women who attended mass meeting after mass meeting could be heard to say, "Just let me touch his garment." Yet Martin appeared to have never lost the common touch. He could calm the rivalries which arose among some of the ministers on occasions. Before MIA board meetings, Martin was always alert to congratulate someone for some deed of kindness. He was jovial, at a well-bred ease and aware of events in the neighborhood, or asking those present about matters which might have escaped him. But those were qualities which were generally not yet realized on the night of the first mass meeting.

Finally, the scheduled time came.

Not only were there thousands of African Americans crowded in and around Holt Street Baptist Church, but also a few whites. The local media and some national media were present. There was an electricity in the air. Such a feeling of unity, success and enthusiasm had never been before in the city of Montgomery, certainly never demonstrated by African Americans. The

White Montgomery high school students protesting desegregation a few years after the bus boycott give a clue to the racial feelings of the era. Photographer Flip Schulke says he often wonders, when he looks at this picture today, if these young women ever outgrew their hatred.

people were together. They were singing. They were praying. They were happy that Mrs. Parks had refused to give up her seat and they were happy that they were a part of a movement that ultimately would eradicate segregation on city buses and would set a precedent for the elimination of segregation in almost every other phase of American life. They clapped and shouted "Amen" as the boycott leaders entered the auditorium. They welcomed their leaders, and they welcomed Mrs. Parks, and as the lawyer I was included in this group.

The high point of the meeting was the speech by Dr. Martin Luther King. This was the first time he had spoken to so many people. It was the first speech of his career as a civil rights leader, later to become an internationally known figure. Each of us listened to his words and waited for his next phrase. My fiancée Bernice was in the audience. She later described how King's inspiring speech ignited the crowd and was the motivating factor that was needed to make the protest successful. It was his message and his encouragement and his speech that gave those thousands of African Americans the courage, the enthusiasm and the desire to stay off the buses.

This mass meeting reminded me of the day of Pentecost as recorded in Acts 2:1-2.

THE CHILDREN COMING ON . . .

. . . [T]hey were all with one accord in one place. And suddenly there came a sound from heaven as of a rushing mighty wind, and it filled all the house where they were sitting.

The second high point of the meeting, of course, was the adoption of the resolution to continue the boycott until we could obtain dignity and until our three demands were met. Pictures and accounts of the mass meeting were subsequently published and broadcast across the nation. The coverage of this event gave additional credibility to the movement and focused the nation's attention on the struggle of African Americans in Montgomery, Alabama, to end segregation on buses.

Hundreds of accounts have been written about the success of the Montgomery Bus Boycott. I believe that one major circumstance helped tremendously in spreading the news about the planned boycott. Initially, the leaders planned to spread the word throughout the African-American community, but not the white community. We realized that this was impossible. Then a front page story appeared in the *Montgomery Advertiser* on Sunday, December 4, 1955, under the byline of Joe Azbell, the newspaper's city editor. Azbell reported that there was a planned boycott and that a mass meeting was scheduled to be held that Monday evening, thus notifying thousands of African Americans who otherwise would never have known about the protest. Joe Azbell was a very good friend of E. D. Nixon. I feel confident that Mr. Nixon discussed our plans with him. Joe Azbell, being the good newspaper reporter that he was, of course, verified the information as best he could and wrote the story.

It was not unusual for leaders of the movement to develop good working relationships with the media. It helped them and it helped us. Early on in the movement, I established a similar working relationship with Frank McGhee, who was then the news director of WSFA-TV, the Montgomery NBC affiliate. As a result of his coverage of the bus boycott, he was later employed by NBC News and went on to become a host of the "Today Show" in New York.

Bus Protest in Progress, December 5, 1955

Five days after the arrest of Rosa Parks, the buses in Montgomery were empty. And for the next fourteen months African Americans stayed off the buses.

None of us realized then that this was the opening event of the modern American civil rights movement. Little did we know that we had set in motion a force that would ripple throughout Alabama, the South, the nation, and even the world. But from the vantage point of almost forty years later, there is a direct correlation between what we started in Montgomery and what has subsequently happened in China, eastern Europe, South Africa, and, even more recently, in Russia. While it is inaccurate to say that we all sat down and deliberately planned a movement that would echo and reverberate around the world, we did work around the clock, planning strategy and creating an atmosphere that gave strength, courage, faith and hope to people of all races, creeds, colors and religions around the world. And it all started on a bus in Montgomery, Alabama, with Rosa Parks on December 1, 1955.

Many African Americans expected that after Mrs. Parks's arrest and the first day of protest that the city officials and the bus company would negotiate a settlement. These expectations rested upon the fact that the three modest requests presented to them could have been granted with little difficulty or inconvenience to the bus system and the city establishment.

Personally, I never shared the view that a settlement could be reached. Knowing white Montgomerians at that time as I did, I knew they would not give in to any demands from African Americans for equal rights. They would reason that "if you give them an inch they will take a mile."

On the other hand, we did not know how the first day of the protest would go. We had high hopes, and as it turned out, the first day was a resounding success; the bus protest was off to a good start. At this juncture I advised the leaders to use the second resolution, demanding three very small actions:

1) all drivers display more courtesy toward the "colored" riders;

2) the seating be arranged on a first-come first-serve basis;

3) the company hire "colored" bus drivers on buses running into areas heavily populated by "colored" people. The population of Montgomery was about one hundred thousand and of that number roughly 40 percent were African Americans.

The actions requested in the resolution were not designed to integrate the buses; rather they were intended as very reasonable reforms. The city officials could have given in to us but they simply refused. Considering the jobs African Americans held in Montgomery prior to the protest, we attempted to make the requests reasonable. White city officials simply dug in their heels and refused to propose an alternate plan. They refused to offer to concede or compromise on any point. We had no choice but to continue the protest. We would have settled for first-come, first-serve seating. Meanwhile, the bus company was losing approximately three thousand dollars a day in fares.

In my opinion, much of the resistance to accepting the resolution was the work of Jack Crenshaw, the attorney for the bus company. He was a product of the times. He simply could not accept the fact that African-American people were not demanding anything from the whites to which they were not entitled. I believe that Crenshaw let his personal feelings interfere with the best interests of his client, the bus company.

In any event, attorney Crenshaw flatly declared that the bus company had no intention of hiring colored bus drivers, and it could not accept the seating arrangement because it violated the law. Of course, I disagreed with him with reference to the seating arrangement. I prepared an exhaustive brief, which pointed out that the seating arrangement did not violate the Alabama segregation laws. The same bus company that owned the buses in Montgomery owned the buses in Mobile. The Mobile buses employed the same type of seating arrangement we were requesting in Montgomery. Thus, as a practical matter, there was no logical reason why the bus company should have rejected our seating proposal.

. . . (While attorney Crenshaw did not agree with any of our proposals,

THE CHILDREN COMING ON . . .

I doubt that he really was anti-African American. It is rather interesting that many years later in the case of Pollard v. United States of America, which is the Tuskegee Syphilis Case, attorney Crenshaw did me a personal favor. After we reached a settlement in the case and I filed a petition for attorney's fees, I was looking for lawyers to testify to substantiate my fee. To my surprise, every lawyer I contacted told me the best person to prove my fee would be Jack Crenshaw. Initially, I was hesitant to ask attorney Crenshaw to testify for me because of my experience with him in the bus protest. Finally I decided I had nothing to lose. To my surprise, he was willing, without hesitation, to testify. He testified in the United States District Court for the Middle District of Alabama before Judge Frank Johnson that I was entitled to a substantial fee in that case. While the Court did not award me as much as Mr. Crenshaw testified that I was entitled to, the fee I received was substantial.)

2

"Another side to Martin Luther King, Jr."

Over the course of the bus protest and other civil rights developments, I had many disagreements with my clients, Dr. Martin Luther King, Jr., and Ralph Abernathy, in my effort to keep them on a sound legal track. There were times when they would consult other attorneys because they did not agree with my advice. It seems as if each time they failed to heed my advice, either one of the two or some other person very important in the Movement would be arrested or end up in jail. Needless to say, they did not hesitate to call me to their rescue when arrested, nor did I hesitate to assist.

Ralph Abernathy once teasingly told me, "Fred, you keep me out of jail and I will keep you out of hell." Ralph, of course, was always getting in jail in connection with the Movement. Later, reflecting on Ralph's comment, I told Bernice, "My job certainly is a lot tougher than his."

In spite of our differences of opinion, Dr. King, Ralph and the other leaders expressed great confidence in my legal abilities and they knew that I was always available, day or night. There were times when Dr. King said, "Fred, I understand what you say the law is, but our conscience says that the law is unjust and we cannot obey it. So, if we are arrested we will be calling on you to defend us." Dr. King frequently introduced me to others saying, "my attorney." I liked that.

There were several similarities between myself and Martin King, even though he was twenty-three months older. He came to Montgomery on September 1, 1954, to begin his pastorship at Dexter Avenue Baptist Church, which was his first church. I was admitted to practice law in Alabama on September 14, 1954. As the young pastor of Dexter Avenue Baptist Church, and as a young lawyer returning home, we developed a close personal friendship. We both have four children, two girls and two boys. Their ages are close together.

It is difficult for persons who did not know Dr. King to understand Martin as I knew him. When I met him, his primary concern was to do a good job as pastor of Dexter Avenue Baptist Church. I had returned to Montgomery with a desire "to destroy everything segregated I could find." Martin was receptive to assisting me in that desire. We joined forces and worked against segregation in Alabama. We had a close friendship during the bus boycott. We were dealing with each other on a day-to-day basis. He was a very kind, compassionate, considerate, easygoing, easy-talking Baptist preacher. He was an easy conversationalist who could talk about anything. Behind his church work and his work with the Movement, there was another side of Martin Luther King Jr. In those quiet moments, you would never think of him as the articulate speaker that he was, with the persuasive power that was able to change people. You wouldn't really think about him in terms of his being a future Nobel Peace Prize winner. He would sit down like you, me, or anyone else in a group and just have a good time and enjoy the fellowship. He never monopolized a conversation. He always listened. He had a tremendous sense of humor and enjoyed telling jokes and listening to jokes. He never met a stranger. He was one of those rare individuals. Nothing you did would upset him. During all of our trials, tribulations, setbacks, and victories I never saw him upset. I never saw him angry. I never saw him display hostility, nor hate toward anyone.

This is even more remarkable when you consider that it is hard even for those of us who knew him and saw him on practically a daily basis to comprehend the pressure he was under. Richmond Smiley was one of Martin's parishioners and they became good friends. Richmond often drove Dr. King to meetings and appointments, because we all recognized that it was dangerous for him to be on the streets alone.

I knew several of those who rode around with Martin from time to time, including the late Cleveland Dennard, who had married Belle Brooks, daughter of the ASU registrar, Dr. J. T. Brooks. Cleveland was later president of a school in Washington, D.C., and still later of Atlanta University. Some thought that those who rode with Martin were bodyguards, but I never knew of Martin saying so. If any of them were ever armed, I'm sure that Martin never knew it.

In addition to the constant danger, Martin's life was also complicated by the incredible weight of the demands on his time. As the Movement intensified and he became more and more famous, he could never really relax at the church or even in his home, the parsonage. He would sometimes escape to Richmond Smiley's house for a little relief from all those who wanted to see him, and sometimes even that did not help. Richmond relates how he answered the doorbell once to find Sander Vanocur of CBS News on his doorstep asking for Dr. King. "I tried to explain to this gentleman that he was not in," Richmond recalled. "He looked at me and asked, 'Is it that he is not here, or is he really not here.' With this I invited him in and said I would check to see if Dr. King was available. Mr. Vanocur was kind enough to wait in my living room until Dr. King got some rest, and then they met." That's the kind of pressure that existed all the time. But despite it all, Martin rarely seemed ruffled. Or at least he didn't let us see it.

Even when his home—the Dexter parsonage on South Jackson Street—was bombed at the height of the Protest, he was a model of restraint. While he was certainly concerned about the well-being of his wife and children, he still maintained his composure. He had been at one of the weekly mass meetings when the bomb went off. Coretta was at home with their infant child and a friend, Mrs. Roscoe Williams, but fortunately they were all in the back part of the house and were not hurt. Of course, this was not clear when Martin got the news. He calmly left the mass meeting and went home. There was already a large crowd gathered outside, and a number of police and city officials were present, trying to control the crowd. Many of the onlookers were very angry and some were armed. It was a volatile situation, and the authorities on the scene were visibly concerned about losing control. After assuring himself that Coretta and the baby were not injured, Martin went back out onto the front porch and gave calming words to the crowd. He told them that no one was hurt. Everything was all right. Don't be violent. Go home and continue to stay off the buses.

Reassured by his manner, his faith, and, I believe, by the hand of God, the crowd calmed and gradually dispersed. This was a dramatic example of Martin's ability to remain true to his faith and his principles, and of his ability to lead others. This does not mean that Martin was never afraid. We all, at certain times during those momentous days, were afraid. But we believed in our cause and we believed in God. Even if it meant death, we were determined to let nothing stop us from carrying out our various goals of ending segregation and discrimination. Martin's innate abilities enabled him to be a true advocate of nonviolence and social change. He talked it, slept it, preached it, and lived it.

Many who were active in the bus protest did not understand when Martin first began to articulate the principle of non-violence. My own brother Tom was a member of the board of the Montgomery Improvement Association. This brought him into the circles of the protest leaders. On a morning after the *Montgomery Advertiser* had carried a story about Martin's recent espousal of the Ghandian and Christian philosophy of "turning the other cheek," Tom went up to him and declared that this was an effective ploy for the news media. "Oh no, Brother Gray, this is no ploy at all," Martin responded. "If we are to succeed, I am now convinced that an absolutely non-violent method must be ours amid the vast hostilities we face." Tom noted Martin's seriousness and decided to drop the subject, because my brother was not personally convinced that he could absolutely follow that doctrine.

Of course, the Movement did result in Martin's death at the hands of a violent person. Incidentally, no one was ever convicted or even arrested for bombing the Dexter parsonage.

At the first meeting of the Montgomery Improvement Association after the bombing, Martin's father, Martin Luther King, Sr., (often called Daddy King) was present, having come over from Atlanta to check on his son. Dr. King Sr. made a fervent plea to the board members, for them to encourage Martin to come home to Atlanta so his son and family could live more safely and more conventionally than in Montgomery. To a person, the board agreed. But Martin would have no part of it. He thanked his father and the rest of the board, but voiced a belief that God could keep him as safe in Montgomery as in any other place, and that he had to be about the business in which we were engaged. As it turned out, he stayed in Montgomery another three years be-

fore moving to Atlanta, and even then he was frequently back in Montgomery and Alabama during key periods, such as the Freedom Riders Riot in 1961 and the Selma-to-Montgomery March in 1965.

The latter occasion provided another example of Martin's great courage and faith, as related by Dr. Emmitt Smiley, a Montgomery dentist and a member of Dexter Avenue Baptist Church. Smiley recalls that at the conclusion of the march, following the mass meeting on the steps of the Alabama capitol, he drove Dr. King back out to the City of St. Jude Catholic complex, which had served as the Montgomery headquarters of the March. St. Jude also housed a hospital and infirmary. Dr. King's feet were hurting after walking fifty miles, and Dr. Smiley drove him to the St. Jude Infirmary. The infirmary was, however, under heavy guard by Alabama state troopers, who were not allowing anyone into the building. One of the troopers drew his weapon and threatened to shoot Dr. Smiley. Dr. King walked up to him, directly in front of the drawn weapon, and said, "Young man, do you know why you are here? You are here to protect us." The officer put up his weapon and Dr. King got treatment for his feet.

The MIA board was more successful in urging its only white member, the Reverend Robert Graetz, to leave town following two massive bombings of his home, the parsonage of Trinity Lutheran Church, on Cleveland (now

Photographer Flip Schulke took this picture of Dr. King, with Andrew Young (on floor) and Hosea Williams in Montgomery in 1965 during the time of the Selma March.

Rosa Parks) Avenue at Mill Street. Graetz was equally willing to remain in Montgomery, but there appeared to be even more hostility toward him—if it was possible—than toward Dr. King at that point. It was thought that this was because Graetz, a white, had allied himself with the black cause, which simply infuriated the most violent of Montgomery's white supremacists. Graetz finally agreed to move to Columbus, Ohio, where he pastored another Lutheran church. Graetz and his famly now live in southeastern Ohio, near the town of Logan.

CHAPTER

3

"Our only hope"

After Mrs. Parks was convicted of disorderly conduct and her case was for the moment basically over, the primary question on everyone's mind was "How long are we going to be able to get the people to stay off the buses?" People must have something to look forward to. Of course, the Parks conviction was on appeal, but that alone would not suffice. The logical thing was to stay off the buses until we could return to them on an integrated basis. Jo Ann Robinson was especially astounded that the city officials were not wise enough to resolve this situation, even on a halfway basis. I was not surprised.

The denial of such simple demands as we had made and the refusal by the white authorities to yield an inch had the effect of unifying the African-American community. It became obvious to everyone that there was no hope of obtaining justice or fair play from the white power structure. I had never thought for a moment that the authorities were going to give in to our small requests. But it was necessary to go through the motions. In the back of my mind I always knew that the matter was going to be resolved in court, and not in an Alabama court, but in federal court. And I started early working in that direction. The shift from the first-come, first-serve seating demand raised in the Parks case, to the demand for full integration of the buses is seen in the next bus case that I handled, *Browder v. Gayle.*

Within two weeks after the Protest started, I began talking to the leadership of the MIA about a new case. I started the research, and talked with other lawyers including Clifford Durr, Robert Carter, and Thurgood Marshall. In *Browder v. Gayle* we asked the Court to declare the segregation statutes unconstitutional and to issue an injunction enjoining the officials from enforcing the segregation statutes. I did not include Rosa Parks as a plaintiff in this case because I feared a question would arise in the federal suit about whether we were trying to circumvent and enjoin the criminal prosecution of Mrs. Parks. Including her would have given the opposition an opportunity to introduce a side issue. I wanted the court to have only one issue to decide—the constitutionality of the laws requiring segregation on the buses in the city of Montgomery.

I had completed much of the advance preparation for the suit by the time Martin's home was bombed on January 30, 1956. We had been waiting for the right moment to file the suit. The Bus Protest was ongoing, but it was a hardship to many people. I knew that we had to give the people something to hang on to so they would continue to make the sacrifice of staying off the buses.

From the outset, I realized that the legal system was against our cause and against me. I knew that as an African-American attorney I had to try every case, whether it was a traffic violation or a matter of race, as if it were going to the United States Supreme Court. We expected to lose in all the local courts. Our only hope was to get our cases eventually to a federal court, where we believed we could get justice.

It was standard procedure in Alabama in those days that if a case could be decided on technicalities, it would never be decided on merit. This was especially true in the segregation cases. In Alabama practice there were many technicalities to trap attorneys, especially attorneys with limited experience. A case could be dismissed because it was not timely filed or because of failure to obtain an extension of time to file transcript, or failure to obtain an extension of time to file the record, failure to state on the record "assignment of errors individually," failure to argue assignment of errors, or even for arguing assignment of errors in bulk. Most of these were administrative or technical matters and had nothing at all to do with the merit of a case. As an African-American lawyer in Alabama, I looked forward to getting cases to the federal courts where the cases could be decided on merit. It was also desirable to be on the offense instead of the defense and thus better positioned to win.

On February 2, 1956, three days after the bombing of the Dexter parsonage, I filed *Browder v. Gayle*. Aurelia Browder was a housewife; W. A. ("Tacky") Gayle was mayor of the City of Montgomery. The case made headlines and provided the encouragement needed for the people to remain off the buses until they could return on an integrated basis.

The suit was filed to declare unconstitutional and a violation of the 14th Amendment to the United States Constitution, ordinances of the City of Montgomery and statutes of the State of Alabama which required segregation of the races on city buses. Joining Mrs. Browder as plaintiffs were Mrs. Susie McDonald, who was seventy-seven years old; Mrs. Jeanetta Reese; Claudette Colvin by Q. P. Colvin, her father; and Mary Louise Smith by Frank Smith, her father. The plaintiffs were selected by the leaders of the Protest. Each plaintiff came to my office and signed a written retainer employing me to file the suit.

In addition to Mayor Gayle, the defendants were Clyde Sellers and Frank Parks, individually and as members of the Board of Commissioners of the City of Montgomery, and Goodwin J. Ruppenthal, individually and as Chief of Police of the City of Montgomery; and the Montgomery City Lines, Inc., as a corporation; James F. Blake and Robert Cleere, bus drivers; and C. C. "Jack" Owen, Jimmy Hitchcock, and Sibyl Pool, as members of the Alabama Public Service Commission. The defendants were represented by Walter Knabe, Drayton N. Hamilton, Herman H. Hamilton, Jr., and Jack Crenshaw.

Joining me as attorneys for the plaintiffs were Charles Langford, Arthur

Shores, Peter Hall, Orzell Billingsley, Jr., Robert Carter, and Thurgood Marshall.

Prior to filing the lawsuit, and during the time I was preparing the suit and discussing it with the officials of MIA, I decided that it would be useful to go to New York and discuss this lawsuit with Thurgood Marshall, the director counsel of the NAACP Legal Defense Fund and Educational Fund, Inc., and Robert Carter, the general counsel for the NAACP. (The NAACP and the Inc. Fund, as it was popularly called, were separate organizations.)

I not only wanted an opportunity to discuss this case with them, but also all of the other legal ramifications involved in the bus boycott. This was the first time that I met Thurgood Marshall, who was later to become U.S. solicitor general and a justice on the United States Supreme Court. From that initial conference throughout the years, I established an excellent working, professional relationship with him and he assisted me in many of the civil rights cases which I filed. It was also during this meeting that I initially met Robert L. Carter. He was also a lawyer from New York. We were to work together on many other cases in years to come. He assisted me in *Browder v. Gayle* and generally gave advice throughout the movement. He later retained me to assist him in representing the NAACP when it was enjoined from doing business in Alabama, beginning on June 1, 1956. He also assisted me in the arguments in the United States Supreme Court in the case of *Gomillion v. Lightfoot*.

This conference with Thurgood Marshall and Robert Carter was the beginning of a long professional relationship with these men, the top lawyers of the two major civil rights organizations in the country, the NAACP Legal Defense and Educational Fund, Inc., and the NAACP itself. I was now in a position that whenever I needed professional assistance in civil rights cases, I had a direct line and the ears of the two major legal civil rights strategists in the nation. This gave me courage, determination and a ready access to all the legal assistance that I would need in connection with all of the subsequent civil rights cases that I've handled. I have maintained that relationship with the appropriate officials of those two organizations over the years.

Shortly after *Browder v. Gayle* was filed, many influential whites in the community contacted me directly and indirectly and attempted to persuade me to drop the case. Numerous local, county, state, and federal officials in all three branches of government attempted to prevail upon me not to pursue the case. Some suggested that I dismiss the case outright because it would only create problems in the community and give me the reputation of an agitator. Others suggested that I agree to let the court pass the case over for a period of time so there would be no ruling on the segregation laws at the time.

When pressed for an answer with respect to a dismissal or to have the case passed over, I did not immediately tell these high public officials "no," but I told them I would confer with my clients. After having conferred with my clients, I told the officials that there was nothing personal involved, but my clients insisted that I pursue the case vigorously.

Some of the officials suggested that if I would get my clients to agree to either dismiss the case or have it passed over, I would not have to worry and they would assure me that from that point forward, I would have all the legal cases I could handle. Of course, I would never have agreed to such an inducement even though those making the offers had the power to deliver. They were capable of referring clients that would enable me to build a substantial practice. Remember, these assurances were made at a time when I had nothing. I did not give them a second thought. Had I accepted their recommendation, I would never have been able to file another suit challenging the segregation laws of the state of Alabama, nor would I have been able to face myself, my family, or those who trusted me. To accept their offers would have been contrary to my goal of "destroying everything segregated I could find."

Since *Browder v. Gayle* challenged the constitutionality of a state statute, a three-judge federal court was convened. The panel consisted of Judge Richard T. Rives, Court of Appeals for the Fifth Circuit, who had practiced law in Montgomery for many years before he was appointed to the bench, and who was a great appeals court judge; Judge Frank M. Johnson, Jr., a November 1955 appointee as United States District Judge for the Middle District of Alabama; and Judge Seybourne Lynne, United States District Judge for the Northern District of Alabama, Birmingham. The case was tried and taken under advisement.

CHAPTER

4

The City's Get-Tough Policy

As the Protest continued and began to broaden its base of support within as well as outside Montgomery, division in the white community became evident. Some whites were sympathetic to our cause and did not oppose equal treatment of whites and blacks in bus transportation. But the overall white resistance drowned out the moderate voices. Remember that the Protest began only eighteen months after the Supreme Court decision in *Brown v. Board of Education*, the momentous school desegregation ruling. Throughout the South, cracks were being seen in the facade of Jim Crow segregation; where no cracks were yet visible, they could be imagined. The segregationists and white supremacists were busily organizing and agitating against any real or perceived threat to the "Southern way of life." Those Southern whites who might have listened to voices of reason were already being intimidated, forced out of public office, threatened economically and sometimes even physically. The oppression of moderate and liberal whites was only a token of what African Americans had to contend with, but it was there and it did have an impact. Of course, the full fury of the resistance still lay ahead.

In Montgomery, Mayor Tacky Gayle led the resistance. He urged white Montgomerians to stop using their automobiles as taxi services for the maids and cooks who worked for them. An article in the January 25, 1956, *Montgomery Advertiser* records Mayor Gayle criticizing whites who did not side with him on the issue. He said the maids and cooks, by boycotting the Montgomery City Lines, were "fighting to destroy our social fabric just as much as the Negro radicals that were leading them." He continued,

> The Negroes are laughing at white people behind their backs. They think it's very funny and amusing that whites who are opposed to the Negro boycott will act as chauffeurs to Negroes who are boycotting the buses. The City Commission urges the white people of Montgomery to cease the practice of paying Negro maids, cooks, or other employees blackmail transportation money in any shape, form, or fashion.

A few years ago, there was a movie in which Whoopi Goldberg played a domestic worker in the household of a white Montgomery woman (Sissy Spacek) during the time of the Bus Protest. This movie, *The Long Walk Home*, was written by John Cork, a white Montgomerian who is the nephew of the present Montgomery mayor, Emory Folmar. Although it is a fictional account, Mr. Cork's screenplay depicts the prevailing attitude and situations in the white community in 1956 quite succinctly.

Early in 1956, Mayor Gayle, other city officials, white business leaders, and white ministers in Montgomery began to publicly announce that they had become members of the White Citizens Council. This was an organization that had begun in Mississippi following the *Brown* decision and had spread rapidly through the South with the stated goal of maintaining racial segregation in both public and private life. White Citizens Council members generally did not approve of the violence of the Ku Klux Klan, yet they were as adamant as the KKK on racial segregation. They did not wear hoods or burn crosses, but they had other weapons. These were often persons of substantial political and economic power in the community. They were the politicians, the city councilmen, the legislators, and the businessmen who were, however, die-hard segregationists.

One of the reasons why the city was unwilling to accept our compromise and grant our three meager requests was the authorities' fear that this would be interpreted as giving in to African Americans, and, in some measure, would signal the beginning of the end of segregation. Therefore, they were determined not to give an inch. For if they gave an inch, they feared we would take a mile. There was no doubt that the City of Montgomery had taken a get-tough stand and had aligned itself with a group notorious for its opposition to the fair and equal treatment of black citizens.

On the other hand, African Americans in Montgomery and across the U.S. saw *Brown v. Board* as a panacea for solving the key racial issues in this nation. This case in effect reversed *Plessy v. Ferguson*, the 1896 Supreme Court decision which established the doctrine of "separate but equal." That doctrine has been plaguing us ever since. Things became separate all right, but there was little equality to be found. With the Supreme Court's decision in *Brown*, African Americans thought they could see coming not only the end of segregated education, but the beginning of the end of segregation in every phase of life.

As a matter of fact, we cited *Brown* as a precedent for *Browder v. Gayle*. The decision in *Brown* had resulted from the work of Thurgood Marshall and other lawyers who had worked with him in the companion cases that were consolidated into the 1954 *Brown* ruling. The architect of the doctrine surrounding *Brown v. Board of Education* was Charles Hamilton Houston, an African-American lawyer who was dean of Howard Law School. He had worked for years with the NAACP and formulated the doctrine which the court initially announced in *Brown v. Board of Education*. He was also one of the professors who taught Thurgood Marshall. Naturally, this legal background was a part of what I was seeking when I visited in New York with Marshall and Robert Carter to enlist their help in the *Browder* case.

Meanwhile, as the segregationist attitudes of the Montgomery authorities were intensifying, so were my own problems as my role in the Bus Protest became more public. Like many activists in the Movement, I suffered my share of harassment, including bomb threats, crank telephone calls, hate letters, and an attempted stabbing. Although I held a 4-D draft status because of my ministerial work, I was suddenly reclassified to 1-A immediately after I filed the lawsuit to integrate the buses. In accordance with the law, I had made periodic reports to the draft board ever since I first registered, stating my ministerial involvement.

My draft matter was presented to the local draft board in Montgomery. I presented evidence to show my past and present ministerial activities. At the time, I was assistant minister of the Holt Street Church of Christ. The elders of the church, Mr. Boise McQueen and Mr. Willard Billingsley, along with the church's secretary, Thomas Gray, testified. The board refused to reconsider. I appealed to higher authorities, and eventually General Lewis Hershey, director of the Selective Service System, blocked the efforts of the Montgomery draft board to send me to military service. Hershey interceded the night before I was to ship out. In protest, draft boards throughout Alabama refused to induct anyone else. Alabama Selective Service officials created a new classification called F-G, and said they would use this deferment for other draftees until Fred Gray was inducted into the service.

I love my country as well as anyone and I did not use my ministerial position for the purpose of evading the draft. I was fully prepared to serve my country immediately upon graduation from law school. But when I made my periodic report to the draft board after returning to Montgomery in 1954, the board was evidently satisfied with my ministerial duties. It was only after I became active in the Bus Protest, and particularly after filing the lawsuit to integrate the buses, that I was reclassified. I fought being drafted because I resented the injustice of using the Selective Service System solely to remove from the Movement the person who was basically responsible for conducting its legal activities.

White politicians probably felt that if they could stop the legal work that I was doing, then they would be in a position to end the Movement or, at least retard the African-American quest for civil rights in Alabama. The conflict and tension over my ministerial deferment continued until I turned twenty-six and thereby became ineligible for the draft.

I was also the victim of a politically motivated criminal prosecution in the March 1956 case of *State of Alabama v. Fred D. Gray*. The Montgomery County Grand Jury indicted me for allegedly representing Jeanetta Reese in a federal desegregation lawsuit without her consent. She claimed she had not retained me, had no knowledge of the lawsuit, and that I had unlawfully and illegally listed her as a plaintiff in *Browder v. Gayle*. In fact, Mrs. Reese had retained me both orally and in writing. As a plaintiff in the case, she had posed in my office for pictures for *Jet* Magazine. I also had tape recordings of our conversations in which she expressed her desire to be a part of the lawsuit and to obtain justice.

I later discovered that Mrs. Reese had worked in the home of a high-ranking Montgomery police official. Her employer and other authorities interrogated her about her involvement in the legal activities, and under that pressure, she disavowed any knowledge of the lawsuit. Even more problematic for her, I later learned, Mrs. Reese had failed to inform her husband that she was a plaintiff in the lawsuit. He was very critical of her when the inevitable harassing calls and other intimidating events began.

Recalling the saying, a lawyer who defends himself has a fool for a client, I did not defend myself against this indictment. Instead, I was defended by a team of African-American Alabama lawyers, Arthur Shores, Orzell Billingsley, Peter Hall, and Charles Langford. This was serious business. The state statute under which I was indicted called for automatic disbarment upon conviction.

I was shocked that the Montgomery County Grand Jury indicted me. However, I should not have been. I knew the authorities would do everything possible to stop the bus boycott. Knowing that, I had been very careful at the time at the outset of the Browder case to document the fact that each plaintfiff had retained me to represent them. I had been extra careful to be sure they understood the problems and the criticisms that would emerge once the lawsuit was filed. In addition, I knew about the earlier use of this statute against attorney Arthur A. Madison, an African-American lawyer who was originally from Montgomery but at the time was practicing law in New York. Madison had returned to Alabama to assist people in becoming registered voters. J. Clay Smith, Jr., in his book, *Emancipation, the Making of a Black Lawyer, 1844-1944* describes attorney Madison's situation.

In 1944, while trying to help blacks register to vote, he was arrested under an Alabama statute that made it a misdemeanor to represent a person without his or her consent. Madison had taken appeals for eight blacks who had been denied the right to vote, but "five (of the eight blacks) made affidavits that they had not employed Madison or authorized him to take the appeals." Madison attempted to obtain a legal decision that the restrictive registration law in Alabama was unconstitutional, but the white power structure, led by United States Senator Lister Hill, was adamant that Madison's efforts to register black voters be stopped by whatever means necessary. As a result of Senator Hill's influence and the pressure brought to bear on the Montgomery County Board of Registrars, Madison was disbarred on July 24, 1945. He relocated to New York City.

This is an example of what had occurred earlier in Montgomery, Alabama, for the purpose of stopping blacks from becoming voters. This type of retaliation was one of the risks that black lawyers encountered in Alabama and the South in representing African Americans in an effort to end racial discrimination. I realized the risks; I wanted to minimize them, but I was prepared to pay the price if it became necessary. However, I am happy it was not necessary.

Either prior to or shortly after filing *Browder v. Gayle*, I personally met attorney Arthur Madison. He was the brother-in-law to Reverend S. S. Seay, my office landlord and my friend and mentor, and thus the uncle of attorney Solomon S. Seay, Jr., who later became one of my law partners. We practiced law together for over thirty year.

After my indictment and prior to the time of my arraignment, I was in the office of U.S. District Judge Frank M. Johnson, Jr., on another matter. When we had completed that matter, Judge Johnson asked how things were going in connection with the prosecution against me.

I responded, "About as well as can be expected."

He parenthetically stated words to the effect of, "You know whatever offense there was, if any, was committed when the lawsuit was filed on the second floor of this courthouse, of which the United States government has exclusive jurisdiction."

I was appreciative to Judge Johnson for his comment. I viewed this as an interesting comment designed to give me a tip if this argument had not been thought of by my defense team. In fact, this very argument had been included by my defense team in a motion to dismiss the case against me. Solicitor William Thetford, at the opening of the hearing in state circuit court, recognized that he could not secure a conviction so he asked the court to dismiss the indictment on the ground that the court did not have jurisdiction and that he would refer the matter to the United States Attorney. I never heard anything else on this matter. This was not the last of the attacks against me as I continued to provide legal services to the Movement.

(All of the civil rights cases I filed in the Middle District of Alabama were decided by [Judge Johnson] or with his participation. Many of these cases were precedent setting cases. He is a man of courage and intestinal fortitude, who interpreted the Constitution in such a manner that it ended segregation in all areas of life in Alabama. But for Judge Johnson's rulings, the realization of the Civil Rights Movement may have been delayed several years if not decades. But for Judge Johnson's rulings, my career likely would not have blossomed so radiantly, or certainly not as early as it did. Even more significantly, his rulings created a new way of life for many Americans. Judge Johnson is the recipient of many honors, awards, and degrees. On May 22, 1992, the Federal Courthouse in Montgomery was named the Frank M. Johnson, Jr. Federal Building and United States Court House. He was honored by the American Bar Association at its convention in August 1993, when he was awarded the Thurgood Marshall Freedom Award.)

During the middle of the Protest, Dr. King asked me to make a speech in Boston in his place because of a conflict in his schedule. I agreed.

My brother Thomas drove me to the Montgomery airport. The plane was delayed, so we took the nearest seats available in the waiting area. Shortly thereafter, a shabbily dressed man asked us to move to the "colored" section of the airport. My brother returned to his automobile. I guess I felt like Mrs. Parks must have when she was asked to give up her bus seat. I was so astonished by such a request that it seemed as if I were paralyzed. I was physically unable to move to the "colored" section. Two police officers arrested me, took me to the city jail, booked and fingerprinted me. When my brother returned to his car, he watched the officers put me in their car. He followed us to the jail to be sure that I arrived safely.

At the jail, a bondsman whom I knew saw me and with great surprise said, "Fred, what are you here for?" He then agreed to sign my release bond. A newspaper reporter took me back to the airport. I caught the delayed plane to Boston and gave the speech. During my speech, I not only discussed what was happening in Montgomery with reference to the Bus Protest, but I also related to my audience my arrest for sitting in the "white" section of the Montgomery airport.

After I returned to Montgomery, I appeared and was tried in the Recorder's Court of the City of Montgomery before Judge D. Eugene Loe. This was the same court where Mrs. Parks was tried on December 5, 1955, and the same court where Martin was tried in 1956 on a charge of speeding as he transported people in the car pool during the Bus Protest. When the case of *City of Montgomery v. Fred Gray* was called, it was dismissed. The judge reasoned that if the plane had been on time there would not have been a problem.

Like all of the leaders in the Movement, I refused to be intimidated by attacks. These had their good side for the Movement, because publicity accompanying these attacks led to more speaking requests and this offered even more opportunity to spread word of the Protest to other parts of the country.

The same grand jury that indicted me in March 1956 for allegedly representing Mrs. Jeanetta Reese without her consent in *Browder v. Gayle*, also returned indictments against ninety-eight participants in the Montgomery Bus Protest. These individuals were indicted for violating the Alabama Anti-Boycott Statute.

We were aware of the anti-boycott statute. The Code of Alabama, Title 14, Section 54 provided the following:

> Two or more persons who, without a just cause or legal excuse for so doing, enter into any combination, conspiracy, agreement, arrangement, or understanding for the purpose of hindering, delaying, or preventing any other persons, firms, corporation, or association of persons from carrying on any lawful business, shall be guilty of a misdemeanor.

It was because of this statute that we never referred to our activities against the buses as a boycott. We always referred to the activities as a Protest because we expected the City of Montgomery would use this statute for criminal prosecutions as well as to enjoin the operation of our car pool. Each of the ninety-eight was charged with violating this statute. They were indicted in small groups. As each person appeared before Judge Eugene Carter, the indictment was read. I entered a plea of "not guilty" on behalf of each.

The arrest process was very unusual. When the sheriff's deputies went to make the arrests, they were very considerate. My brother Thomas recalls that he was arrested at home but was allowed to go by his place of business and explain to his employees why he was being arrested. The deputy sheriff then stopped to arrest Reverend A. W. Wilson, the pastor of Holt Street Baptist Church. Reverend Wilson told the deputy he was busy, but he would go to the jail later and be booked. And he did.

When the indictments were returned, people went to the jail voluntarily

THE CHILDREN COMING ON . . .

and offered to be arrested. Some were disappointed because they had not been indicted.

Ironically, as the word spread that ninety-eight* persons were indicted, including many African-American preachers, it became a real honor to have been indicted and arrested. Soon, deputies did not have to go out to make arrests; protest leaders and ministers voluntarily went down to the jail to see if they had been indicted and offered to be arrested. Any number of persons who were not indicted were very disappointed because they knew they were involved as much as the ones who were indicted. They felt that they had been somewhat insulted by not having been arrested for exercising their constitutional rights. One of these persons was Richard Harris, one of the unsung heroes of the Protest.

Harris was the owner of Dean Drug Store, located on the corner of Monroe and Lawrence streets; his father had operated that store before him, and Dean Drug was a fixture in the African-American community. Harris and his wife, Vera, lived two doors from Dr. King on South Jackson Street. Richard Harris was one of the key persons behind-the-scenes, truly a "mover and shaker" during the Protest. His drug store had a lunch counter and was a gathering place for the leaders of the Movement. It was located half a block from my office. Richard Harris served as my personal adviser on many matters, from "Don't let your clients stop and talk to you on the street, take them to your office," to advising me as to how to invest my money once I made some, what type of automobiles to purchase, and the type of tires to put on them.

Richard Harris was also known as "Dr. Harris" or, for those closest to him, "Rich Harris." His major Protest role was to solve problems, particularly in the transportation system. As long as the transportation system worked well and everyone was being transported, Rich Harris felt good and felt there was nothing for him to do other than to keep communication flowing between the various parties. In a real sense, Rich Harris at Dean Drug Store was the nerve center for all major problems. Whenever a problem needed resolution, whether it was a problem with transportation, or someone had been arrested or harassed, or just to get a message from one person to another, we would always call Rich Harris at Dean Drug Store. He was always there and could always make the contact and get the problem solved. Rich Harris spread the news of my arrest and indictment for representing Jeanetta Reese without her consent. He was looking out his drug store window and saw a deputy's car pass with me in the back seat and he knew something was wrong. I was immediately released on bond, but if I had not been, help would have soon arrived. Harris would have seen to it. He had two dedicated employees, Annie Birch and Alberta "Peaches" Williams, who also assisted in the Movement.

Rich Harris was one of those disappointed because he was not indicted with the ninety-eight. Robert Nesbitt, an insurance company executive, was not indicted, but he contributed substantially to the Movement. He was responsible for recruiting Dr. King to Montgomery to become the pastor of Dexter Avenue Baptist Church. Another unsung hero who was indicted was Dr. Moses William Jones, a well-respected physician and a member of the

MIA board, who attended all of the mass meetings. He, too, is one of the unsung heroes of the Movement. There were many.

Judge Eugene Carter presided over the anti-boycott cases. Judge Carter and Judge W. B. Jones were the two state circuit court judges in Montgomery at that time. These courts were part of Alabama's statewide judicial system, though they operated at the county level. They were the next courts up from the local recorder's or municipal courts such as the one where Mrs. Parks had been convicted of disorderly conduct and where my airport seating case had been dismissed. Recorder's court cases could be appealed to the circuit courts. Above the circuit courts were the state courts of civil and criminal appeals, and above them was the Alabama Supreme Court. Appeals beyond the state level went to the federal courts.

Judge Carter has since retired and still lives in the Chisholm Community in Montgomery. He and the former sheriff, Mac Sim Butler, still meet at the Courthouse for coffee with some of the old-time lawyers. Judge Jones died many years ago.

While Judge Jones and Judge Carter were the two circuit judges, the old-time lawyers around the courthouse knew that the person who really ran the Circuit Court of Montgomery County was the circuit clerk, John Matthews. Mr. Matthews was truly a Southern gentleman. Early in my practice, I established a very good working relationship with him. While I am of the opinion that he believed in segregation, as did most white people at that time, he went out of his way to be fair with me and to show me that he treated me with the same type of courtesy and dignity that he treated white lawyers. It is important that a lawyer, and particularly a young lawyer, establish and maintain a good working relationship with the clerks of the courts because clerks can tell you how to file your documents, where to file your documents, exactly what should be included in them, and offer valuable tips that are not found on the faces of the judges or in the state code and law books.

I talked with Mr. Matthews on many occasions about my cases. When I would get a new type case and I didn't know exactly how to prepare the papers, I would go to Mr. Matthews and tell him that I had a case and I wasn't sure how to draft the documents.

He would say, "Fred, what kind of case do you have?"

I would describe the case. He would go in the files and pull out a case with similar facts, and I would use that case as a guide. At various times during my practice, I have raised almost every conceivable issue involving discrimination and segregation based on race. I have always presented each issue in a professional manner and have always enjoyed the respect of the bench, the bar, and the persons with whom I came in contact.

5

The Trial of Martin Luther King, Jr.

Charles Langford, Arthur Shores, Peter Hall, Orzell Billingsley and I represented those charged with violating the anti-boycott statute. The prosecutors were William Thetford, Robert D Stewart, and Maury B Smith. It was a challenge to plan strategy to defend ninety-eight persons indicted for allegedly violating the anti-boycott statute. Even though our clients were indicted in groups, there were still sixteen individual cases. Early on, the opposing counsel and the court agreed that only one case would be tried and that would be the case against Dr. King. The other cases would be resolved depending on the outcome of his case.

There had been no violation of the Alabama anti-boycott statute. The statute in effect said that if a person, without just cause or legal excuse, boycotted a business, then there was a violation. While we believed that the statute was unconstitutional on its face, according to *Thornhill v. Alabama*, a case in which the U.S. Supreme Court declared unconstitutional an Alabama anti-picketing statute similar to the one here, certainly it was unconstitutional as applied to our clients. We further believed that there was no violation because we had legal excuse and just cause for failing to ride segregated buses, particularly where we had been mistreated and humiliated.

In preparation for the trial, we filed a number of pretrial motions, namely a motion to dismiss, a motion to quash the indictment, and almost any other motion we could think of, including a motion to integrate the courtroom. As expected, all motions filed were denied. The motions were filed not so much because of the likelihood of success, but rather for the purpose of preserving the record. This is the manner in which African-American lawyers knew we had to conduct all cases, even misdemeanor traffic offenses.

The case was ultimately tried without a jury. Judge Carter, as we expected, found Dr. King guilty and fined him five hundred dollars. Our motion for a new trial was denied. We appealed. The case ultimately, like most of our other cases, was never decided on the merits, but was dismissed on a technicality.

Subsequently, all of the other cases were dismissed. No fine was ever paid and no one served any time as a result of these indictments.

Amidst the trials, tribulations, and protests, there were good times. The high point for Bernice Hill and me was our marriage. Bernice and her friends sent out two thousand invitations. When people sent word that they had not received an invitation, we went around and retrieved invitations from our close relatives and friends for those people who indicated they wanted to be invited. We wanted anyone who wanted an invitation to have one. I was considered most everybody's lawyer in the local African-American community, so a lot of people wanted to come.

We were married June 17, 1956, in the Holt Street Baptist Church. Our own church, the Holt Street Church of Christ, was constructing a new building and was not large enough for the crowd we expected. The wedding was to be at 6 p.m. The church was filled by 3 p.m. It was just like a mass meeting. People came early so they could get a seat. In the mass meetings, the people would get off work and bring their dinner so that they could get a seat. That is what they did for our wedding. It must have been the largest wedding ever held in Montgomery up to that time. Maybe it still is.

It was a Protest wedding; that's what we called it. Everybody pitched in to help us because we surely did not have that kind of money. The baker, Mr. Shaw, made a huge cake and did not charge the regular price. For something borrowed, Bernice wore Dr. Hagalyn Seay Wilson's wedding dress. She was the daughter of Reverend Seay and the sister of attorney Seay. I purchased Bernice's ring from Mrs. Frances Burk's husband, the owner of Burk's Jewelry, with a special discount. The church was decorated by my brother, Hugh, who still owns a floral shop in Montgomery. My childhood friend, K. K. Mitchell, minister of Holt Street Church of Christ, performed the wedding ceremony. The reception was at the Derby Supper Club, owned by D. Caffey, who served as a personal bondsman for many of the ninety-eight who were honored by being arrested for allegedly conducting an illegal boycott. Caffey was also the uncle of attorney Calvin Pryor who later became one of my law partners and recently retired from his position as assistant U.S. Attorney. Another of Caffey's nephews was Dr. Julius Pryor, a noted surgeon, who was also my mother's surgeon. All of the arrangements for the wedding were done by African Americans.

The day after the wedding, Bernice and I left for a working honeymoon. My step-brother Curtis Arms, and his wife, Minnie, accompanied us to Cleveland for a reception and then to San Francisco, where I was the Montgomery Branch delegate to the annual convention of the NAACP. Our honeymoon was cut short because the Alabama draft board ordered me to report for a physical examination in preparation for my induction into the army.

Meanwhile, two days after our wedding, on June 19, 1956, the United States Court for the Middle District of Alabama ruled in *Browder v. Gayle* that the city ordinances and the state statute requiring segregation on Montgomery buses were unconstitutional. As you can imagine, this was quite a wedding gift.

This was a day of rejoicing for the Movement and a great day for African-American people in Alabama. The ruling provided the impetus needed to keep the protest alive. In a broader sense, this was a great day for all the people in America. For the first time, a court had declared unconstitutional city ordinances and state statutes requiring segregation on city buses. The court used *Brown v. Board of Education* (the school desegregation case) as precedent for declaring segregation laws on buses unconstitutional. *Browder v. Gayle* is a landmark case and has been used many, many times as precedent for declaring segregation in other areas unconstitutional. The case is also significant in that it is the first civil rights case handled by Judge Frank M. Johnson, Jr. It was also significant to me because it was the first civil rights case that I won, making the first step toward realization of my goal to "destroy everything segregated I could find."

However, the white power structure would not be outdone. They appealed to the U. S. Supreme Court. Therefore, our people still had to remain off the buses until the case was decided by the U. S. Supreme Court. The Bus Protest continued.

Montgomery's African Americans had been walking or car pooling for 192 days. There had been twenty-eight mass meetings and one mass wedding. The Montgomery City Lines had lost hundreds of thousands of fares. There had been a dozen bombings, any number of physical attacks by whites on blacks, untold incidents of petty harassment, firings, foreclosures, etc. Several hundred people had been arrested. The legal expenses on both sides must have been substantial.

We were not even tired.

So, the legal work went on. Whites employed many schemes to break the protest, including the refusal of the white-owned insurance companies to insure automobiles operated by the car pool drivers and protesters. Money had poured in from throughout the United States to finance our transportation system. A number of station wagons had been purchased and Rufus Lewis and his assistants had organized what amounted to a private, city-wide transportation company. The sudden inability to get insurance on these vehicles was a big crisis. When no one else would or could help, Martin called upon Mr. T. M. Alexander, a successful African-American insurance businessman of Atlanta. Mr. Alexander placed insurance coverage for Dr. King and the Montgomery Movement with Lloyd's of London. Alexander was no stranger to Montgomery. He was born in Montgomery. His father had been a contractor whose company had relocated Jefferson Davis's Confederate White House to its present site adjacent to the Alabama State Capitol. Martin's ability to reach out to successful African Americans outside Montgomery was a testament to his growing national prominence and influence, but it was also a sign of how hungry African Americans were across the country to strike a blow in the heart of Jim Crow.

Alexander's connection with Lloyd's of London got us past that crisis, but there were others. In another attempt to end the Bus Protest, the City of Montgomery filed a lawsuit on November 5, 1956, against the Montgomery Improvement Association, in the Circuit Court of Montgomery County, to enjoin the operation of the car pool. The City was represented by Walter J Knabe. Judge Eugene Carter presided in the case. The lawsuit was against Dr. King, the MIA, and the leaders of the Bus Protest. It is interesting that the city had not filed such a lawsuit earlier. If such a case had been filed in December 1955 or January 1956, the Bus Protest perhaps might never have garnered the necessary support, financial or otherwise, to sustain itself.

While this trial was in progress, on November 13, 1956, there was suddenly quite a stir and a lot of whispering in the courtroom. I was handed a note signed by WSFA-TV newsman Frank McGee, which stated "I need to see you immediately outside the courtroom." The case was in progress, but I excused myself. I went outside, and Frank said he had just received word over the wire service that the United States Supreme Court had just affirmed the local federal court in *Browder v. Gayle*, and he wanted me to comment on that decision. I told Frank I was very happy about the decision but I would have to go back into the courtroom, and after the session I would be glad to give him an on-camera reaction. I returned to the courtroom immediately.

Judge Carter immediately recessed court and never reconvened for the conclusion of the case against the car pool operators. I never received another notice from the clerk about this case. I assume Judge Carter entered an order of dismissal.

In any event, the battle was won. Segregated seating on city buses, at least, had been destroyed.

The news from the Supreme Court was not only music to my ears, but also to those of all the leaders—Mrs. Parks, Dr. King, E. D. Nixon, and others; we were all elated that the three-judge district court decision had been affirmed. We knew that segregated seating was wrong, and we believed that it was unconstitutional. Now the highest court in the land had upheld our position. It was sweet vindication.

At the time Frank handed me the note, all of the lawyers who were working with me on the case were present—Orzell Billingsley, Peter Hall, and Arthur Shores. When I returned to the courtroom, I whispered to them what Frank McGhee had told me. And of course we were all very happy. When Judge Carter recessed court he never indicated the reason for the recess, but naturally the news spread like wildfire.

The white court officials, the deputy sheriffs, and the white community, to put it mildly, were generally not pleased. The African-American community was ecstatic. We knew that we would be able to ride the buses on an integrated basis. Even more importantly, I think, our people realized that as we had won this battle involving segregation of the buses in Montgomery, there were other battles to fight, and we would also be successful in them.

Even though the Supreme Court had affirmed the decision of the three-judge federal district court panel declaring state segregation laws unconstitutional, it was thirty-seven more days before the official paperwork arrived in Montgomery. So the Bus Protest continued for a little longer. Finally, on December 20, 1956, the long-awaited day arrived. The MIA and the African-American residents of Montgomery ended their protest.

The three-judge district court entered an order acknowledging receipt

THE CHILDREN COMING ON . . .

of the mandate from the Supreme Court, officially ending the case of *Browder v. Gayle*. Not only did it end the case of *Browder v. Gayle*, but upon the arrival of the mandate, Dr. King, Mrs. Parks, and others boarded a bus in downtown Montgomery and rode it on an integrated basis. With the court decree in place and our people able to ride the bus as they elected, there was no longer any need for the Bus Protest, per se. Even though some of the meetings continued for a period of time, the Protest officially ended. The transportation system was dismantled, and the station wagons were donated to the various churches.

This was the end of one mighty struggle, but only the beginning of others. There were many more desegregation cases to come. Nevertheless, I had realized a personal milestone toward my goal to "destroy everything segregated I could find."

6

"Many outstanding accomplishments"

There were many outstanding accomplishments as a result of the Montgomery Bus Protest. Mrs. Rosa Parks triggered the Protest, and she became the heroine of the Movement because of the beauty of her character. Also, she brings to mind the words concerning the woman found in Mark 14:8, "She hath done what she could . . ." to restore dignity and command respect for African-American people. Mrs. Parks is a glowing figure who has earned a place in history because of what she started on a bus. Her resistance to dehumanization gave courage to the forty thousand African Americans who united to make the protest effective. Her example has empowered many other peoples throughout the world to stand against oppression and to overcome it.

The arrest of Mrs. Parks set in motion the modern-day civil rights movement and gave birth to a world leader, Dr. Martin Luther King, Jr., a future Nobel Peace Prize laureate. King was the type who attracted other leaders and potential leaders. Though King was never annointed a king, he was appointed one by the people of Montgomery, Atlanta, and later, America and the world.

As a result of *Browder v. Gayle*, the United States Supreme Court held that certain segregation laws in the City of Montgomery violated the due process and equal protection clauses of the 14th Amendment to the United States Constitution. This was the first case to establish such a precedent. And, in helping to keep the community together and motivated in Montgomery during the Bus Protest, Browder v. Gayle showed to the emerging civil rights movement the political usefulness of litigation strategies.

A young, newly appointed federal judge with only three months on the federal bench was given an opportunity to demonstrate to the world that justice could be obtained even in Montgomery, Alabama, the Cradle of the Confederacy. *Browder v. Gayle* was the first major civil rights case in the career of Judge Frank M. Johnson, Jr. He went on to preside over many, many others. There is little doubt that he was the most significant federal district judge in U.S. history on civil rights issues.

On a personal note, the Bus Protest and the related legal cases provided me an opportunity not only to begin fulfilling my ambition to "destroy everything segregated I could find," but the cases helped to establish my legal practice. The crowds attending the many trials which transpired during the Bus Protest saw my legal skills first-hand. Consequently, my case load became very demanding. The days when I could have a leisurely lunch with Rosa Parks and discuss youth work were long gone.

THE CHILDREN COMING ON . . .

It is rather interesting to note that most of the high-profile participants in the Bus Protest were in Montgomery during that period for specific purposes or to some degree became involved in the bus boycott by coincidence. However, in my case, I had intentionally left Montgomery for the purpose of becoming a lawyer. I returned to Montgomery to attack segregation. My involvement in the Montgomery Bus Protest was but the beginning of my putting thoughts and dreams of this goal into actions. The Bus Protest marked the beginning of my forty-year career to "destroy everything segregated I could find." By the way, I'm still on the job.

One could say that Mrs. Parks's refusal to surrender her seat on a Montgomery bus created an ever-widening ripple of change throughout the world. Her quiet exemplification of courage, dignity, and determination mobilized persons of various philosophies:

Martin Luther King—nonviolence
Clifford Durr—civil liberties
Fred Gray—integrated society
Jo Ann Robinson—courtesy and fair play
E. D. Nixon—everybody is somebody

A pebble cast in the segregated waters of Montgomery, Alabama, created a human rights tidal wave that changed America and eventually washed up on the shores of such far away places as the Bahamas, China, South Africa, and the Soviet Union.

And it all started on a bus.

Montgomery Voices

III

Thelma Glass:

Well, I'm a native Mobilian and a product of the public schools in Mobile, Alabama, a graduate of Alabama State 1941, valedictorian. And then to Columbia University for a Master's Degree and some later study at the University of Minnesota.

I give credit to Alabama State University, leaders of Alabama State University, and especially the late H. Councill Trenholm, who was president when I came and who taught me as a student and sent me to every job I've ever had. I had two (teaching jobs)—one at Henry County Training School and West Charlotte High School and then he brought both my husband and me back here to Alabama State in '47.

. . . Well, I think the returning veteran was one who felt, many of them, that they had made a contribution and they were entitled to a better life. Just equal opportunities. My husband was one of those veterans who came back. He had served. And I remember once when we first came riding on the streetcar, he didn't want to take a seat in the rear. And I said to him—before we get in trouble, we just gonna have to try to get some kind of an automobile. And it ended up then, you know, you couldn't buy new automobiles. We ended up with a secondhand Chevrolet, but he was one of those who was resentful of treatment and felt that there should be something better. And actually, my interest in things that were going on I felt that there was a political way to do it and on campus was a friend that I had known, a native Montgomerian, Dr. Mary Frances Burks, who was outstanding. She had a Master's, I believe, at 19. And, of course, when she died, she was a Ph.D. from Columbia University in English. But she was one who was a creator and initiator and an organizer. And those are big words. And somehow I feel that she has never been given the credit for he many things that she did.

For example, on campus, she had the idea of Club 21, all veterans who returned. We organized and worked with them to vote. Rufus Lewis was, you know, working on the side and everything. He was one of the hardest workers in voter registration that I've ever met in my life. And then, at that time, for example . . . everything was separate. And blacks had no opportunity to participate in elections. Electing a mayor and all of these kinds of things. And Mary Frances organized what we call "Youth City" and the singers from three high schools—Alabama State (high school), Carver and Booker Washington—were invited to "Youth City" and this was their first introduction (to democracy). We had them go do all the things . . . how to—they elected a youth mayor and made bills and all of these kind of things. It was, I believe, a two or three-day performance. The activities were mostly at the Alabama State campus. And we were interested then especially in getting the young started right. And then those who were ready to become active—and of course, voting councils and working with voter registration, all of that—from Rufus Lewis to M.L. King when he came, because I worked with him in all the clinics and things and what not. Because we were determined that if we could get them registered to vote, some things could be changed. And it would mean a better life for all of us.

. . . I was one of the women in the Women's Political Council movement. And it all started with Dr. Mary Frances Burkes. She was the first president of this organization and then Jo Ann (Robinson) became the second president.

We had two very strong chapters going, but the whole idea was to have a political council in each area of Montgomery. Four, I think, was in the original plan: east, west, north and south, with its own membership and what not. I worked all the time with the original chapter that was started, you know, mostly made up of persons like me who were in at the University and school teachers and others in the city and what not—and some outstanding religious leaders—women who had always shown interest in making things better. And we got ready—we were—after a series of things which really shook us up, you know, like people getting hurt on the bus and I can't remember all the details—somebody was killed—I can go back in my notes and find it. People were being mistreated. Closing the parks and all these things. Well, we were just—decided that we would get together. And I think the thing that pulled all of us together was the fact that everybody used the bus. And it's the only thing that I know of where people have been as united as they have. The success of it was a fact that it touched everybody. The one thing that they had. And that so many people had been embarrassed and hurt. And we tried all kinds of ways, the city you remember—the story is much too long (to tell all of it now)—said they didn't own the buses and the bus was owned by some company, I've forgotten where it was. We tried to negotiate with them and all of these kinds of things. But the women in the council had really organized the plan of what would happen if we had a boycott. And the late—and we invited the late E.D. Nixon into our meetings at that time, you know. To take care of every (traffic) citation . . . the city began to retaliate. We began to lose members, they got threats—if they stayed in the council, (they'd lose) their teaching jobs—people had children to feed and all that, and you know, about that situation. So gradually, membership just dropped and dropped until on campus I remember there were just four of us left, Jo Ann Robinson, and J. E. Pierce and Mary Frances Burkes and myself. That was the nucleus.

. . . (We had many leaders). . . . Rev. Vernon Johns . . . was one of the forerunners. . . . He was the one who started the store here. And it was located right there next to his house. . . . [He was] one of the most gifted men that I've ever met. Lecturer, orator—could just stand up and quote chapters—looked like to me—from the Bible. One of those kind of individuals. A person who was interested in black enterprise and development. With the common man's touch. He'd put on his overhauls and go up to Virginia and bring hams back and things and put them in the store. And that kind of thing. And a very outspoken person at injustice. His wife worked with me at the college. She was a musician, a brilliant woman too. Altrona Trent Johns. Brilliant musician, especially in children's music. And he had some gifted children. One or two of them finished Phi Beta Kappa and what not.

Alfreida Dean Thomas:

I met Dr. King when he became pastor of our church, Dexter Avenue Baptist. I don't remember the year. I was a member of this church, and he came down for a trial sermon—as they call it.

At the time I was in high school, and as a young person in high school I was very impressed because he related to us—I say "us" because there were other children in my Sunday School class and we would discuss things, whether or not we liked or did not like them. We were all very impressed with Dr. King.

. . . he never looked above you, or around you, but right at you every time. He would always speak your name loud and clear and would always make some personal comment which was very elevating or would give some word of encouragement or ask how you were at school, or how was your family. This was just the initial greeting.

Shortly after he came, I graduated from high school, and he started this scholarship fund. I was one of the first recipients of the scholarship fund, and he, of course, awarded it to me.

. . . Well, it was easy to feel that you knew Dr. King personally at church; he just made you feel that way. However, later after Mrs. King joined our congregation, I got to know her very well because by then I was in college and was a music major. I became very attached to her, and through her I got to know him much better than I had just being at church.

From the very beginning he made you know him personally. I suspect that we always felt very attached to both him and the family from the very beginning. I always say this because I grew very, very attached to Mrs. King. Sometimes I would forget that she was Martin Luther King's wife. I never called her Coretta, but to me she was "Coretta." I knew him, like I said, through her. All the time I always felt very, very close to him from the very beginning until the time that he left. Even after he left, I felt that anytime I went to Atlanta I would call. I almost felt like a member of the family with Yoki and

Mrs. King and Dr. King. I saw him more when I would come to the meetings than I did when I was in the home because I was always with the children—with Yoki or Marty—or with Mrs. King or some of the other girls who were there.

I was closest to him, I would say, if you were speaking in a spiritual sense, during the sermons in church. I just always felt that everything that he said was directly related to me, as well as the other people, but very, very directly related to me and very much an influence on my life. So I don't really know any special period of time when I felt closest; I always felt close to him. I just can't say like 1959 or 1955; I always felt close to him. It's like I said, there was a very quick identity with Mrs. King which naturally meant that I was identified with Martin Luther King.

I felt that Mrs. King was a very, very strong person; from the very beginning, this is what impressed me—I suppose because I was insecure and a teenager and at that time I needed someone strong. Of course, there was my mother—there is always your mother—but you need an outside figure to identify with I think also. Your family you accept and you know what they're like, but then you've got to go into the outside world.

I've always felt that she was the backbone, as most wives are. I've always felt that she was always the strength of Dr. King—always—more than normal. I know his family was always there. Although everybody made sacrifices in the protest, I think that the sacrifices that she made personally were very great. I mean, I don't know that much intimately, but I mean as a wife. Now that I'm married, when my husband goes away to school for a month, I'm about ready to say, "Look, forget school. It's not that important." But I think that the fact that she had children—he was away when she was expecting Yolanda. Even after Yolanda, he was away and she had many anxieties. Yet she held up so well—not just in public—it was even at home. She was able to give strength when everybody else was anxious and afraid. I have never seen Coretta afraid—never, never, never.

I'm sure they complemented each other. I'm sure that he must have been the same kind of person—like I say, I didn't know him that well. But I do know that she was very strong. I don't know why she was strong. Maybe this was her personality. I remember reading where she said that her experiences at Antioch College prepared her for this. She was, and I'm sure she still is, a tremendously strong person.

First of all, she had just graduated from Boston Conservatory, and at that time I was gung-ho on opera and wanted so much to continue my studies in music. I was a music major (piano major). To me, anyone who had a strong love of music I liked. She had a love of music. I would talk to her, and I would sing solos. She was a very warm person, too, from the very beginning.

She was a consistent person—very consistent, very true, and, I don't know, somehow very pure. She came across to me very, very early as being an unflinching, true person.

Of course, he was the same way. I suppose then that I identified more with women at that time because of my upbringing—my grandmother had raised me.

Like I said before, I really think that she was the strength. I think that if she had been kind of fickle-minded—which in no way describes her—or the kind of whining wife or whining mate, I'm not so sure that he would have had the happiness and encouragement to go on the way he did. I know this discussion has shifted from Dr. King to her, but I really knew her well.

. . . He would always refer to her as "Corrie." When I was at their home, it was all "Corrie," "Corrie," "Corrie," "Corrie," all the time. Just the few things that I could gather—and, of course, at that time I was a teenager—I just had the feeling that when he would walk in the door, he would have a relaxed countenance and just a love for her. I really do. I remember that a few times when I would ask him something, he would always say, "Ask Corrie, Alfreida, ask Corrie." He would say, "Gee, I don't know, ask Corrie." I have the feeling that every decision that he made, he consulted Mrs. King first.

I do remember a few discussions—of course, other people were there—when some of the others were getting weary. I remember specifically because I was keeping Yoki at the time. There were some anxious moments, but instead of her being anxious she would be angry. She would say, "Well, I don't see why this has to be or that has to be." She really meant it; she wasn't really afraid at all. I remember once when someone said, "Well, I'm afraid to say this on the telephone." After hanging up, she said, "How can people be afraid to say things on the telephone?"

Whatever it was on the other end, someone must have been very anxious about Dr. King or something. But I don't think she was ever afraid.

Other members of the family would occasionally come over. I didn't get to know any of them personally. They would also make you feel very warm; they would always say, "Hello, Alfreida" and were very warm.

I remember that whenever they would come over it was such a beautiful family relationship. They were all just so relaxed and so wonderful. Like I said, I really wasn't involved in their family relationships, but I was struck by the warmth that they all portrayed to each other. They'd all sit down—Dad, Mother, Christine—and I thought, "Gee, with all of the degrees how will they relate to each other? Are they any different from everybody else?" But no, they were warm just like any other family. I couldn't tell you any specific influence because I just don't know. And besides, at that time I was a teenager and like, you know, in my own world anyhow.

. . . The mass meetings were very really something to look forward to. There was such a feeling of unity that I had never felt in Montgomery before. There were all kinds of people. For such a small town, there was so much division among people just on the basis of "Did you work here," "Did you work there," "Who is your mother," and "Who is your father?" that it was unbelievable. I felt for the first time that here were people who had been separated just on really fictitious reasons but were not together in oneness of purpose. This alone was enough to make a good feeling.

The meetings were carried on in the traditional Baptist way. The meeting would start with someone singing and handclapping—unaccompanied singing. Someone would start a good old hymn, and then it would go into spirituals. There would be no plan—nothing planned—prior to the coming of the speakers. When the speakers, either Abernathy or King, would come in, the people would stand and clap. When the speakers would make their speeches, people would give very warm responses of "Yes, yes, yes" to whatever was said. There was no holding back on anybody's part. There were even whites in the group who would, of course, stand back in corners. But for the first time I felt that Blacks did not care. People, you know, who on street corners would be afraid to say anything, absolutely did not care. There was religious fervor during the meetings, but this is very traditional of any church gathering in Montgomery, I think. This is just a way of letting off steam; this is typical. But I thought it was very good.

If the mass meetings would start at eight o'clock, people would start pouring in at four to get seats. By six o'clock if you weren't there, then there was standing room only on the outside. It didn't matter where the mass meetings were held.

. . . I don't know how local whites reacted to Dr. King, but I do remember two occasions during the boycott mass meeting. In one, a man came up during contribution time and put some money on the table. The lady who was taking it up was shocked. I looked at her and people asked, "Well, how much did he give?" He had given $50; then he went out. Others that I would see were really listening; they were really listening. They may have been coming to keep an eye on what was going on, but I have a feeling that they were really moved. Now I don't know what they did when they went out, but I had the feeling that they were really, really moved.

. . . I think Dr. King's—his greatest contribution was himself, and that encompasses everything—and what he was and what he was willing to give, what he had, not just to the blacks, but to all of us. I think his greatest contribution was the uplifting of people, period: the uplifting of their spirits and their souls to becoming aware that there is oneness in all of us. In this oneness, I think, he gave to us the fact that we could reach this oneness which is eventually God. I feel that in all of these protests and these movements and his speeches, his greatest contribution was to bring us all together, which I feel is God—oneness.

I think that what was motiving him to do the things that he did was something which I think we all have, but I think that we're not willing to listen as he was. I think he was disciplined to listen from his experiences and from his training, and I think he was more willing to hear. He was probably more capable of hearing. He was willing, I would say. For this reason I would say that he had a sense of destiny. I know that I have read this many times, but I think he was more willing to listen than many people are.

I've read that he had a destiny, and I've heard others who were closer to God and to destiny than I am. I don't know; I really don't. But he was more willing to be an instrument, a true instrument, not just a speaker—but I mean a really true instrument.

Idessa Williams Redden:

As a child growing up, I was born on Hill Street, I was from a very poor family. My great-grandmother reared me up. Her nephews was the one that took care of her—and her nieces. So this is how we lived. And they took care of my grandmother so therefore they took care of me. I was able, I went to— well, at that time I couldn't go to a public school because we was considered out of the city limits—and I went to a little one-room school on Hall Hill. I can't recall the name of that street now, but—I had a man teacher—at that time we was going to school about six months out of the year. Of course all this is in the city limits now.

Back in those days, black people thought they had to, I'll use the word, "knuckle under" whites to survive. And that just wasn't my thinking. And of course I was considered as radical. And of course I will admit to a certain extent I am, because I just couldn't see myself [shufflin']. I can recall, if you don't mind me telling it: I was working the night shift as the floor lady. That morning [there was a] young man who was a bundle boy, named George Edwards. He told me, Mr. Geeson wants to see you. Don't leave until he gets here. So I waited and waited and after everybody's shift came on for the 7 o'clock and the 7:30 came, 8, and he hadn't come around to talk to me, so I start out the door. So he sent him to catch me. So I went back and we sat down and he started to telling me about if, uh, the girls could do better work if they didn't go to BT's. Well, BT had a nightclub on the corner of Jeff Davis and Dawson Street. So I had three answers for him.

These are the answers. I said: "Now, I'm going to tell you, first of all, the reason why I will not sit and talk to you about my people—although they are your employees—I have too much race pride. Secondly, is because you are not going to come and talk to me about neither one of those women up there in that front office (and those women was white women). And thirdly, when these Reliance Manufacturing employees leave this property, you do not have control over them. So they can go where they please. We are not in slavery."

And he told me I needed to go up North to live because I had too much hate in me to live in the South. My answer was to him that I'm going to stay right here in Montgomery, Alabama, to try to help straighten it out. And one day I met him in a grocery store, Delchamps, on Court Street, and he always called me, you know, "little girl", and he said, "How are you?" I told him I was fine. So he said, "You look well, are you driving that car out there?". I said," Yes." He was driving a Cadillac. Of course, not that I ever expect to own one, I told him, "Yeah, one day I'm going to be driving one of those things that you are driving." So he just laughed and he went on.

. . . By living in Montgomery as a child, I always felt there was a need for something, but as a child I didn't realize what this need was for. I worked on a job that I couldn't understand why blacks—at that time, it was "Negroes" or "Niggers"— were treated the way they were being treated.

. . . The evening after Mrs. Parks was arrested, my cousin, Mrs. Consuela Quitton came in and told me—she was teaching at St. Jude Catholic School—

that we was not supposed to ride the bus on Monday, my reply to her was this: "Oh girl, that's not going to work." So that Monday morning, the bus was one block over from where I lived. And I went around the corner and I stood there to watch the buses as they passed. And to my surprise, nobody was on the bus. So I went back home amazed and said to myself, "Maybe these people do mean business."

That Monday afternoon when she came in from school, she said, "There's going to be a mass meeting tonight. Do you want to go?" I said, "Sure. About what time." She said, "We'll go up there about a quarter to 7." So we left home about 6:30. Well, it didn't take us fifteen minutes to walk to the church, which was Holt Street Baptist Church. And when we got there, we just did get a seat in the balcony. And of course when the meeting started, I had never even heard of Martin Luther King—cause at that time I had been out of town during the summer working jobs while my husband did construction work in various parts of the country.

So when I heard Dr. King speak that night—and I had never in my lifetime got emotional in a church—I screamed to the top of my voice, "Lord, you have sent us a leader." It was just something about him that was different from all other ministers that I had heard. Now there are people—I will only say here in Montgomery, not only in Montgomery but around this country— that seemingly want to discredit him but they can't do it, because, in my judgment, Dr. King was a born leader and a born prophet.

During my lifetime and some others' lifetimes, there will never be a leader, not in this century, for the blacks, like Martin Luther King was. After that Monday night at the meeting, that particular meeting—my first meeting—it wasn't a meeting that I missed until I would go out of town in April and come back in November. Then I would come home and if it was meeting twice a week, you know, we would go to church at 3 o'clock in the evening for a 7 o'clock meeting. Because I had to sit on the front seat, so I thought.

And I can recall one night at which I was very ugly. I did ugly things. The reporters was at First Baptist Church here in Montgomery, Alabama, and they were sitting all in the aisles. Of course, this was the devil. I looked at them and I said to myself, "We can't go in their church, so why do they come here and sit anywhere they want to." And I just got up and started to stepping over them without saying "please," "excuse me." The next day Dr. King's secretary called me and she told me, "Dr. King wants you to come over to the office." So I said, "Hazel, I have just left." She said, "Well, he wants you back over here." So when I went in, he asked me to sit down and I sat down. He said, "Mrs. Williams, we've got to love our white brothers and sisters." But I think it was the look that I would give the whites when they would come in the church that he could tell that I still had hate in me. So I promised him. I said, "No, I don't promise you right now that I can start loving right away, but I am going to try to get some of this hate out of me."

. . . And of course, being treated like I had been treated from the whites, I couldn't help but to have it. I recall I was coming from State Normal School when I was in high school and a white man told me—there was street cars back then—and he pulled me off the street car when I stepped on the street car in front of him and he told me that no nigger supposed to get up on the street car before him. But I had an umbrella and I just wore the umbrella out on him. 'Course that wasn't what Dr. King wanted. 'Course I didn't know Dr. King at that time. I was a child. So when I went home and told my aunt and uncle about it—they reared me; my mother died when I was two. And they was so afraid that the Ku Klux Klan was coming to the house that night.

But I didn't have that fear. I guess it was just a part of me not to be fearful. And I don't intend to be fearful at this age. I wasn't fearful when I was a child and I'm not going to be fearful now. So with the Movement started, it gave me the opportunity to express and do some of the things I would like to have done in the past but I did not have a leader that I felt like wouldn't get me out in the middle of the stream and leave us there. And that was what he didn't do.

. . . So from there on (after the boycott), every move that Dr. King made, I tried to be there. And the first voter registration drive in 1960 in Selma, Alabama, I was there. And a dear soul that would go with me the minute I called and said, "let's go to Selma"—Mrs. Virginia Relf—she's deceased now. But I could call her at any time and say, "do you want a ride." And in '66 and '65, (we went , too). And (in '65, it was) a beautiful sight—well, I had just gotten home that afternoon—and Hazel Gregory, who was secretary for the MIA, called me and said—Martin had made an appeal to the National Council of Churches—"300 clergymen will be in here tonight." I said, "Well, Hazel, I don't know whether I'm going to be able to do all that driving tonight." She said, "we going to have to get those clergymen to Selma." So the first group came in around 9 o'clock. And I want to tell you it was a beautiful sight to see all those mens in their clergymen clothes. And I had a 1965 station wagon and the fellow that was killed—I took him to Selma from the airport here in Montgomery—Rev. (James) Reeb. So the next day, well, I drove that night from 9 o'clock to 4 o'clock the next morning meeting chartered planes. So the next day I had to go back to the airport with others who was driving. I picked up a rabbi, it was four a.m.—but this particular rabbi, he said that when he got the news of what Dr. King had asked for, he just told his secretary to call his wife and tell her that he was on his way to Alabama. So while going down the Selma highway, he said, "so this is the highway that George Wallace said we couldn't march up"—the Selma highway. And [a few days later] of course, to see the National Guards out there, you know, clearing the path to keep the Ku Klux from hiding in all the trees and things, it made me feel very good for Judge Frank Johnson to give us that protection—because he had federalized the Alabama National Guards, at that time.

PART 4

THE FEDERAL JUDGE

By Frank Sikora

From

The Judge:
The Life and Opinions of Alabama's
Frank M. Johnson.,Jr.

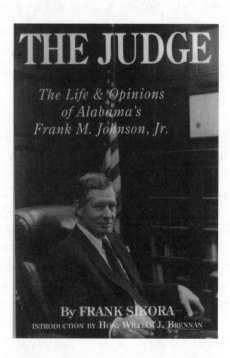

The material in this section is excerpted with permission from THE JUDGE: THE LIFE & OPINIONS OF ALABAMA'S FRANK M. JOHNSON, JR. *(Montgomery: Black Belt Press, 1992. 340 pages, $28.50. ISBN 0-9622815-9-X)*

1

"A powder keg of human discontent"

Wednesday, March 2, 1955, was balmy and spring-like in Montgomery; the magnolia trees were in bloom, and around the Alabama State Capitol building, jonquils lined the winding sidewalks. But the sun was hazed by gathering clouds that signalled rain or thundershowers by nightfall. That afternoon, as usual, black students from Booker T. Washington High School stood along the cobblestone streets downtown waiting to catch a bus home. Among them was Claudette Colvin, a sophomore, age fifteen, a slim girl standing five-foot-three and weighing about one hundred and fifteen pounds.

She boarded the Highland Avenue bus, made her way to the back, noting the seats for "Colored" were full. However, the last seat in the "White" section was vacant. She hesitated a moment, then suddenly sat down there. A short time later, a pregnant black woman named Hamilton followed and sat beside her.

It didn't take the driver, Robert Cleer, long to spot them in the rear view mirror. He ordered them to stand and let a white woman have the seat. In those days, Southern bus drivers had almost as much power as police officers. But on this day, the two blacks remained in the seat.

Angered, Cleer parked the bus and summoned police. Minutes later officers Paul Headley and T. J. Ward came aboard and made their way down the aisle. After some exchange of words, a black man stood and Mrs. Hamilton moved and took his seat in the "Colored" section. Miss Colvin, however, remained. The officers warned her that she was in violation of state and city codes which declared there was to be segregated seating ("It's the law," one of them said.)

Still, she didn't move. Then, according to the police report filed later, she "struggled and kicked and scratched" as they forcibly pulled her from the seat and removed her from the bus. Sobbing, she was handcuffed and taken to jail.

The incident had occurred near the heart of downtown, called Court Square. It was just down the street from the imposing Capitol where Jefferson Davis had been inaugurated President of the Confederacy. The square had once been the site of the county courthouse; a century earlier, it had been the city's main slave auction block.

Miss Colvin was booked, held in jail for a short time, then released on bond. She would later be tried in city court, found guilty and placed on probation, a ward of the state.

Her solitary protest on that bus had come nearly a century after a civil war and laws that were supposed to give black people full freedom. It would be the first salvo of what would become a legal-social revolution. The Thirteenth, Fourteenth and Fifteenth Amendments of the Constitution had ended slavery, given blacks citizenship and the right to vote. Yet, one decision by the Supreme Court of the United States effectively froze those laws and the rights they carried.

It was the 1896 case styled *Plessy vs. Ferguson* in which the court upheld the State of Louisiana's right to segregate its public transportation facilities. But far more sweeping was the doctrinal trend it carried — separate but equal.

That case allowed Southern politicians and Southern society to oppress blacks along every avenue of day-to-day life, restraining them as second-class citizens. "Separate but equal" became the misguided beacon for life in the South and would go unchallenged for more than half a century.

But Miss Colvin, the school girl, would contest it, and so would others after her. Her action was the beginning of what would become the most dramatic American story in the post-Civil War century. This plaintive cry for full freedom was not unlike that which had sparked the War Between the States nearly a hundred years before. And the backlash against it would be much the same as the terror that flamed across the Southern states during Reconstruction.

At the time, it seemed unlikely that Miss Colvin's arrest could in any way be affected by Frank Minis Johnson, Jr., then thirty-six years old. Johnson was a resident of Jasper, a coal-mining town in Walker County. He was also the United States Attorney for the Northern District of Alabama, with his main office in Birmingham. Montgomery was in the Middle District, out of his territory. Johnson was a tall, rangy man, standing six-foot-two and weighing a hundred and eighty pounds. He had thick brown hair which sometimes fell over his right forehead; the cheekbones were high, the jaw firm; his nose was long and hawklike; his brown eyes were narrow and piercing, glinting darkly when he was riled, twinkling when he found something amusing. There was something of the frontier about the man. He liked country music and buck dancing. He hated hunting, but loved to spend a cool spring morning fishing.

Like most attorneys, he knew change was coming across the land. The year before, in May of 1954, the U.S. Supreme Court had decided in *Brown vs. Board of Education* that racial segregation in the public school systems was unconstitutional. It would only be a matter of time, he felt, before the effects of that ruling would cut across the entire social, political and economic fiber of the country.

Johnson hadn't heard the first thing about the arrest of the black girl on the Montgomery bus. But fate would put Johnson and Miss Colvin on a course that would ignite the start of dramatic change to the Southern way of life.

On June 6, 1955, U.S. District Judge Charles Kennamer of Montgomery, the lone judge in the state's Middle District, died at the age of eighty-four. Almost from that instant rumors began that Johnson would be considered to fill the vacancy. A few days later he received a telephone call from the Republican party chairman in Alabama, Claude Vardaman, who asked if he would be interested in the job. Johnson said he would be.

JOHNSON

At that time I was a rather scarce item in Alabama — a Republican. My family came from Winston County, in the northwest section of the state, a county which had historic ties with the GOP dating back to the Civil War. We were what I call Lincoln Republicans. I had played a small part in politics; I hadn't sought any elected office myself. When Dwight Eisenhower ran for President in 1952, I had headed the Alabama Veterans for Ike and had been a campaign worker for him. In the national convention in 1948, I had been a delegate.

When Ike was elected President, he chose me in 1953 to be the United States Attorney for Alabama's Northern District. I had not planned to make a career of federal service. I figured I'd be back in private practice in a few years. But when the judgeship came open, it put a different slant on my future. It was a lifetime appointment. Most lawyers desire, I think, to be a federal judge. I was no different.

On September 26, 1955, Eisenhower suffered a heart attack while in Colorado; things like naming federal judges took a back seat. Then, on a Saturday night in late October, Johnson received a telephone call at his home in Jasper, Alabama, about forty miles northwest of Birmingham. The caller was a reporter from the *Birmingham News*.

"Mr. Johnson," the reporter said, "we have an AP story out of Denver here that says President Eisenhower has named you the federal judge for the Middle District of Alabama. We want to know what your reaction is."

"I haven't heard a thing," Johnson said. "You guys know more than I do."

"It's an authentic story," the reporter said.

"Well, if it's true, then you can just say that I am very pleased," Johnson said.

The following Monday, the Justice Department called him to confirm the report. The job was his. He was asked when he could take over and he replied, "I'll go to Montgomery as soon as I can, but I still have one very important bank robbery case up in Anniston to be prosecuted."

On November 7, 1955, eight days after he had turned thirty-seven, Johnson and his wife, Ruth, and their son, Johnny, eight, whom they had adopted at infancy, drove to Montgomery for the ceremony inducting him as a federal judge.

A city of 123,000, Montgomery was the heart of the Alabama Black Belt, the old plantation section curving across the middle of the state from Georgia to Mississippi, an area where cotton was still king. In the autumn months, before the harvest was complete, the cotton looked like snow lying on the reposing, amber meadows. On the low horizon were narrow hardwood thickets, aging fences and stately mansions which contrasted sharply with the shanties where the black tenants lived.

Most of those blacks, as well as those living in places like Selma, Union Springs, Marion and Tuskegee, could not vote, could not serve on juries, could not run for political office, could not get a Coca-Cola at a soda fountain and drink it there, had separate but unequal water fountains and restrooms at public places, and could not go to the same school with white children, not to mention that they had to ride in the back of public buses and stand while white people sat.

In Alabama and other Southern states, "separate but equal" was more than a malady in the education system: it was woven through the entire fabric of life, touching every aspect of society. Johnson was not sure the nation would ever really comprehend what it did to the black people who endured it all those years. Slavery might have ended nearly ninety years earlier, but in 1955 the black people living below the Mason-Dixon Line truly were not free . . . .

JOHNSON

I took the oath of office at 10 a.m. that day. Ruth and Johnny stayed for lunch, then drove back to our home in Jasper. Until school was out and we could buy a home in Montgomery, I would stay with my parents who had lived in Montgomery since World War Two, and Ruth and Johnny would stay in Jasper.

There was concern among the local people about me being the new judge; the Montgomery newspapers referred to me as an outsider, "a foreigner" from the hill country of Northwest Alabama; even called me a Yankee.

It went back to my Winston County heritage. During the Civil War, Winston had refused to fight against the Union and had, in effect, "seceded" from the State of Alabama. Most of the men there and in Fayette County, including great-grandfather James Johnson, had fought for the Union. Only a few people in Winston had owned any slaves. When I was growing up in the 1920s and 1930s, I remember only about a dozen black families in the whole county, so the caste system that marked much of life in the South was not a part of my upbringing. I just never thought about it in terms of racial discrimination (even though the few black children who lived there were not able to send their children to the same school with whites).

He was still getting settled into the new job when the sputtering fuse lighted by Claudette Colvin's arrest ignited a powder keg of human discontent.

2

"Long enough to need a law clerk"

On Thursday, December 1, 1955, less than a month after Johnson had become a federal judge, there was another incident on a Montgomery city bus. A woman named Rosa Parks, forty-two, was arrested after she refused to stand and give her seat to a white man. It was the final straw as far as black people were concerned. Overnight the word crackled like electricity across the city that some action was imminent. By Saturday, December 3, leaflets were being circulated in Negro neighborhoods reading, "Don't ride the bus on Monday."

At churches that Sunday morning, ministers called from the pulpit for the people to unite and "walk in dignity rather than ride in shame . . . ." After generations of segregation, something in the soul and heart of black Southerners had stirred. As one minister told his people, "This is God's movement."

It would prove to be a brilliant strategy, using the churches and the religious approach, especially so in the Deep South where the church was such a part of life for black people. In its Sunday editions, The *Montgomery Advertiser* ran a front-page story headlined "Negro Groups Ready Boycott of City Lines." (Carried as an expose, the story actually helped spread the word of the action to those black people who might not have gone to church or otherwise heard the word).

The boycott was the brainchild of E. D. Nixon, a tall, muscular man who was head of the Sleeping Car Porters Union and an NAACP official. He had signed bond to get Mrs. Parks out of jail, after obtaining legal guidance from white attorney Clifford Durr. Durr and his wife, Virginia, had accompanied him to the police station that night. When Nixon told his wife about the plans to boycott, she skeptically replied, "Cold as it is?"

On Monday morning, December 5, the city editor of The *Advertiser*, Joe Azbell, drove to downtown before five-thirty a.m. to see if the boycott would develop. He chose Court Square as the likely place . . . also the place with historic ties.

A misting rain glazed the streets; the wind, raw and whistling, rattled signs and rustled the Christmas decorations. Across the street was the National Shirt Factory, the building from where, in 1861, the Provisional Confederate government had wired the orders to troops in South Carolina to open fire on Fort Sumter.

Azbell spotted a solitary black man walking toward him. The man stopped by a shed adorned with a sign printed in crude lettering: "Remember it is for our cause that you do not ride the buses today."

Finally, from around the corner, one of the yellow buses came, easing down the brick-and-stone cobbled street. It stopped. The door opened. Azbell watched in fascination as one of the pivotal moments in the fledgling Civil Rights Movement began to unfold. The black man stood tensely in the moist chill, staring at the white bus driver.

"You gonna get on?" the driver asked.

Silence.

Again: "You gonna get on?"

"I ain't gettin' on," the man shot back, "until Jim Crow gets off."

For a moment there was no reaction from the driver; then, suddenly, he tilted his head back, roaring with laughter. The bus lumbered off. Azbell would later lament that he failed to get the name of either man. As a gray, somber dawn broke, the story was the same: buses would roll to a halt, the door would open, clusters of Negro men and women, some clutching brown paper bags, would stand stoically in the wind. The buses would roll away empty.

Some of the Negroes took taxi cabs or caught rides with people they knew. Most waited. Or walked. Then, around 7:30 a.m., the makeshift bus system devised by the newly formed Montgomery Improvement Association—headed by the Reverend Martin Luther King, Jr.,—swung into action.

That same day, in city court, Mrs. Parks was found guilty; it was appealed to the state court system.

Johnson's view of the boycott was limited. He saw scores of blacks walking as he drove to work in the mornings, huddled in the chill, waiting for a ride. And he read newspaper accounts of their rallies at the churches. The national press was already taking note of the Reverend King, then only twenty-seven.

The judge told his wife that the issue was bound to come before him, sooner or later. It didn't take a crystal ball to know that. He would see his wife on weekends, driving to Jasper every Friday night and staying until Sunday night. The Johnsons still hadn't found a house in Montgomery.

As 1956 began, the boycott movement continued; the transit system, minus about thirty-thousand black riders each day, slipped into a precarious financial position. White resistance began to stiffen; King and about a hundred other black ministers were arrested for violating an Alabama anti-boycott law. Mrs. Parks, meanwhile, went before Montgomery County Circuit Judge Eugene Carter and was found guilty. Said the judge: "And the defendant, asked why this sentence should not be pronounced upon her, says nothing." She was given fifty-six days of hard labor.

But the sentence was put on hold because, on February 1,1956, attorneys for Claudette Colvin—the teenage girl arrested the year before—and other black women, came to the federal building and filed suit challenging the state's segregation code which required separate seating on buses. The case would be styled *Browder vs. Gayle*, after Mrs. Aurelia Browder, a black woman made to stand on a bus, and W. A. Gayle, Montgomery's mayor.

JOHNSON

That same day I wrote Judge Joseph Hutchenson, the chief judge of the U. S. Fifth Circuit, telling him a state law was being challenged which would require a panel of three judges to hear it. He must have thought me brash; a few days later he wrote back, brusquely noting that "it doesn't take a three-judge panel to hear a matter of local law." I sat down and fired off another letter, telling him the State of Alabama's segregation laws were overriding the city's bus segregation ordinance.

Hutchenson shot back a tersely worded message which, in effect, said "I beg to differ with you about the state's role." He told me to hear the case alone.

Finally, after a third letter, one which ran three pages single-spaced, the judge relented, agreeing that it would take a three-judge panel. He named Appellate Judge Richard Rives of Montgomery and District Judge Seybourn Lynne of Birmingham to hear it with me.

Hutchenson seemed to take a dim view of all my requests; when I had written him seeking permission to hire a law clerk, he popped back a quick reply: "You haven't been out of law school long enough to need a law clerk."

When the bus boycott began, the Reverend King and others pointed out the abusive treatment they had been subjected to on the Montgomery buses.

There were cases of pregnant black women being forced to stand. Negroes were expected to have the exact change; if they didn't, irate drivers often told them to get off.

There was the incident where a young Negro woman boarded with two small children and, while she hurriedly rummaged through her purse for change, had placed the youngsters in the front seat. The driver ordered her to move them. She asked for a few seconds. In anger, he sent the bus forward, sending the woman off balance. Then, he braked to a sudden halt; it threw the children out of the seat and onto the floor. In humiliation, the woman picked them up and asked to be let off.

Blacks, after paying their fare, were often told to leave the front entrance and enter through the second door, located about halfway back. There were cases, they said, where the driver would hurry away before they could get to the second entry point, leaving them on the sidewalk, minus their money.

But Claudette Colvin had challenged the system and so had Rosa Parks. On their behalf, and others similarly situated, the case had come to the federal court. It was set to be heard May 11, 1956.

Several days before, Judge Lynne came to Montgomery to join Judge Rives and Judge Johnson in preparation for the hearing.

In the meantime, the city of Montgomery had filed suit in state court asking that segregation laws be declared in force (this after the Chicago-based firm that owned the local transit system said it wanted to end segregated seating).

THE CHILDREN COMING ON . . .

Montgomery County Circuit Judge Walter B. Jones — whose father Thomas Goode Jones, had carried the white truce flag at Appomattox — quickly issued a ruling, saying segregation was the law in Montgomery. Rives, Lynne and Johnson were going to lunch that day (May 9) when they saw the headlines in the *Alabama Journal*.

In his ruling, Judge Jones had said, "Where in the United States Constitution is there one word, one sentence, one paragraph that says . . . the sovereign states cannot make reasonable rules pertaining to the separation of the races in public transportation?"

The three federal judges read the story with interest, then put it aside for lunch.

CHAPTER

3

"We represented ourselves"

May 11, 1956, the day of the hearing.

It was a sparkling morning; the magnolia trees near the entrance of the federal building shimmered in the sunlight. Blacks began gathering in front before 8 a.m. Most were tall, spare men in dark suits, and women in their Sunday dresses.

Johnson was joined in his chambers by Judges Rives and Lynne. Rives, the senior judge, was a member of the U.S. Fifth Circuit Court of Appeals. A minute or so after 9 a.m. a U.S. marshal popped his head in the door and asked, "Ready, your honors?"

Rives nodded. "Let's go," he said, beckoning for Lynne and Johnson to follow to the courtroom. They took their seats behind the sturdy oak bench, which measured about twenty feet in length. Johnson sat on the left, nearest the witness stand; Lynne was on the right, and Rives in the middle. As they waited, some of the spectators were still filing in.

It wasn't that large of a courtroom, with room for about two hundred. Johnson saw people shooting hurried glances over the place. The walls were beige, the drapes a pale yellow; the windows were high, the carpeting a soft green. Behind the judges' bench was a clock with Roman numerals, set against a backing of blue draping adorned with silver stars.

Within the restraining rail, NAACP attorneys Fred Gray and Charles Langford of Montgomery, and Charles Carter of New York, watched the crowd fill the seats. Across from them, Montgomery city attorney Walter Knabe, a short, slim man with close-cropped sandy hair, studied his notes. Also defending the City of Montgomery and State of Alabama were Truman Hobbs, who years later would become a federal judge, and Alabama Attorney General John Patterson, who would later be governor. Rives read the complaint. Then he turned to Gray and said, "Call your first witness." Aurelia Browder, a widow, was thirty-four, a nurse's aide, the mother of four, and a student at Alabama State University.

"Would you state your name, please?" Gray asked.

"Aurelia Browder."

"Where do you live, Miss Browder?"

"I live at Ten-twelve Highland Avenue."

"Prior to December fifth, did you live here in Montgomery?"

"Yes."

"And prior to that date did you ride the city buses?"

"Yes. Sometimes two or three times a day."

"Have you been riding the buses since December fifth?"

"No."

"Why did you stop riding them?"

"I had stopped riding because I wanted better treatment. I knew if I would cooperate with my color, I would finally get it."

"Have you experienced any difficulty on the bus in connection with the seating arrangements?"

"Yes," she answered, nodding for emphasis. "Several times I have."

"Will you please tell the court what happened?"

She replied, "April twenty-nine of last year and I was on the Day Street bus. I got a transfer from Oak Park bus in front of Price Drug Store. I was going to get off and go to the dry cleaner, where I would get out on Court and Day. After I rode up by the Alabama Gas Company the bus driver had three of us to get up and stand and let a white man and a white lady sit down."

"When you say three of you, do you mean yourself and . . . along with two other Negroes?"

"Myself and two other Negroes," she said. "I was sitting in a seat and another lady beside me and the seat just across from me there was just one colored person in there. And he made all three of us get up because he said we was in the white section of the bus."

Gray nodded. "If you were permitted to sit any place you wanted on the bus, would you ride . . . would be willing to ride it again?"

"Yes, I would."

"That is all."

Rives glanced at Knabe. "You may cross examine."

The Montgomery city attorney, a soft-spoken sort, rose, paused for a moment while he scanned his notes, then moved forward slowly, rolling a pencil in his hands. "You say you stopped riding the buses about December the fifth, 1955, is that correct?"

"Yes sir."

"And I believe you said you stopped riding at that time . . . because you wanted better treatment, is that correct?"

"That is right."

Knabe strolled about, his eyes on the floor. "It is a fact, is it not, that at that time the Reverend King and several others so-called Improvement Association, I believe, made such a demand? Is that right?"

"No." She shook her head slightly.

"They did make some request, did they not?"

"I would not call it that."

"What would you call it then?"

"We, the Negroes," she said, clasping her hands tightly in her lap, "request the Reverend King, and he not over us."

Knabe shrugged. "You didn't understand my question. Did Negro King ask three certain things at that time, did he not? One was, you said, for more courteous treatment on the part of the bus drivers. That is correct, isn't it?"

"That is correct."

"And you then asked for seating first come, first served, didn't you?"

"Yes."

"And that . . . you said unless you were granted all three of them, you would not return to riding on the bus, is that correct?"

"Yes," she said.

"In other words," he continued, "you did not stop on account of segregation, but you stopped riding before the segregation issue was ever raied; that is correct, isn't it?"

"It is the segregation laws of Alabama that cause all of it," she announced.

"Just answer the question," he snapped. "Isn't it a fact that your mouthpiece put into—"

"No!" she cried. "He did not put it into us—"

"—is it not true," he persisted, his voice rising, "that he put into the newspaper a statement of his requests, and he specifically stated in that that the segregation statutes were not involved?" A puzzled frown knitted her forehead. "Do you know that?" he quizzed. "Didn't you read what he put in the papers?"

"Yes, I did."

"And that was in there, wasn't it?"

She stared at him a moment. "Yes."

"And also your attorney sitting there," and Knabe turned to gesture, "attorney Gray, also at the meeting . . . put out a statement that the segregation laws were in effect. That is correct, isn't it?"

"Yes."

"And you had the bus boycott on at the time. That is correct, isn't it?"

"That is correct."

Actually, Knabe's argument was a play on words: Blacks wanted better treatment, black drivers, and seating first-come, first-served: i.e., meaning no segregation.

The next witness was Mrs. Susie McDonald, seventy-seven, who testified that she had lived all her life in Montgomery and had been a regular rider on the city buses until December 5.

"Why did you stop riding the buses?" Gray asked her.

"Well, I stopped because we were asking for it, but we didn't expect to get it, we didn't. We all had to stop, so I thought I would stop, too."

"Were you involved in some incident on the bus?"

"Only I had to get up and let some white people sit down," she said. "I was asked to move."

"You were asked to get up?" Gray asked slowly.

"The . . . yes, by the Cleveland Avenue bus driver. I don't know who they are. They asked me to move. I had to get up."

"That is all."

Rives glanced at Alabama Attorney General John Patterson: "Mr.

Patterson?" he invited. "Cross examine?"

"No questions."

"Mr. Knabe?"

"Yes, sir." Knabe questioned the elderly witness about King's involvement in the boycott.

She shook her head. "I couldn't tell you much about that."

"Now, when you stopped riding the buses on December fifth, there was no agitation of any type among Negroes for a change in segregation laws, or an interpretation of them, was there?"

"Well, there wasn't any court orders, but we have been mistreated for some time."

"That is not the reason you stopped riding the buses?"

Langford rose. "Your honor, I think all these questions are irrelevant. It is not what the Negroes in Montgomery have done or will do, is not an issue in this case. The question is whether or not this particular person is one who has been injured in being subjected to segregation."

Rives shrugged. "You have alleged the people stopped riding the buses for a particular reason," he said, directing the words to Langford, "and if segregation laws were declared (unconstitutional) in the matter that they would commence. I overrule your objection."

Knabe shot a glance at Langford, then turned again to face Mrs. McDonald. "You stopped riding the buses prior to the time any reference was made to any change in the segregation laws, is that right?"

"I had to," she said. "I was sick. I couldn't go."

"You stopped riding because of ill health?" There was surprise in his voice.

"No, not altogether. I was often mistreated."

"You stopped at the time there was agitation among the Negroes to stop, didn't you?"

"I didn't follow the others," she replied firmly. "I reached my own judgment. I stopped because I thought it was right and because we were mistreated."

"But you stopped at the same time the others stopped, didn't you? And their grievance at that time said they wanted more courteous treatment. That was one of the main things, wasn't it?"

A long pause. "Yes, sir."

"And that had nothing whatsoever to do with segregation law issues, did it?"

There was the first murmur from the crowd, an uneasy ripple that flowed through the courtroom.

"That is what we asked for," Mrs. McDonald responded, appearing to be slightly confused. "We didn't want no social equality. We wanted what we asked for. We wanted recognition."

"I see," Knabe said, "in other words, you stopped . . . you did not want equality of any type, but you merely wanted recognition?"

"That's right."

"No further questions."

Gray was on his feet. "Mrs. McDonald . . . will you ride the buses if segregation is removed?"

"We object to the question," Knabe said.

Rives shook his head. "She has said she will. Overruled."

"That's all," said Gray.

Mary Louise Smith, nineteen, the third plaintiff, took the stand. Langford questioned her, receiving responses that she had, like the others, stopped riding the buses on December 5.

"Now, prior to that time, have you had anything happen to you in any way . . . or any incidents?"

"Yes."

"Please tell the court what . . . just what happened."

Her eyes lifted for a moment, studying the ceiling of the high room. "Well, this particular incident took place on Highland Avenue bus on October twenty-first, 1955. I was riding the bus and I was sitting on the bus side reserved for 'white and colored.' I was sitting behind the sign that said for 'colored.' At this particular moment a white lady got on the bus and she asked the bus driver to tell me to move out of my seat for her to sit there and he asked me to move three times. And I refused. So he got up and said he would call the cops. And he asked me to move." Her eyes narrowed; her voice became more intense. "And I told him . . . I told him, 'I am not going to move out of my seat. I am not going to move anywhere. I got the privilege to sit here like anybody else does.' So he say I was under arrest, and he took me to the station."

"You were arrested at that time?"

"Yes, sir, I was." She said it in such a way to reveal that she was still perplexed by the incident.

"What happened after that?" Langford asked.

"Well," she said, "they arrested me and they kept me in jail for about two hours or more longer, and then they charged me five dollars and cost of court."

"You were subsequently tried in city court?"

"Yes. And they fined me nine dollars."

"As I understand it," he said, moving closer to her, "the bus on which you were riding had a sign, 'white' on one side and 'colored' on the other?"

"Yes, sir," she replied quickly, nodding her head. She gestured. "The card said this side was for white, and an arrow pointed to the back for colored."

"That, in effect, was a segregated bus?"

"Yes."

"You are a Negro," he said, "and you were required to move from that seat to allow a white woman to sit down?"

"That's right."

"Had it not been for the rule . . . , no I'm sorry. I will ask you this: Do you know what you were convicted of at the time they took you from the bus?"

"We think the record will speak for that," Knabe said. "We object to that."

"I asked her if she knew," Langford said. "Do you know what you were convicted of?"

She glanced up at Rives. He nodded at her. "Just answer yes or no," he said.

"No," she said. "No, I don't know."

"Would you ride the buses again," Langford asked, "if the laws were changed?"

She nodded. "I would ride the city buses provided we had no segregation on the buses . . . the city buses."

She watched warily as Knabe approached. "You say you were arrested back in October?"

"October twenty-first, 1955," she answered.

"Did you have a lawyer?"

"No."

He seemed surprised. "You didn't have a lawyer?"

"No," she repeated.

"You didn't appeal the case?"

"No, sir," she said, "I did not."

He examined his notes for a moment. "You were not interested at that time in the question of segregation, were you?"

She stared evenly at him. "I have always been interested, all of my life, because I have grown up in a period—"

"When did you first employ attorney Gray in this case?" he snapped, cutting her off.

Gray objected. "When she employed me has nothing to do with it."

"One of our contentions," the Montgomery city attorney said, his voice growing testy, "is that all this is one scheme and plan. These people have had the opportunity when this woman was in there to have tested everything they asked for today. And we are trying to find out if at that time she was in contact with him (Gray) and why it couldn't have gone in the usual course of procedure."

Shaking his head, Gray countered: "Your honors, whether or not she decided to exhaust the state judicial remedy under the federal code is a question of law and not a question of fact."

Rives sustained Gray's objection.

Knabe continued: "Now, you said on this incident you mentioned here, you said, 'he' said you are under arrest. Who is 'he'?"

"Policeman."

"Policeman? Of the city of Montgomery?"

"Yes."

"It wasn't the driver of the bus, was it?"

She shrugged. "Yes. He first tells me to get up and move."

Knabe scanned his notes, then: "Are you riding free at this time?"

"No. I'm not riding at all."

Again the surprise: "You are not riding any of the free buses that the churches are furnishing you?"

"We don't have no free buses."

"You mean you pay for the buses when you ride on them?"

She seemed puzzled. "What bus?"

"Those station wagons," he said quickly, exasperation in his voice.

"No. We ride those free."

"Now, you are riding those free then, aren't you?"

"Yes, I am."

He nodded. "Now, you said you stopped riding on December fifth. Why did you happen to decide on that particular day?"

"Well, I think one person has been treated wrong and somebody else had been treated wrong." She paused, her eyes playing over the crowd. "I just feel like I want to cooperate and do what I can to help them."

"You say," Knabe pursued mildly, "that you feel you should cooperate. Who are you cooperating with?"

"With the colored people of Montgomery."

"Did you get together and agree to stop riding on December fifth?"

"No, we didn't get together. We just stopped ourselves."

"You must have had a meeting," he said. "Who gave you instructions to stop on December fifth? Did you just say to one another, 'I am going to stop riding' and everybody at one time stopped?"

A silence. Then: "They must have said because nobody went back on the bus."

"Now, somebody said, 'Let's stop on a certain day.' Who was that?"

"I really don't know."

"But that was at the time when you had your first negotiations with the bus company and with the city, wasn't it? That you stopped, is that correct? That was December fifth, that is the time you stopped riding the buses, wasn't it?"

"Yes."

"And at that time nothing was said about segregation, whatsoever, was there?"

"Something was said about segregation," she replied sharply. "As long as I have been living I have known myself."

"Well, you didn't represent to anybody anything about segregation, did you, to any officials at all?"

"Well, I still—"

"Just answer the question," he instructed. "You, yourself, did not at any time say anything about segregation to any of the officials . . . the city officials, did you?"

"I did not say anything to them," she said.

"As a matter of fact," Knabe persisted, "Reverend King represented you, didn't he?"

"No. He didn't represent no one. We represented ourselves. We appointed him our leader."

"You appointed him as your leader—"

"Our leader," she corrected.

"But he did represent the colored people. He was the spokesman for the colored people?"

She nodded. "Yes . . . he and his assistants."

"That is all," he said, turning abruptly from her.

Gray rose. "Miss Smith, do you object to segregation?"

"Yes."

"Do the rest of the Negroes in the Montgomery section object to segregation, Miss Smith?"

"Yes, they do."

"We object," Knabe intoned.

"Overruled," Rives said, matter of factly. "Anything else of this witness?"

"No, your honor," Gray said.

"You may step down," the judge said. "Call your next witness, Mr. Gray."

4

"We were treated wrong"

If there was to be a star witness in the boycott case, it had to be Claudette Colvin, then sixteen. The blue dress she wore accentuated the firm dark skin. She walked up to the witness stand timidly, her eyes darting over the three judges.

"Where do you live, Miss Colvin?" Gray asked.

"I live at 658 Dixie Drive," she replied.

"And you stopped riding the buses on December fifth?"

"Yes, sir."

"Before that date, did you experience any incident on a bus?"

"The bus . . . yes, sir."

"Tell us about it, please," he invited.

"It was on March second, 1955. I was on my way home from school. It was the Highland Avenue bus."

"Tell us about . . . tell the court what happened, please."

She nodded, speaking in a soft voice. "I rode the bus and it was turning in on Perry and Dexter Avenue, and me and some other school children . . . well, I sit on the seat on the left hand side," and she gestured briefly, "on the seat just above the emergency door, me and another girl beside me."

"You say another girl was sitting by you and another girl was sitting across from you: Do you mean those two girls were Negroes?"

"Yes, sir," she said. "And he drove on down to the next block and by the time all the people get in there, he seen there were no more vacant seats . . . he asked us to get up and . . . and the big girl got up but I didn't. So he drove on down into the square and some more colored people boarded the bus. So Mrs. Hamilton, she got on the bus, and she sat down beside me . . . and that leaves the other seat vacant."

Gray raised a hand to halt her. "You mean that from across the aisle the other two girls had gotten up when the bus driver asked them to?"

"Yes, sir. So, he looked back through the window and saw us, and he was surprised to see we was sitting down, too. He asked her to get up, then. And he asked us both to get up. She (Mrs. Hamilton) said she was not going to get up and that she paid her fare and that she didn't feel like standing. So I told him I was not going to get up. So he said, 'If you are not going to get up I will get a policeman.' So he went somewhere and got a policeman."

As she related the eent, her voice achieved a subdued intensity. "The first policeman came in and asked who it was. So he told the policeman who I was. 'Why are you not going to get up? It's against the law here.' So I told him that I didn't know that it was a law that a colored person had to get up and give a white person a seat when there were not any more vacant seats and colored people were standing up. And so he got off. And then two more policemen come on. He said, 'Who is it?' And he was very angry about it. He said that is not new that 'I had trouble with that thing before.' So then he said, 'Aren't you going to get up?' He didn't say anything to Mrs. Hamilton, just to me. He said, 'Aren't you going to get up?' I said, 'No.' He saw Mrs. Hamilon but was afraid to ask her to get up. He said, 'If any of you are not gentlemen enough to give a lady a seat, you should be put in jail yourself.' And so a Mr. Harris, he got up and gave her a seat and got off the bus. And so she (Mrs. Hamilton) taken his seat and so the policeman again asked me if I was going to get up. I said, 'No, sir,' and I was . . . I was crying then—"

"Oh, God!" a woman in the crowd wailed.

Miss Colvin continued: "I was very hurt because I didn't know that white people would act like that and I . . . I was crying." She shrugged. "And (the policeman) said, 'I will have to take you off.' So I didn't move, I didn't move at all. So I just acted like a big baby. So he kicked me—"

Again the wail from the woman in the audience.

"—and one got on one side of me and one got the other arm and they just drug me out. And so I was very pitiful." She paused, shaking her head slowly, looking out over the crowd. "It really hurt me to see that I have to give a person a seat, when all those colored people were standing and there were not any more vacant seats . . . I had never seen nothing like that. Well, they take me on down, they put me in a car and one of the motorcycle men, he says, 'I am sorry to have to take you down like this.' So they put handcuffs on me through the window . . . ."

There was a hush in the room; she sat there shaking her head slowly, blinking, studying the floor. Several seconds went by. Then Gray asked: "And where did they take you, Claudette?"

Her eyes lifted and there was a trace of a smile tugged at the corners of her mouth. "City Hall. And from there I went to jail."

"Did they mention anything to you about the juvenile court or . . . well, instead of jail?"

She nodded. "One of the policemen, yes, sir. And they put me in jail and lock me up."

"Thank you," said Gray. "That's all."

Knabe drummed the pencil on the desk for a second or two, studying his notes; then he rose and walked slowly in front of the bench.

He spoke somewhat hesitantly. "You have changed . . . that is, you and the other Negroes have changed your ideas since December fifth, have you not?"

"No, sir," she said, shaking her head. "We haven't changed our ideas. It has been in me ever since I was born."

"But the group stopped riding the buses for certain named things . . . that is correct, isn't it?"

"For what?"

"For certain things that Reverend King said were the things they objected to."

"No, sir. It was in the beginning when they arrested me, when they seen how dirty they treated the Negro girls here, that they had began to feel like that all the time, although some of us just didn't have the guts to stand up."

"Did you have a leader?" he asked.

She puzzled for a few seconds. "Did we have a leader? Our leaders is just we, ourselves. We are just a group of people."

"But somebody," he insisted, "spoke for the group."

"I don't know. We all spoke for ourselves."

"Did you select anyone to represent you?" he pressed. "Like the Reverend King?"

She turned her head to one side, thinking. "We did select . . . quite naturally we are not going to have any ignorant person to lead us and . . . we have to have someone who is strong enough to speak up . . . someone with intelligence enough . . . we have got to have someone who can stand up and who knows the law and who knows . . . it is quite natural that we are not going to get up there ourselves and some of them can't even read or write . . . but they knew they were being treated wrong."

Knabe folded his arms. "Is the Reverend King the one you selected?"

"We didn't elect him," she said.

"You said you selected somebody who was better informed to represent you," he reminded her. "Now who did you select?"

"Well, I don't know anything about selections, but we all just got together—"

"But somebody spoke for your group," he snapped. "Now who was it?"

"I don't know," she said. "We all spoke for ourselves."

"Now just a minute ago I understood you to say that you selected somebody that knew the law better. Now . . . now who was that person?"

"Who knew the law better?" she asked, her eyes wide. "Now a lot of people know the laws better. Now, are you trying to say that Reverend King is the leader of the whole thing?"

Knabe rubbed his head in a gesture of exasperation. Then, with exaggerated patience, he said: "I am merely asking if Reverend King was one of the leaders who represented your group at that time, and expressed to the city commission what the Negroes wanted."

"Probably," she said slowly, "he was one of them who went to the city commission, but I don't know."

"You don't know at all then?"

She shrugged. "I don't know nothing."

"Now, was attorney Gray here one of those whom you felt knew the laws?"

She gazed at him, then shifted her eyes to Gray. "Yes, quite naturally . . .

he is a lawyer."

"Did you know at that time," Knabe said, his voice rising, "that he sustained that the state law didn't apply at all in the city of Montgomery?"

She shook her head, perhaps confused by his question. "I go to school myself and I know there is a lot of law, state law, national law and local law."

The attorney at one point asked the judges to instruct her to be more direct in her answers, and Rives said: "If you know the answers, just answer 'yes' or 'no'; don't make speeches."

For the next several minutes she replied curtly with either one or the other. Then Knabe asked: "Why did you stop riding on December the fifth?"

"Because," she said, her eyes narrowing, "we were treated wrong, dirty and nasty."

That comment drew murmurs of agreement from the crowd and a warning look from Rives. The girl returned to her seat.

Montgomery Mayor W.A. Gayle, one of the defendants, was called as a hostile witness by the plaintiffs. Langford questioned him.

"Mayor Gayle, what instructions, if any, have you given to the city police with respect to enforcing segregation?"

"We have told them to enforce all laws and ordinances that are on the books."

"I am talking about policemen now, with respect to segregation in the buses," the attorney said.

"That is one of the laws," the mayor said, "and I believe in segregation and I believe in enforcing the city ordinance concerning it."

Langford nodded. "One further question, Mayor Gayle. I think you have answered it, but I want to make it clear for the record. Your instructions with respect to enforcing segregation laws, is to arrest persons who violate its operation now and in the future, is that correct?"

"That is right," the mayor said, nodding to reinforce it. "That is the law and that is the way we enforce the laws."

"Your witness," the attorney said, turning to Knabe, who rose and moved forward.

"Mayor, did you, prior to the time of entering suit with this suit, have conferences with the various leaders . . . Negro leaders, including Reverend King?"

"Yes."

"And at that time did they make certain requests and state that those were the reasons for which the bus boycott had been begun?"

"That is right."

"Did they at any time say that there was any complaint with reference to segregation?"

"Reverend King made the statement and there was no reference to segregation even on December the fifth," Gayle replied.

"Since the bus boycott there . . . has there been disorder in Montgomery due to racial conditions?"

"We are trying to hold it down as much as we can," the mayor said, "but there is danger of bloodshed or something like that unless we can strictly enforce the segregation laws."

Knabe paused for a moment, then returned to his seat. Rives watched him. "Any further questions?"

"Yes, sir, your honor," Langford said, popping up, and moving quickly around the table. "Mayor, how did you know there was going to be bloodshed if segregation laws were not enforced? Have you taken a survey, too?"

Gayle shrugged. "It is my responsibility to look after the welfare and comfort of the people and if I anticipate anything I try to avoid it before it gets here . . . we don't wait until it happens."

Langford raised both hands in a gesture of bewilderment. "Well, people have not been riding the buses for about six months now and nothing untoward has happened, has it?"

"Well . . . they had shooting in the buses, knocked the windows out, and beating up the colored women and quite a number of things like that," the mayor said. "Are you familiar with what has been going on in Montgomery?"

"I am afraid I am not."

"You mention the people not riding the buses," Gayle continued. "I can cite you in my own mother-in-law's cook, who was cut up and beat up on account of it."

"Now, mayor," Langford said, "it is my understanding . . . I may be wrong . . . but the bus company, on or about April twenty-fourth, issued instructions that there was going to be no segregation on the buses—"

"And we warned them to cancel that order, too," the mayor injected.

"During those days of April twenty-four or April twenty-five, when the bus company issued orders that there would be no segregation," Langford said, "was there any bloodshed or violence?"

"None that I know of."

"That's all."

Knabe rose, a hand lifted to indicate further questions. Rives nodded. "Mayor, you said there were some Negroes who were injured during the time of this bus boycott. Who injured these people? Was it white or colored people?"

"It was colored people."

"Is it true that they were Negroes who were causing bloodshed because they objected to other Negroes riding the buses?"

"That is right."

"From your experience, is it your opinion that there will be violence in the event that segregation is permitted . . . I mean, that non-segregation is permitted?"

"In my opinion it would."

"Do you think the violence would be severe?" Knabe asked.

"I don't know what it would be," the mayor said, "but it would be dangerous."

Langford bolted up from his chair. "Mayor, do you know how many incidents of shooting, beating and knifing have been introduced?"

"No." The answer was hesitant.

"Well, if I told you that only two Negroes said they had been molested,"

THE CHILDREN COMING ON . . .

the attorney said, "would you accept that, Mayor Gayle? Only two out of the twenty-thousand or more Negroes in Montgomery?"

Gayle fixed a testy gaze on Langford. "Do you say we had no bombings?" he demanded. "Do you say we had no bombings, either? The only one I know of is the one that happened to my mother-in-law's cook. The rest were routine . . . that happened as the enforcement of the law."

"Well, the fact of the matter is," Langford said briskly, "you don't know how many shootings that have been as interference of Negroes riding the buses, do you?"

"I know some have called me and said they wanted to get back on the buses but they were afraid of a 'goon squad' who would hurt them."

"But you don't know for sure how many incidents there have been?"

"Not for sure."

There were other witnesses who, like the mayor, felt that if segregation laws were not enforced, there would be a dangerous situation not only in Montgomery, but throughout Alabama. One of them was city commissioner Clyde Sellers who predicted, "If segregation barriers are lifted, violence will be the order of the day."

To which Judge Rives puzzled aloud: "Can you command one man to surrender his constitutional rights — if they are his constitutional rights — to prevent another man from committing a crime?"

The hearing ended late in the afternoon; it was with an air of uncertainty that both sides left the federal building.

CHAPTER

5

"We're getting on this horse now"

For a case that the history books would call a landmark, it had occurred
with incredible swiftness — less than five hours, all told. And while it would
take several weeks to write and announce the opinion, the actual decision
took only ten minutes.

JOHNSON

Actually, none of us knew how the others felt at first. During the
hearing both Judge Rives and Judge Lynne had made comments that
they were not sure the Supreme Court had ended segregation in society
with its decision on schools (in Brown). I had not said the first word
during the hearing. I just sat there listening.

So we went into my chambers after it was over and sat there for a few
moments. Finally Judge Rives says to me, "Well, Frank, you're the junior
judge here. You vote first. What do you think?"

It was tradition that the junior member of a panel vote first so as not
to be swayed by the senior judges.

"Judge," I said, after thinking it over for a moment or two, "as far as
I'm concerned, state-imposed segregation on public facilities violates the
Constitution. I'm going to rule with the plaintiffs here."

And right away Judge Lynne shakes his head, no. But he doesn't speak.

Instead, Judge Rives looks at me and nods. "You know, I feel the same
way as you."

Judge Lynne continues shaking his head. "I don't reach it that way,"
he says. "The (Supreme) Court has already spoken on this issue in *Plessy*.
It's the law and we're bound by it until it's changed."

He had a tenable position, too, because, as he said, the Supreme Court
had ruled in Plessy that segregation was valid provided "whites and
coloreds" had "separate but equal" facilities in public transportation.

But I told Judge Lynne that there was no way to reconcile the *Plessy*
case in light of the more recent *Brown* decision. I couldn't reconcile it in
my mind how, on the one hand, the Court could put the stamp of approval on segregation as in Plessy, while, on the other, mandating the

     THE CHILDREN COMING ON . . .

desegregation of the races in public schools, to wit, the *Brown* case.

In the way it spelled out the *Brown* decision, the Supreme Court had confined the ruling to schools alone, not desegregation in other areas of public life. The wording applied to children and how segregation had a psychological impact on black children. But while it was narrowed to the school issue, it nonetheless set a doctrinal trend as far as Judge Rives and I were concerned. While it said nothing about transportation, it suggested that courts should now conclude that *Plessy* was no longer valid. Judge Lynne on the other hand, felt the Supreme Court had not intended *Brown* to be applied in other areas. And he was on sound legal ground, too, because he had a Supreme Court decision directly on point that backed him up.

As far as I was concerned, it wasn't a dificult case to decide. There were no conflicting constitutional questions at issue. The long and short of it was that there was a state law that said Negroes — simply because they were Negroes — had to ride in the back of a bus and had been extended to say they had to get up when white folks wanted their seat. Now (Montgomery County Circuit) Judge Walter Jones had asked the question, "Where in the Constitution is there one word, one sentence, one paragraph" that says you couldn't segregate folks in public transportation? My question was, "Where in the Constitution is thre anything that says you can segregate them?" It just isn't there. To the contrary, it specifically says you can't abridge the freedoms of the individual. The boycott case was a simple case of legal and human rights being denied.

The testimony of the four women — Miss Colvin and the others — merely reinforced that position. What was going to be unusual was the fact that our decision would, in effect, overturn a Supreme Court decision, namely the *Plessy* case of 1896. That was what made it a novel decision. A lower court had never done that before.

I point out for the record that my vote in favor of the plaintiffs in the case was not based on any personal feeling that segregation was wrong: it was based on the law, that the state imposing segregation violated my interpretation of the Constitution of the United States. It wasn't for a judge to decide on the morality question, but rather the law.

Actually, there hadbeen another suit filed regarding segregation on buses. A black woman in Columbia, South Carolina, had filed it but it was not a class-action suit. It simply asked damages for her as an individual and in July, 1955, the Fourth Circuit Court of Appeals in Richmond had upheld her claim. But that case was not a pervasive precedent on the matter. It certainly didn't pave the way for the decision that Judge Rives and I made.

At that time, the issue of segregation on public facilities was not getting clear-cut decisions from the courts. The day after the Fourth Circuit ruled on the Columbia case, it alsoruled that Prince Edward County, Virginia school system could continue racial segregation, using the puzzling argument that to enforce integration immediately was not consistent with the Supreme Court guide regarding "all deliberate speed."

Georgia Governor Marvin Griffith reflected the mood of the white South after the Supreme Court issued a ruling November 7, 1955 — the day Johnson was sworn in — which struck down segregation on the city-owned golf courses of Atlanta. Said the governor, "Any decision respecting segregation is designed . . . to force intermarriage (of the races). The state will get out of the park business before allowing a breakdown in seregation in the intimacy of the playground."

Johnson was sympathetic to the plight of blacks, but his vote was not based on emotion. He recognized, too, that the social customs of the South were going to be upended. But the pressure would be much greater on Judge Rives, because he was a native of Montgomery, a "hometown boy." Johnson was "the foreigner." The Montgomery decision was made public on June 5, 1956. It was a cloudy, cool day. The reporters had been told that the order was going to be released and they had gathered around the district clerk's office at the federal building.

Judge Rives was working on another case; Judge Lynne was back in Birmingham. Johnson had the order in his office and reread it a final time, then called in his first law clerk, Syd Fuller. As he handed him the order, Johnson said, "Well, Sydney, we're getting on this horse now. Let's ride it."

Fuller carried the opinion down to the office of the U.S. Clerk to have copies made. As he entered that office, news photographers in the hallways snapped his picture, getting the back of his head. "It was history," he would say later, "and they got the back of my head."

Some news accounts would say Rives and Johnson had stopped Southern tradition in its tracks. Johnson's own view was less cavalier: what he and Rives had done, he said, was correct a denial of full freedoms.

In part, the order read:

> We hold that the statutes and ordinances requiring segregation of the white and colored races on the motor buses of a common carrier of passengers in the city of Montgomery and its police jurisdiction . . . violates thedue process and equal protection of the law . . . under the 14th Amendmentof the Constitution of the United States.
>
> The 'separate but equal' doctrine set forth by the Supreme Court in 1896 in the case of *Plessy vs. Ferguson* can no longer be applied.
>
> There is no rational basis upon which the 'separate but equal' doctrine can validly be applied to public transportation in the city of Montgomery. In their private affairs, in the conduct of their private business, it is clear that the people themselves have the liberty to select their own associates and the persons with whom they will do business, unimpaired by the 14th Amendment. Indeed, we think that such liberty is guaranteed by the due process clause of that Amendment. There is, however, a difference, a constitutional difference, between voluntary adherence to custom and the perpetuation and enforcement of that custom by law . . .
>
> We cannot, in good conscience, perform our duty as judges by blindly following the precedent of *Plessy vs. Ferguson* of 'separate but equal'.

An opposing view was taken by Judge Lynne who wrote:

Only a profound philosophical disagreement with the majority that the 'separate but equal' doctrine can no longer be safely followed as a constitutional statement of the law would prompt this, my first dissent.

In issuing the opinion, Rives and Johnson said the injunction against segregation would not become effective for two weeks, to allow the city and state time to file an appeal.

Mayor Gayle said he didn't need two weeks; he had no comment for reporters other than to say the case would be appealed to the Supreme Court.

The Reverend King was pleased with the decision. But the boycott would continue, he said, pending the outcome at the Supreme Court.

In Alabama, white resistance to the Civil Rights Movement began even before the boycott itself.

In 1953, a year before the Supreme Court's *Brown* ruling, the Alabama Legislature, "that august body," Johnson called it, named a committee to "prepare any such legislation as may be required . . . to protect the citizens of this state" in the event of a court decision "which destroys the principle of separation of the races . . . ."

To be sure, Alabama's lawmakers had been very active before that. In 1947 they had passed a bill "empowering any motor transport company to provide separate ticket windows and waiting rooms for whites and coloreds" whether interstate or intrastate.

Even on buses operated by Greyhound or Trailways, blacks often suffered at Alabama terminals; while cities like Birmingham and Montgomery and others had dual waiting rooms, smaller towns did not, and blacks would have to wait sometimes for thirty minutes before the bus even resumed its journey.

In 1949, the Legislature had a bill which stated with dubious wisdom that "segregation is well established and favored by a large majority of both races as being a measure for preventing racial animosities and violence . . . ."

That same session also rapped Congressional probes of the violence caused "by hooded men in Alabama," and knocked President Truman's civil rights program which included an anti-lynching law.

It added that the effort by the Congress and the President to desegregate was not only "unwise" but also "unAmerican."

And to ice the posture of the state, when the Supreme Court ruling was handed down in 1954, the Alabama Legislature simply declared it to be "null and void."

Still, there had been some courageous voices in those times. One was Governor Jim Folsom who, in 1950, noted in a speech that "all men should have equal rights" and pointed out that Negroes made up thirty-five percent of the state's population, yet had not a single park where they could take their children. Further, he had said, even though many Negroes were qualified to vote, they had "maliciously been kept from exercising their right." The speech was given a cool reception. Then, the legislators responded by making Robert E. Lee's birthday a state holiday "reaffirming the belief in the principles of Southern Civilization." They also refused to approve a scholarship program for Negro nursing students, then authorized the stamping of "Heart of Dixie" on auto license plates.

Folsom was a man ahead of his time; he had proposed "one man-one vote," revenue sharing, and the abolition of the state poll tax, one of the measures used to discourage blacks from trying to become voters.

The impact of the bus boycott decision began bouncing across the South; in Delray Beach, Florida, the city council voted four-to-one to exclude a black neighborhood from the city.

In Birmingham, police commissioner Robert Lindberg confidently said "we don't anticipate or contemplate any change being made now or in the future as far as segregation on buses is concerned." But blacks were already preparing to test the issue there.

In Montgomery, a telephone heckling campaign against King and other Negro leaders intensified; white women, who drove to pick up their maids and return them home in the evening, were also victimized by such calls.

Judge Johnson and his wife began receiving prank phone calls and threatening letters. One of the letters received came from Bullock County, dated June 6, the day following the decision. It read: "If I had been in your shoes before I would have rulled (sic) as you did, I would rather have had my right arm cut off. I trust that you will get on your knees and pray to Almighty God to forgive you for the mistake that you have made."

A photographer from Savannah, Georgia, wrote: "If you ever show up in Savannah, don't expect our photographers for *The Evening Dispatch* to snap your best side."

JOHNSON

A day or two after the decision, I dropped by my parents' home and my mother was in the kitchen cooking supper. They had moved to Montgomery some years earlier. When she saw me she kind of nodded, kept on cutting carrots. Then she said, "Well, son, you got them on the buses, didn't you?"

I never got into debates with my mother; I just grinned, sat down beside her, took a bite of a carrot and waited.

"Well, I'll tell you one thing," she said. "You may have gotten them on the buses, but you'll never get them into the schools. The people of this state just won't put up with it."

Mother wasn't a segregationist; never had much to say about racial matters other than the fact that all people should be treated equally. She was a tough woman; tough, I mean, in her convictions and the way she viewed the world around her. She was stating what she considered the reality of the situation — not what she considered right. I told her when the school situation developed — as it surely would — I would deal with it. So she didn't say anymore. Just kept working on the carrots, looking at me every once in a while.

THE CHILDREN COMING ON . . .

CHAPTER

6

"Weary feet and weary souls"

On November 13, 1956, the Supreme Court of the United States upheld the June 5 decision of Rives and Johnson which banned segregation on Montgomery city buses. The impact in the city was like an electric shock; blacks gathered again for a mass rally at Dexter Avenue Baptist Church where King, now clearly a leader of national import, cautioned them. "We'll have to wait and see," he said. The city's mayor had not yet received the notification. Meanwhile, the State of Alabama asked for a rehearing by the Supreme Court; it was denied. On December 20, more than a year after the arrest of Rosa Parks, a U.S. marshal served the city and state officials with the federal injunction prohibiting segregation on the buses. "I guess we'll have to abide by it," Mayor Gayle said dejectedly, "because it's the law."

That night, more than fifteen hundred blacks collected at the Holt Street Baptist Church for a rally; the inside was packed, and people were spilled out onto the street for more than a block in each direction; loudspeakers affixed to the front carried the sounds of the freedom songs and the spirituals wafting through the winter night air.

"We sang "Swing Low, Sweet Chariot" and "This Little Light of Mine, I'm Gonna Let It Shine," and a whole lot of others," said Georgia Gilmore, then in her thirties. "Weary feet and weary souls were lightened. It was such a night. We didn't have to walk no more. Even before Martin Luther King got up there and told us it was over, we knew it was over and we knew we had won."

Bernice Robertson, seven, and her sisters, Rosetta, nine, and Naomi, ten, felt that triumph, too, as they sang. For more than a year they had walked more than eight miles a day, twice a week, just to take piano lessons, she said. "We had walked because it was right and because it was wrong to get on the bus. And it wasn't easy, either . . . because sometimes white folks would go by and blow the horn or yell things at us, because they knew what we were a part of, what we were doing."

At that rally King announced that the boycott would end.

"We must not take this as a victory," he said, "but merely with dignity. When we go back to the buses, go back with a quiet pride. Don't push your way. Just sit where there is a vacant seat. If someone pushes you, don't push back. We must have the courage to refuse to hit . . . we must continue to resist segregation non-violently. This dynamic unity, this amazing self-respect will soon cause the oppressor to become ashamed." He also praised the efforts of some whites. "If there had not been some discipline among them, some sense of moral responsibility, some sensitivity from the white community, there would have been more violence. We must return to the buses and we must be courteous."

The next day King, Nixon, Mrs. Parks and others boarded the buses for the first time in three hundred and eighty-one days. Most whites stared straight ahead in stony silence; but some spoke or nodded; it was reported widely in the press that one white man remarked to Mrs. Parks and some of the others, "Looks like it'll be a nice day."

(It's interesting that Claudette Colvin was not in the group and rarely, if ever, rode a bus again in Montgomery. After her arrest and late appearance in the court hearing, she was more or less forgotten. Later she would tell a reporter that she would sometime attend the rallies at the churches. "I would sit in the back," she said, "and no one would even know I was there." She would, within a few years, leave Montgomery, going to New York as a domestic worker.)

JOHNSON

> I remember that evening Ruth and I went to a Christmas Party at a home in the neighborhood. My mother was at home caring for Johnny. So right in the middle of the party mother calls and says, "Son, I think you better come on home."

> So we hurried back there, it was just a block or so away, and saw a fire flickering in the front yard. Somebody had put up a crude little cross there. It didn't bother me and it didn't bother Ruth. She's from Winston County and doesn't scare that easily.

> People are always asking me what I thought when I saw that cross. I didn't think anything. I guess I was supposed to say something; perhaps strike a dramatic pose, point, and in a falsetto declare, "Oh, look at that cross burning."

A few days later, the FBI picked up two juveniles; they were charged with disturbing the peace. It was passed off as a prank. But elsewhere the discontent was measured in more menacing tones. Early on the morning of December 23, a shotgun blast riddled the King home. No one was hurt.

The events in Montgomery again made ripples around the South; in Birmingham, the Reverend Fred Shuttlesworth, president of the Alabama Christian Movement, asked the city commission to lift segregation and when he was refused, he told them, "We plan to ride the buses in an unsegregated fashion." On Christmas night, his parsonage at the Bethel Baptist Church was bombed; his wife and children suffered minor injuries.

The spectre of violence haunted Alabama; on December 28, there were two buses fired upon by snipers; later, that same day, a third bus was riddled with bullets. Two shots struck a black woman, Mrs. Rosa Jordan; she was carried sobbing from the vehicle with wounds in both legs.

As the new year dawned, Montgomery was bristling with racial tension. The homes of King and Abernathy were bombed, and two black churches were heavily damaged by explosions.

And a black truck driver, Willie Edwards, Jr., the father of two, was pulled over one night by four Klansmen, driven to a bridge on U.S. Highway 231 north of Montgomery, and forced to jump into the cold waters of the Alabama River. He was accused of making remarks to a white woman. (He was driving the truck that night as a substitute for the regular driver, also a black; later, it was determined the Klansmen had gotten the wrong man). Edwards' body was found three months later, lodged against a log in his native Lowndes County, fifty miles downriver.

There were distressing times for Aurelia Browder, one of the four plaintiffs in the bus boycott case. There were phone calls through the endless nights, she said: harassing, threatening, frightening. Her daughter, Manervia, nine, would always remember the lights burning in the front bedroom, as her mother sat up studying. One night the girl was awakened by the phone ringing; she ran through the hallway to answer. "Your house is gonna be blowed sky high!" a voice said. She became hysterical. Her mother grabbed the telephone, and told the caller, "Blow it up. I need a new house, anyway."

By early spring of 1957, tempers in Montgomery began to cool; the integration of the buses gradually became accepted — or, at least, tolerated — by whites. The first crack in the wall of segregation in the South had been made.

7

John Kennedy's inaugural address

It was during the boycott that another racial situation brought national attention to Alabama. In Birmingham, U.S. District Judge Hobart Grooms issued an order requiring the University of Alabama at Tuscaloosa to admit a black, Authurine Lucy. There was such a venomous reaction that Judge Grooms, a stately gentleman with graying hair, would go to bed each night with a shotgun within easy reach. He later became ill and was hospitalized.

Miss Lucy, meanwhile, was chased about the campus by a virtual lynch mob; she was the target of stone-throwing and racial slurs. One night the campus broke out into rioting and a mob tried to get into the dormitory where she lived. She was later expelled.

JOHNSON

Years later, in 1970 or so, I went to a football game at Tuscaloosa and watched Wilbur Jackson, the first black to start in the Crimson Tide backfield, run for a sixty-yard touchdown. The people went wild. And I could only shake my head in amazement. All this cheering at a place where Authurine Lucy had been stoned and driven away because she was black. If she had been able to play football, she might have made it.

But as for segregation, it was an American problem, not just one unique to the South. I used to ride a train from Montgomery to Washington and I never noticed that much difference in the seating arrangements once we crossed the Mason-Dixon Line.

As long as there are people, there will be discrimination of some type. Prejudice doesn't depend entirely on race, it's not always a black-and-white issue. It can be just as vicious and hateful among different ethnic or religious groups.

This country's great social problem, however, was race; for decades we kept it buried under the sand, trying to hide the stench. But it finally came to the surface, and permeated the country. Even when the Supreme Court issued the Brown ruling, the leadership of the country failed to tackle the problem of racial discrimination head-on. The churches failed, the lawyers failed, even the President of the United States, Dwight

Eisenhower, to some degree defaulted on leadership when it came to civil rights.

When the movement began in Alabama, and then spread across the South, he could have provided some leadership for the nation in the area of racial equality. He could have been more aggressive with the Congress, trying to push through legislation in the rights area. He could have even issued executive orders. But he did nothing. His only action in the cvil rights field was at Little Rock, Arkansas, when he sent federal troops there to enforce a court order on desegregating Central High School in September, 1957. And the only reason he did that was because he had no choice. Attorney General Herbert Brownell in a formal opinion had spelled out for him in detail what his duties were.

When John Kennedy was elected in 1960 and sworn in, there was almost an immediate and dramatic change. He was like electricity compared to Eisenhower. His inaugural address, I felt, put the nation on notice that there were changes that were long overdue.

JOHNSON

I avoided the word "integration" in my court orders, preferring to use "desegregation" instead. To desegregate means to open a public facility to all people, or rather, to prohibit one race from denying another race entry into a public facility because of the racial factor. Integrate, on the other hand, means the social interaction between members of different races. I think of it in more social terms. My purpose in the school cases was not to integrate the school system — putting blacks in just to be putting them in — but rather to disestablish an illegal system, which is what the segregated system was.

I was sensitive to the interchangeable uses of the words, and there was some conflict within the federal judiciary itself. For instance, the U.S. Fourth Circuit Court of Appeals in Richmond was of the opinion that *Brown* simply said a system could not deny black children from entering because of their color. But the U.S. Fifth Circuit in New Orleans shot that down by saying the fulfillment of *Brown* went beyond that. The Fifth said the states were REQUIRED to disestablish a segregated system. The Fifth's interpretation called for an affirmative effort to bring blacks into previously all-white schools.

. . . Despite the determination and courage of those black children at Tuskegee, Mobile and Birmingham, the schools of Alabama remained basically segregated for several more years. But in March of 1967, Johnson was joined by Judge Rives and U. S. District Judge Hobart Grooms in issuing a statewide desegregation order that applied to all school systems, except some in Huntsville that were doing it on their own.

The reaction was hysteric; whites lamented that all the treasured traditions of high school — the senior prom, the sockhops and such — were a thing of the past; that whites would not be safe with blacks in the same schools.

There was open defiance from the state's leadership; in some school systems, particularly in the state's Black Belt counties, private schools sprung up like mushrooms, almost overnight. White parents feared their daughters would be raped.

JOHNSON

I could not personally buy those arguments. In my mind, if security could be maintained in a school hall for white children alone, it could be maintained on the same basis if black students were there as well.

Ed Livingston, the chief justice of the Alabama Supreme Court, declared: "I'm for segregation and I don't care who knows it. I'd close every school from the highest to the lowest before I would go to school with colored people."

Governor Lurleen Wallace, in April 1967, addressed the Legislature; so wrapped up emotionally was she that she stamped her feet and said state leaders and parents would "go to jail before permitting their children to attend desegregated schools." While the legislators whooped, stomped their feet and issued rebel yells, she added that Johnson's court orders "were the final step toward a complete takeover of our children's hearts and minds." She equated the court order to a decree by Hitler. "They've made their decree . . . now let them enforce it."

The state's superintendent of education, Austin Meadows, went on to explain that "segregation was a perfectly good word" and added that the Lord "segregated fruit in the Garden of Eden." To explain further to the unenlightened, he said, "Red birds mate with red birds."

It was against this background that, on the night of April 25, 1967, a bomb exploded at the home of Johnson's mother.

JOHNSON

I lived about six blocks from her home and at about ten p.m. was in bed nearly asleep when the telephone rang. It was my sister, Ellen Harvill.

"F. M., get on over to Mother's," she said. "There's been an explosion."

Johnny had picked up the extension in his bedroom and heard her. He and I quickly dressed and sped over there. At first I thought it might have been a gas explosion or the hot water heater. I wasn't sure.

The first thing we saw was the red lights flashing on the fire trucks and the police cars. Johnny shouted that he saw his grandmother standing in the yard. "You OK?" I asked. She nodded.

Mother was unhurt, but angry. A fireman told me he thought the explosion was caused by dynamite. I was enraged.

"Give me your flashlight," I told him and started poking around the wreckage to look for clues, although I'm not sure I could spot anything.

I was sure the bomb was meant for me. My telephone was unlisted, but Mother's was still listed in the directory under my father's name, "Frank M. Johnson." Some deranged person or persons thought it was my address. The device had been placed on the ground near the house. Mother had just left the kitchen and gone upstairs to her bedroom when it exploded.

THE CHILDREN COMING ON . . .

The force of it swept all the way through the downstairs, tore the carpet up, broke windows, knocked the chandelier down from the ceiling of the dining room. Mother was living alone then. Daddy had died two years before. But she was rational; it didn't scare her. The news reporters and FBI agents were milling around and poking into things and that added to her discontent.

Some of the agents began boarding up the windows, sweeping up the glass and other debris. One of them came up to Mother and said, "Miz Johnson, don't you want to go somewhere and spend the night?"

"Absolutely not," she said. "They're not going to run me away from my home. I'm staying right here."

She even turned me down when I suggested she come stay with Ruth and me for a few days.

She was mad, too, because some of her plants and flowers outside had been ravaged by the explosion.

The agents and the U.S. marshals told me they'd post a couple of people out there and keep watch to make sure the bombers didn't return.

Mother tolerated that for a few nights, but it soon began to wear on her nerves. She didn't like looking out the windows at night and seeing them prowling around, shining their flashlights about. Mother was a very courageous and cool woman.

A couple of days after the explosion I went by to see her and she said to me, "When are you going to take them away?"

I told her they wanted to stay for a few more nights to assure that nothing else happened.

"Well, they're bothering me," she said. "All night long they go around looking, opening and closing doors . . ."

The cowardly act directed at my mother burned me, made me want to get my hands on the person or persons responsible. I knew the bomb had been intended for me. I had been aware for several years that I might be a target for some lunatic. The murder of President Kennedy in November, 1963, had heightened that possibility. But I didn't run from shadows; you can't live in fear of a sniper or a bomber.

The FBI from the early 1960s kept me supplied with a list of known KKK members. That list gave their name, address, employer. The list was given to me after undercover agents had overheard KKK members discussing the prospects of bombing my home. While it never happened, the explosion at my mother's house made it clear that it could happen. I can't say the Klan bombed mother's house, because no one was ever arrested and brought to trial.

A few days after the bombing, Governor Lurleen Wallace issued a statement calling the act a "cowardly deed" and offered a reward leading to the arrest and conviction of the person or persons responsible.

It was of little consolation to me. It would have been far too little had my mother been killed or injured. The only thing that saved her was the fact that she had gone to bed. Had she been sitting in the living room she might have been seriously or fatally injured.

. . . When Robert Kennedy and Martin Luther King, Jr., were shot and killed, and later when George Wallace was severely wounded, I felt the same sense of outrage that most Americans felt.

I first heard about Bobby being shot when I awoke the morning of June 6, 1968, and heard the news reports. I felt disbelief, shock and a deep agony about what was happening in a country which has laws to protect human liberties and human life. He and I had been friends and he had been a courageous leader, especially in the field of civil rights. His brother John, the President, had been a strong leader in that area, too.

My feelings about King's assassination were a little more mixed, I suppose. I hadn't known him on a personal basis. I had admired his courage, but at the same time took a dim view of some of his methods. This had nothing to do with the sorrow I felt when he was shot. He was a leader.

Wallace's wounding was also a terrible thing and reflected some of the sickness in the country. In all three cases — King, Kennedy, Wallace — I could not accept the rationalization that a "demented" person had committed the deed.

MONTGOMERY VOICES

IV

Gwen Patton:

My name is Gwendolyn Marie Patton, and I was born October 14, 1943, in Detroit, Michigan, but my upbringing was in a small town called Inkster, Michigan, during the time it was a village. My father was very active in the community.

Each summer I would come to Montgomery. I enjoyed the South. I found it fascinating. I found it romantic. I just liked it, and the parties and the petticoats and the crinolines and all of that, so I enjoyed it.

One year when we were here — I was about nine years old — and every Sunday we would go for this bus ride. My grandmother's bus was fifteen cents. You could get on in front of the house and ride to the end of the line and come back. We decided to stop off in town, right down where the fountain is, and there was—where there's One Court Plaza—there was a little shopping area there, and they had a Ligget's Drug Store. I wanted to go get a cup of water, and they charged me three cents for this cup of water, and I decided to sit down and drink my water, and they told me I couldn't do that. So I looked at them like they were crazy, poured my cup of water on the counter, and promised them that we were going to do something—I don't know, whatever a nine-year-old kid — I remember some words being exchanged. My brother, and my first cousin brother, Al, just got me out and we got back on the bus and went on home. There was not anything said about that.

. . . At sixteen I came to the South to live. My father decided that I needed feminine input in order to direct my life. Mother had passed. Plus I was angry with my father, too — I also came out of rebellion. It was the summer of 1960.

Back when I was 13 years old I was in direct contact with the Montgomery bus boycott via phone, because my grandparents on both sides, and relatives were here. We had a direct line as to what was going on to what we saw on television. In the eighth grade I wrote a paper on the Montgomery bus boycott for my civics class, and I anticipated a victory for the boycott.

. . . Now an interesting thing about the bus boycott and my grandmother:

that following summer—we did not come to the South in the summer of 1956, cause they were afraid that something would happen. But I came the winter of 1957. On the bus with my grandmother. She would always go to the back, and I would be sitting up front. Don't let anybody white be there, I sit right there. So one time, no white folks were on the bus, so I went to the back with my grandmother. I said: "Mommie, you all fought so hard and people suffered and went to jail. Why are you sitting in the back of the bus? What was the struggle about?" And she had a tight lean look about herself. I have to give you some character background of this lady. She had that tight little lip, and she called me Gwendolyn. She said: "Gwendolyn, the boycott—the Movement—wasn't about sitting next to white folks. It was about sitting anywhere you please. Now, I choose to sit here."

That helped me to look at the Movement from another point of view, too. The Movement was about widening the options. It was not about trailing some honkey or some racist, though if you want to do that, you have the right to do that too. The crux of the Movement was about the options to be free. I'll never forget her for that.

So when I came to Montgomery at 16 to live, my first thing was to go to the M.I.A. office—Montgomery Improvement Association. It was on Dorsey Street. I went every day. I just assumed being a staff member. And I've always loved older people and that's when I met Hazel Gregory and Mrs. Idessa Williams at that time, she's since married Mr. Redden. Bertha Smith. And what amazed me was that these ladies were hair dressers, which meant that they were independent. They generated their own revenue, their own survival, and gave them that kind of freedom. I just loved . . . I just worshipped them. And I remember Mr. Rufus Lewis, the coach, and he was like a towering something that you couldn't approach, but that you respected tremendously. I remember Mr. E.D. Nixon, not as much, but I remember seeing him, because he too was a massive man, and being a child, everybody looked bigger then. I remember folding papers. I learned Movement organization in terms of how you do a mailing, and how you set up assembly lines and all of that.

. . . So, soon after M.I.A., Dr. King had pulled together the Southern Christian Leadership Conference in Atlanta. . . . (Later in the 60s) Bevel (an SCLC staff member) had come into town, Jim Bevel. James Orange. So I worked with them (and SCLC). I remember going to the Projects . Organizing the Projects and teaching freedom songs, and Bevel was living in an apartment, and he wasn't comfortable with that. My grandmother had another house, and I talked to my grandmother and said, "Mommie, let this house be the 'Freedom House'." . . . See, my grandmother was a block captain and very much involved in the struggle (and her house became the Freedom House).

[in 1965, after a serious ilness] . . . when I returned back to Tuskegee, [I'm] back into the honor dorm again, SNCC comes again. This time I cannot remain aloof. You see, I was confused as to my allegiance. SNCC had begun to make waves in the SCLC. The primary question, I think, was we should have the right to help set policy and plan strategy. And that what you [in SCLC] do, you all go in your closed rooms, determine the program, and then call us—the shock troopers—to go and do the grassroots work, and SNCC no longer felt that was fair. And since they had arrived at that position, I felt comfortable with SNCC.

We decided . . . you see, SNCC had become not only mentors to the students at Tuskegee Institute, but models too—in terms of what is a commitment. Now I had some misgivings about a lot of things — particularly Stokley [Carmichael, now Kwame Toure] and I probably still have some differences on this — I did not think students had to quit college to be full-time freedom fighters. In fact, I found the two to be complementary. And so, that disturbed me. Secondly, I was always—at that point I had become concerned about the war, and the draft and where were black men going, because I've always had a great passion for black men. I haven't seen a set of men since. And also within SNCC.

I saw some contradictions with some SNCC guys and I used to talk about this a lot with Fred Mealey from Philadelphia. That, who are the SNCC people? Are they first generation so-called formally educated? are they second generation? Are they people who couldn't fit in the mainstream? Could they hang out on the block? Could they hang? You had the son of a psychiatrist in the person of Stu House. You had the son of a ghetto youth in the person of Stokley Carmichael. And then everything in between. I found it to be the most wholesome group of people I've ever seen in my life, and that there was no caste system imposed. After we got to know each other fairly well, it was dismissed, [so] that we somehow looked like a new slate, and that our growth and development started from that point on in the collective. You could fuss at people and nobody took it personally. Later on it degenerated into that, but in the initial stages . . . And the fierceness of it all—just the fierceness — impressed me.

So when SNCC said, we're gonna join in Selma on the march, and we argued the logistics of how to do that and worked out the program . . . we were gonna do that. When I saw students like Sammy Younge and Eldridge Burns, and all the kids that were going off to prep schools call up and tell their white friends to send them some money down here 'cause we got to get us some buses. And when I saw the determination of just stopping cars cold in the street to take up our collection in the buckets, I just knew that we were on the right road. And we did that in a matter of about two weeks. And it was organized . . . .

Tuskegee had the most unusual set of kids, of course I'm romanticizing because they're my peers. But we never were daunted by anything. Whatever—we worked to do that. But there was sense of organization. There was such brilliance.

George Ware's a brilliant man. First thing to do was take over student government. First, the respect for protocol. "First," they said, "we will go through the bureaucracy," which we did. And they didn't get the favorable response, like okay, student government will finance our going. So then, what do you do? Then we'd get back . . . we'd regroup. Then we'd say, this is the problem, then everybody can talk on this particular problem. Three-hour discussion. Then we'd work out a strategy as to how we're gonna achieve the goal. That strategy was to get the president of [Tuskegee student government] to physically abdicate his role since he has already spiritually, philosophically done that by not giving us money. Now he just needs to vacate—make it total. So that was a scheme to do that, and George Ware was declared interim student body president. Just that simple. We've always had that kind of knack, which then meant that his struggle had to be to control the budget. And the administration had never met any Negroes like us before either, and they don't understand. He goes: "I'm student body president. I have the prerogative to work out the budget." And later on, I can tell you about my student body presidency, that really blew their minds.

We couldn't get any money so we had to become creative. So we stopped cars and called folks around the country, and so forth and so on. We always had a romantic feeling, probably romantic, for helping, you know, for example, the dining hall workers, the cafeteria workers, the laundry workers. And that was because we had come to raise the contradiction. You see the struggle in Tuskegee was not about racism, it was a class struggle. You had middle-class youth—the NOW generation, at least second generation educated, at least. Most of us were third and fourth generation, but we were all at least second. Our parents were all college graduates. And we had said "no" to their value system.

The way *that* was posed was—why did the cafeteria workers' children swim in the Negro pool on Wednesday and the campus and VA kids swim in the same Negro pool on Thursday? Now what was that about? See, we challenged that. We [also] stopped a Christmas party—told [Tuskegee President] Dr. Foster he couldn't have a Christmas party if he couldn't have one big Christmas party for everybody. Don't have one for the workers and then another for the professionals—cause we would picket. And that's another thing about our generation that makes it so difficult for us to adjust, because, our motivation was never to adjust to the environment—it was to master and to give direction to the environment. So we got a collision of missions right there. And then you have to understand, we had all day to make [picket] signs. See our whole minds . . . we were just totally preoccupied.

I'll never forget my senior paper for Victorian Lit. You had to be in orals and you had to defend it. It was on whether or not the romantic poet . . . no, it was how I would view the romantic poets' participation in the death of Sammy Younge [in Tuskegee]. I went through the whole thing from Longfellow and pulled stuff out and said that Keats could probably respond to that and Byron. Coleridge would probably just trip out on cocaine or dope or whatever—it would be too much for him. You know Longfellow probably would write to daffodils and so forth. But anyway—our whole life was centered around this single issue of freedom. Everything was secondary to that. And it worked.

So when we got the money [to join in the Selma march] and got the cafeteria workers to pack us a bologna sandwich and an apple and we had these white kids [to] carry over [for the march]—and now I don't want to say anything that would take away, but during COFO [Council of Federated Organizations] we understood that in order to bring light to our legitimate struggle, we're gonna need white presence. Cause racism is too steep. White presence might bring—prick the conscience. We had St. Olaf students who were from St. Clair, Minnesota—they probably ain't got no black folks up there; I been up there—who were part of this, and Charlene Krantz and some other folks who came out of the Washington scene—the ADA scene, Americans for Democratic Action. And we went to Montgomery. We went to Montgomery with no fear. We fortified ourselves with Movement songs. We were naive. We really thought we were gonna see the governor. I mean, how do you deny Tuskegee Institute students? That was—so many variations in the development of a Tuske . . . I mean they instilled in us a dignity, almost to the point where people who don't understand — a Tuskegee student could be confused with arrogance.

Fifteen hundred of us [Tuskegee students] out of an enrollment of 2,300 [marched]. There were all kinds of threats of *in loco parentis*, expulsion—all kinds of threats.

We came down and went to First Baptist—Reverend Abernathy's church. Now you have to remember that we thought the world was coming with us because the march had been set on the day. Judge Johnson had some kind of injunction or something to cancel the march. Dr. King had sent a telegram to Dr. Foster, president of Tuskegee Institute, asking us not to demonstrate, because whoever the SNCC representatives were—in the pow-wow meetings up in Birmingham—had relayed that Tuskegee kids are gonna march. They had to see how they could stop it. And Dr. Foster duplicated Dr. King's telegram and had it placed at all of the seats in the dining hall. And we looked at it. And we had already made a decision. We thought that this had been set, and that Judge Johnson didn't have a right to set the logistics for black folks' struggle for freedom, and that this kind of thing should not be a circus . . . it should have the character—and I think we even articulated words using this type of vocabulary—that it should have the "character of struggle." What do we need with portable toilets and helicopters flying over us?

You know black folks are used to struggle. You go and pee behind a tree, [if] that's what you gotta do. And also the whole black culture, if you got to do more than that, people let you go in their houses and use the toilet or go to the outhouse. Bathroom privileges have never been a problem in terms of just the physical elimination. So what's with all of this ?—so we couldn't buy into that. And so we had a rebellion in the dining hall. See we had a thing—by that time we were so organiz . . . we were just an organized group of students and we were young, we were creative and we were a collective. SNCC had modeled that for us—that's what we saw. If one of the leaders—and we had about 50 million leaders for each group—if he or she started beating on the table with a fork, then everybody would do that. And we used to have a little thing, if we were in any kind of group mass setting, and one of us stomped our foot, that meant that we were getting ready to get up and leave out of there. We had gotten to a point of non-verbal communication. The school didn't know what to do with us.

Getting back to the march. ASU students had come to join us, and the school has sanctioned—by default—so Dean Phillips who was the Dean of Students (and we love him dearly and we loved him then) was there. So now we get into all this discussion about who's gon' do the demonstration, who's gonna be on the front. And it looked like every preacher, even those who thought they would be a preacher in the future, wanted to opt for that role. I didn't even want to be bothered with the discussion. I left that discussion with George Ware, George Davis and all them SNCC folk. So they worked out something. So here we are, we're coming on around Ripley Street come on up to Dexter Avenue—big, strong . . . we were at least 2,000 folks. And we get to the capitol. Well the first thing is that we see two sets of cops. We see cops in blue, and we see cops in brown. We see cops on horses, standing by motorcycles and then just standing up. So we stopped. Forman is really the guy. He's like almost a guru. James Forman. And we had lots of confidence in Forman.

So we get there, and we dispatch our student leaders to go take the petition to Gov. Wallace. We *really* thought we were gonna meet—we were naive. We were idealistic. And again, you have to understand, we weren't angry or pissed off with white people as we were hurt that we couldn't get the approval of our black elders. See that was the struggle at Tuskegee Institute—to convince our elders that we were right and [for them] to join us—to share with us. We never really had any animosity toward Gov. Wallace because we didn't expect any differently from him. But we did think he would meet with us—after all, we *are* Tuskegee Institute, I mean the President, Dr. Foster, meets with us, why can't he meet with us?

So when George Ware, no George Davis, and Pinkey, I think it was, attempted to deliver the petition and were coming back — [and] they had been denied a meeting with the governor — they wouldn't let George and Pinkey back into the circle. So, and then they carted George and them off to the paddy wagon and the word filtered that we had a city permit, but we didn't have a state permit—so if you were standing on state property you were probably trespassing.

. . . We sought refuge in Dexter Avenue [Baptist Church some hours later] because it was right at the bottom of the hill. And we were tired. So we just sought sleep anywhere, and we did. And when we woke up. When the lights wouldn't come on, you couldn't flush the toilets because somebody had all of the utilities cut off . . . .I think that was the point I really made my commitment to SNCC because I was still straddling the fence—working with both groups [SCLCand SNCC].

There was this debate going on in the basement of the church with Bevel and Jim Forman. Bevel was trying to say that the Tuskegee kids had no business coming. And we were arguing our position, and that also did something with the student leadership between Gwen Patton, George Ware, George Davis and so forth. George Ware did not disagree that we should not have come, though in essence that's what he meant. But being a scientist, he's a chemist, he really felt that we should have thought out all of the contingencies, in case this happened and so forth and so on. He was coming mainly from a planning question. My position is that there was no way we could anticipate . . . .how do you anticipate evil if you're not evil? How can you foresee? How do we—you know we really thought we were gonna see the governor.

We had planned to come down here, go see the governor, give him our petition and go back to Tuskegee. We did anticipate folks going to jail, and so we had a little bond money and we had who to call and that kind of stuff, but we didn't anticipate not seeing the governor, or at least a representative. What could be more democratic than to petition your government?—to support the Selma-Montgomery march and to give us our voting rights—to be in accord with the [at the time proposed] voting rights [bill] of 1965—that he would go on record being supportive and that he would enforce it if that becomes law, that black folks will have the right to vote. And we didn't see anything ominous about that. So George's argument to me was what I call the argument of the beard. And Forman won that argument. When we went back to Tuskegee, and at Tuskegee we were power . . . well the Montgomery community at that point had still been about consultation—mass meetings, mass meetings, and SNCC reenforced it. And so we went back and had great debates. That thing created such a stir that we decided that we ought not even have school anymore. And the first moratorium that was called in this country in the [1960s]was at Tuskegee Institute. Not at Berkeley and not during the Vietnam War—Peace Movement. And Luther Foster, the president, had to get this guy named Haverhurst—who's supposed to be a renowned somebody in Chicago. And we had a moratorium.

. . . Then I thought about running for student body president and I didn't ever think that I was a woman. I just decided I would do that—why not. There were three guys who ran against me, and the student body president had been in the hands of the Kappas—this fraternity. The thing that helped me win—first of all, I'm an organized person. My father's a union man so I grew up with that sense of organization too. I had a budget—a line item budget. And I decided that my signs would be made of of wood with water-proof paint—indelible paint. They were attractive. I got the squarest boy on campus to be my campaign manager. He was very smart—but he was also square. Then I had coalitions of folks. I had somebody over in the married student dorms to work on my campaign—special interest groups. All those folks made up my little consulting board as to how I was gonna run my campaign—parades . . . just like politicians do.

News Clippings

Montgomery Advertiser 12-4-55

Negro Groups Ready Boycott Of City Lines

By JOE AZBELL
Advertiser City Editor

A "top secret" meeting of Montgomery Negroes who plan a boycott of city busses Monday is scheduled at 7 p.m. Monday at the Holt Street Baptist Church for "further instructions" in an "economic reprisal" campaign against segregation on city busses. The Advertiser learned last night.

The campaign, modelled along the lines of the White Citizens Council program, was initiated by unidentified Negro leaders after a Negro woman, Rosa Parks, was arrested by city police Thursday on a charge of violating segregation laws by sitting in the white section of a city bus.

Yesterday Negro sections were flooded with thousands of copies of mimeographed or typed letters asking Negroes to refrain from riding city busses Monday.

SECOND TIME

The letter states:

"Another Negro woman has been arrested and thrown into jail because she refused to get up out of her seat on the bus and give it to a white person. It is the second time since the Claudette Colbert case that a Negro has been arrested for the same thing. This must be stopped. Negroes are citizens and have rights.

"Until we do something to stop these arrests, they will continue. The next time it may be you, or you or you. This woman's case will come up Monday. We are, therefore, asking every Negro to stay off the busses on Monday in protest of the arrest and trial. Don't ride the busses to work, to town, to school or anywhere on Monday. You can afford to stay out of school for one day if you have no other way to go except by bus. If you work, take a cab or walk, but please, children and grownups, don't get on a bus at

(See NEGRO, Page 6A)

---

all on Monday. Please stay off the busses Monday."

WOULDN'T GIVE NAMES

The Rev. A. W. Wilson, pastor fo the Hold Street Baptist

(Continued From Page 1)

Church, said he would not divulge under "any circumstances" the names of the Negroes who asked permission to use the church facilities for the meeting.

"I don't feel I should give their names out for publication. But the meeting will be open and public and the doors will not be closed to Negroes or whites," he said.

Asked why he would not provide the names of the leaders of the boycott campaign and the meeting, the Rev. Wilson said that he didn't know enough about the meeting or the campaign to provide the information.

"Under no circumstance will I give you the names," he told The Advertiser.

First reports of the boycott came to The Advertiser Friday afternoon when white women reported their maids had asked for Monday off so they could "boycott the city busses" because "we have been asked to do it."

In the letter circularized yesterday, it was not stated what "for further instructions, attend the mass meeting" was intended to mean. The Rev. Wilson said "further instructions" doesn't mean anything except "just further instructions."

NO COMMENT

In Friday's attempts to locate Negro leaders backing the boycott

---

plan, The Advertiser met with "no comment" and replies of "no knowledge."

In the Thursday night arrest of Rosa Parks, 634 Cleveland Ct., city policemen acted under authority of Section II, Chapter 6 of the Montgomery City Code.

J. F. Blake, 27 N. Lewis St., City Lines bus driver, said the Parks woman refused to accept a seat in the Negro section assigned to her and instead seated herself in the white section. Blake called city police who took the Negro woman to police headquarters and charged her with violation of the segregation law. She will get a Recorder's Court hearing Monday.

J. H. Bagley, manager of the bus company, issued this statement after learing of the circulars:

"The Montgomery City Lines is sorry if anyone expects us to be exempt from any state or city law. We are sorry that the colored people blames us for any state or city ordinance which we didn't have passed. We have to obey all laws just like any other citizen. We had nothing to do with the laws being passed, but we expect to abide by all laws, city or state, to the best of our ability."

Bagley said he first learned of the circulars today when a woman informed him her maid had brought one of the circulars to work with her. Bagley said he immediately went to the woman's house and obtained the circular and turned the matter over to the firm's attorney, Jack Crenshaw.

HAWK IS GUEST

WORCESTER, Mass. — (UP)— Carl Anderson's unusual pet is a broadwing hawk. Fund injured,

Negress Draws Fine In Segregation Case Involving Bus Ride

Alabama Journal
12-4-1955

(Potos On Page 5-B)
By BUNNY HONICKER

A Negro woman was fined $10 and cost in police court here today for violating a state law requiring racial segregation on city buses.

Rosa Parks, 634 Cleveland Ave., a seamstress at a downtown store, did not testify.

Negro Atty. Fred D. Gray informed Recorder's Court Judge John B. Scott he would appeal the decision to Montgomery Circuit Court. A few minutes later, Gray signed a $100 appeal bond for his client.

Also signing the woman's appeal bond was E. D. Nixon of Montgomery, a former state president of the National Assn. for the Advancement of Colored People.

Gray had entered a plea of innocent for his client, who stood silent throughout the hearing.

BUS DRIVER TESTIFIES

City Prosecutor Eugene Loe called Montgomery City Lines bus driver J. F. Blake to the stand to open the city's case. Blake briefly told how Rosa Parks refused to move to the rear of his bus last Thursday night after he had requested her and several others to move to make room for white passengers he was taking on near the Empire Theater.

Blake said there were 22 Negroes and 14 whites seated in the 36-seat bus and that he asked several of the Negroes to move to the rear in order to equalize the seating.

CHARGE AMENDED

At the outset, Loe moved to amend the charge against Rosa Parks, making the warrant read a violation of the state law instead of the city ordinance. Gray objected by Judge Scott allowed the amendment. The state law merely sets forth as unlawful any failure for a person to comply with the assignment or re-assignment order of a bus driver.

Gray said the law was not a city law and would not apply to his client.

Loe said the state law referred to all transportation.

Gray declined to say specifically whether the state law would be attacked as unconstitutional on appeal. But he made this suggestive comment:

"Every legal issue will be raised that I think is necessary to defend my client."

The question of constitutionality was not raised in Recorder's Court

Judge Scott Scott shooed away photographers.

90 PER CENT BOYCOTT

The steps leading into the north side of the courtroom and the sidewalk, along with the corridors leading into the east entrance of the courtroom, all were jammed with spectators and witnesses.

Meanwhile, Montgomery City Lines Manager J. H. Bagley this afternoon estimated that some 90 per cent of the Negroes were refusing to ride the buses in protest of today's hearing.

The boycott was uncovered Saturday after thousands of unsigned circulars were reportedly being spread throughout the Negro districts in Montgomery.

ONE INCIDENT

Acting upon the orders of Police Commissioner Clyde Sellers that there was to be no violence today, patrolmen arrested a 19-year-old Negro youth who allegedly tried to restrain a Negro woman from getting on one of the morning buses.

Fred Daniel, 19, of 1646 Hall St., was jailed on a charge of disorderly conduct, according to Police Chief G. J. Ruppenthal. Arresting Patrolmen R. M. Hammonds and C. A. Weaver said Daniel grabbed a Negro woman by the arm about 7:15 a.m. at the intersection of Hall and Thurman and pulled her away from a City Lines bus she was attempting to board.

NEGRO TAXI CABS BUSY

All Negro taxi cab operators in the city reportedly told their drivers to charge only 10 cents a head today from the hours 4 a.m. to 9 a.m. and from 3 p.m. until 11 p.m. in an effort to make the bus boycott effective.

Several buses seen on downtown streets today carried nothing but white passengers from front to rear.

Several thousand Negroes use the buses on a normal day.

Police cars and motorcycles followed the buses periodically to prevent trouble after Sellers said some Negroes reported they were threatened with violence if they rode buses today.

MASS MEETING TONIGHT

A mass meeting of Negroes has also been scheduled tonight at the Holt Street Baptist Church to discuss "further instructions" in the "economic reprisal" campaign against the Montgomery City Bus Lines.

The circulars distributed in Negro residential districts Saturday urging the boycott today in protest to the arrest of Rosa Parks were not signed. Rev. A. W. Wilson, pastor of the Negro church where the meeting is to be held, said he would not disclose "under any circumstances" the names of those who asked permission to use the church for the meeting.

He said the meeting would be open to whites as well as Negroes.

Earlier, Bagley had issued a statement saying the bus company "is sorry if anyone expects us to be exempt from any state or city law."

In the Rosa Parks case today, the city was prepared to offer testimony from 11 witnesses. Only three, Blake and two women passengers, testified. One of the women said there was an empty seat where Rosa Parks could have sat if she had moved to the rear.

Alabama Journal 12-5.

Negro Rule In Boycott Is To Walk

By JOE AZBELL

At 5:30 a.m. today the big yellow busses of the Montgomery City Lines began pulling into Court Square to pick up passengers.

Generally a swarm of Negro passengers are waiting at the stop for the busses to take them to the railroad shops, private homes, laundries, factories and jobs throughout the city.

POSTER TORN DOWN

As the first bus arrived, the driver noticed a sign tacked to the wall at the bus shed:

"Remember it is for our cause that you do not ride the bus today." It meant the Negro boycott of busses was on.

The sign was printed in illegible hand with shoe polish on a white cardboard. A policeman tore down the poster and took it to police headquarters.

Negroes were on almost every corner in the downtown area, silent, waiting for rides or moving about to keep warm, but few got on busses. Negro cabs were packed tight and it seemed as if they stopped to pick up more passengers at every corner. Some appeared as if they would burst open if another passenger got in.

WAIT FOR RIDE

The Negroes were hunkered down in overcoats or jackets as the wind was crisp and biting. They stood on the corner for as long as 30 minutes and an hour waiting for a ride.

None thumbed rides. As each car passed the Negro driver would inquire of the men and women on the street-corner where they was going. If they were going in the same direction, they loaded in.

Scores of Negroes were walking, their lunches in brown paper sacks under their arms. None spoke to white people. They exchanged little talk among themselves. It was an event almost solemn.

The policeman at the Court Square said only two Negroes had gotten off busses up to 7 a.m. and about four of five Negroes had gotten on. Generally the busses are packed with Negroes going and coming at that time. A driver said one Negro rode his bus "trembling with fear."

WHITE MAN GETS LOAD

He said traffic was extremely heavy because many employers of Negroes were on the streets in their automobiles fetching their employes along with the Negro motorists. Wildcat "taxi services" were operating. At least one white man was carrying Negroes in his automobiles and parked in the downtown area until he got a load.

The motorcycle corps of the police department moved out about 6:30 a.m., and it appeared every vehicle in the department was being used. The motorcycle policemen buzzed up and down the streets and remained near most busses as they entered Negro sections.

SOME DEFY BOYCOTT

Most of the Negroes who rode the busses in defiance of the boycott order were elderly. One Negro woman standing at Court Square alone waiting for the bus as other Negroes stared at her, said she thought the whole thing was "silly."

"I've got to get to work if I want to keep my job and my young 'uns come before all of this mess," she said. "If anybody fools with me I'll crown 'em." She raised her umbrella in rehearsal.

WALK TO SCHOOL

Negro children walked to school, some for more than a mile or more. They turned their backs when busses passed and parents accompanied some of them.

In Washington Park, there was moving about at 7 a.m. as people signalled for rides and old pick up trucks hauled Negroes down the street, the crisp cold air causing them to hide behind the hoods.

At 7:30 a.m. in Newtown and along North Ripley Street there was a long line of Negroes on foot walking to their jobs in the downtown area or other sections.

At 8 a.m., more than 50 Negroes had gathered at the police headquarters at the rear of which is Recorder's Court where a hearing for Rosa Parks was set. The crowd swelled to 200 before court opened.

Prominent among the early arrivals were members and officials of the National Association for the Advancement of Colored People and Montgomery Progressive Democratic Association. Several of those attending the hearing were students or teachers at Alabama State College for Negroes.

E. D. Nixon, president of the Negro Democratic Association and former state NAACP, accompanied Rosa Parks to the courtroom along with her attorney, Fred Gray, and an unidentified Negro woman. The crowd dispersed after the conviction, but none took busses home.

The Rev. King Is Boycott Boss

27-Year-Old Baptist Pastor Seems To Be Deferred To By Other Leaders; He Says, Surprisingly, NAACP 'Looks Down Nose' At Boycott

By Tom Johnson

THERE seems to be uncertainty in the minds of the white community of Montgomery over the identity of the director of the bus boycott. Who is the acknowledged boycott leader? He seems to be the Rev. Martin Luther King Jr., a 27-year-old Negro Baptist preacher.

The Rev. King does not speculate on the ultimate fruits of the Negro movement, but he does declare the current boycott is directed solely toward obtaining a better seating arrangement for Negro passengers. However he is frank to admit that his own views are more ambitious.

"Frankly," he says, "I am for immediate integration. Segregation is evil, and I cannot, as a minister, condone evil."

King is pastor of the Dexter Avenue Baptist Church, whose congregation includes 375 "professional people" on a "higher economic level." Many of his members come from Alabama State College. The president of the college, Dr. H. Council Trenholm, is a deacon in the church.

King is a member of the Montgomery Improvement Association, a Negro organization of some 50 members which has been active in the conduct of the boycott. King, as spokesman for the association, has also served as spokesman for the protesting bus riders.

The association, apparently, is handling the boycott funds. Recently, a check for $5,017 was made payable to King, who, it is said, transferred the money to an out-of-town bank because the organization feared its funds might get "tied up" in the local bank. This I was told by an associate of King.

At all meetings where the boycott has been discussed, is the one who has enunciated the Negro demands for better seating, more courtesy and the hiring of Negro drivers on predominantly Negro routes. His remarks on these occasions have never been challenged or countered by other Negro ministers, who accord him a deference that is surprising in view of his youth and relatively short residence in Montgomery.

Seems Older

KING had his 27th birthday Sunday. (He looks and acts older. Most people would guess him to be about 35.) He holds degrees from Morehouse College, Crozer Theological Seminary and Boston College, where he earned his doctorate. His title is Doctor of Systematic Theology, for which he wrote the dissertation, *A Comparison Of The Conceptions Of God In The Thinking Of Paul Tillich And Henry Nelson Wieman.* His wife, a native of Marion, attended Antioch Co-

King speaks openly and with an authoritative air on the Negro view of the bus boycott. He is convinced the boycott will not end so long as the present arrangement exists. Moreover, whatever effect the boycott has had on the bus company and on race relations in Montgomery, King says the Negro has profited—he has gained a "dignity" that he never knew before. He has discovered the voice of the protestant.

NAACP Disdains Boycott

KING says the National Association for the Advancement of Colored People has made not so much as a "small contribution" to the boycott. In fact, he says, the NAACP looks down its nose at the puny, deviationist efforts of local Negroes.

The goal of the NAACP is to gain full race mixing; it, therefore, sanctions no movement such as the local boycott which, King says, aims merely at achieving a "better form of segregation" within existing segregation laws.

To be sure, many Negroes involved in the boycott are members of the NAACP. ("Most well-thinking Negroes are members. If one tells you he is not, he is being dishonest.") And some of them have contributed money, but King says no help has come from the organization itself.

Admires Hegel's Philosophy

KING, who is from Atlanta, is motivated in his racial activities by what he terms the "social gospel," as distinguished from the gospel of personal salvation. He says:

"A minister should attempt to improve social conditions of men at every point where they are not proper—educational, cultural and economic. He must not only change a man's soul but a man's environment, too."

It is evident that he feels it folly to resist the changes that the Supreme Court decision gave momentum to. This is how he sees the boycott:

"It is part of a world-wide movement. Look at just about any place in the world and the exploited people are rising against their exploiters. This seems to be the outstanding characteristic of our generation. Why it had to happen at this time in history, I don't know. But it's happening."

Besides the religious philosophers, King was particularly interested in the German philosophers Kant and Hegel. The latter, his favorite, fathered the "dialectical process" which holds that change is the cardinal principle of life and that in every stage of things there is a contradiction which only the "strife of opposites" can resolve.

Further, as Will Durant, in his *Story Of Philosophy* defined dialectics: "Struggle is the law of growth; character is built in the storm and stress of the world; and a man reaches his full height only through compulsions, responsibilities and suffering."

King said he tries to translate the teachings of philosophy to his congregation.

Came Here In 1954

HE WOULD NOT comment on the possibility of a compromise settlement of the bus boycott, except to say: "We began with a compromise when we didn't ask for complete integration. Now we're asked to compromise on the compromise."

As an ardent member of the NAACP, King was asked to state his definition of the difference between the White Citizens Council, a champion of one race, and the NAACP, the champion of another.

The aims of the NAACP, he said, are "to get full rights for Negroes, to abolish injustice, to obtain the vote, to obtain protective legislation, improve the cultural life of Negroes and stop lynching," and to do all this through the courts.

On the other hand, the WCC "seems to be an organization to preserve the status quo and to buck the law of the land." King wasn't sure where the WCC stands on violence (he is opposed to it) and how it plans to achieve its goals. All official WCC statements reject violence of any kind.

In short, he thinks the aim of the NAACP is "constructive," the aim of the WCC to "block progress in race relations."

The Dexter Avenue church is King's first congregation. He came here full-time in September, 1954, after getting his doctorate. From 1948 to 1953, he was assistant pastor of Ebenezer Church in Atlanta. His father has been pastor there since 1932 and before that, his maternal grandfather was pastor of the church for 37 years.

Mobile Pn. 3-2-5-6

Montgomery Mayor Fed Up With Biracial Plans; Little Hope Seen For Success Of Folsom Proposal

Gayle Says Negroes Out To Destroy South's Social Fabric

By TED PEARSON
Press Staff Reporter

MONTGOMERY — Complete failure of truce attempts by biracial committees is indelibly written into the record of the now-famous Montgomery bus boycott.

Time and again, since the city's Negro populace quit riding the buses on Dec. 5 in protest against segregation practices, such racial committees have attempted to settle the issue through compromise.

And each time these attempts have fallen through, principally because of the unequivocal refusal of the boycott leaders to accept any plan short of their demands for an end to segregation in the municipal transit system.

HERE IS RECORD

Here is the record:

On Dec. 1, 1955, a Negro woman named Rosa Parks was arrested on a charge of refusing to accept a seat assigned to her by a City Lines driver, thus violating the city's segregation laws.

Two days later, hundreds of unsigned circulars began being passed from door to door in the Negro sections of the city, urging all the Negro populace to protest by refusing to patronize the City Lines.

On Dec. 5, the day the Parks woman was fined in city police

CONFERENCE IN MOBILE TONIGHT

Discussion on Mayor Joseph N. Langan's proposal to establish a biracial committee on human relations in Mobile will be held at 7:30 p.m. Friday at an open meeting in the Council Chamber of City Hall.

Langan said his proposal for the meeting came after a long study of similar groups in other localities and after he had received requests from "many interested citizens" that such a group be established here.

Since his original announcement of the meeting earlier this week, Langan said he had received "numerous telephone calls and letters" from Mobilians who had expressed their intentions of attending. Representatives of government, education, labor, business, religion, women's activities and others are expected. Both whites and Negroes are invited.

"I feel that if a group of our Mobile citizens—men and women of fairness, justice and good will—would form an organization to consider areas of possible conflict, study situations and conditions which could precipitate conflicts and then make recommendations to the public, business, church and government bodies for the elimination of such conditions, much could be accomplished toward elimination of strife in our community," Langan said.

court, the boycott became full-blown. At that time fully 90 per cent of the bus company's usual Negro patronage had fallen off.

On Dec. 8, a delegation of Negro leaders led by the Rev. Martin Luther King met for four

Efforts To Compromise Bus Boycott Fall Flat At Capital

hours with a committee of white officials of the City Lines, but to no avail. King said the boycott would continue until a "satisfactory" seating arrangement was devised. He proposed that bus patrons be seated on a first come, first served basis with no sections reserved for either race, pointing out that Negroes would continue to seat from the rear and whites from the front with no reassignment of seats once the buses were loaded.

King specified two other demands: More courteous treatment of the Negroes, and hiring of Negro drivers on predominantly Negro routes.

On Dec. 17, Mayor W. A. Gayle named a committee of 16 members—eight white and eight Negroes—to try to reach a compromise to settle the dispute.

'COOL OFF' FAILS

The committee met that afternoon and failed in trying to agree to a "cooling off" period.

Two days later, this same committee again sat down together. Again, no agreement. Said a

(Continued on Page 8, Col. 1)

MOBILE PRESS

MAR 2 1956

THE CHILDREN COMING ON . . .

Ala Ju. 3-21-56

Judge Overrules Defense Motion To Acquit King In Boycott Trial

.The state completed its case in the first of Montgomery's bus boycott trials today and Negro defense attorneys immediately sought to throw out all of the prosecution evidence as insufficient to prove any unlawful act, but the trial judge overruled them.

Circuit Judge Eugene Carter dismissed a motion which sought to exclude all of the state's testimony and halt the trial of Rev. Martin Luther King Jr. with a verdict of acquittal.

Defense attorney Fred D. Gray of Montgomery argued that the state had completely failed to prove that King violated Alabama's anti-boycott law which prohibits a conspiracy or agreement to hinder the operation of a lawful business "without just cause or legal excuse."

CLAIMS STATE FAILED

Gray insisted the state failed to show that King or anyone connected with him committed any unlawful acts; did any act whatever to prevent Montgomery City Lines from operating buses, or entered into any agreement or conspiracy.

The Negro lawyer said that whatever action Negroes took in refusing to ride the segregated buses was taken among themselves and that they made no effort to stop the bus company from operating its business.

Even if the state had proved such actions, Gray continued, no evidence was produced to show the Negroes didn't have a just cause or legal excuse.

That was a reference to cross-examination of state witnesses in an effort to show that the bus boycott was started after the Negroes had failed by other means to get relief from what they called "unfair treatment."

SAYS LAW INVALID

Gray also argued that the law itself under which King was brought to trial is unconstitutional and that it violates the defendant's right of free speech, freedom of assembly and freedom to petition for redress.

Pursuing the theme that Negroes were justified in refusing to ride buses, defense attorneys produced witnesses who testified that they had made complaints about mistreatment long before the boycott began on Dec. 5.

They said they had protested to the city commission as well as to bus company officials about seating conditions, particularly where Negroes were required to stand while there were vacant seats in the white section of buses. In some instances, the said, they were required to vacate seats to let white passengers occupy them.

BUS TREATMENT HIT

One witness, Georgia Gilmore, testified that she stopped riding the buses last October because she said she suffered from the treatment she received.

At one point in her testimony, she made this observation: "When you pay your fare and they count the money, they don't know the Negro money from white money.

Circuit Solicitor William F. Thetford rested his case after the manager of the bus company, Montgomery City Lines, Inc., had been recalled to the witness stand for further cross-examination by Negro defense attorneys.

BOTH RACES ARRESTED

The bus company official, J. H. Bagley, testified that white passengers as well as Negroes have been arrested for refusing to comply with segregated seating arrangements on Montgomery buses.

It was the arrest of a Negro seamstress, Rosa P a r k s, that led to the boycott last Dec. 5.

She was fined $14 for refusing to move to the Negro section of a

Special File — Library
Department of Archives and History
Montgomery, Alabama

Montgomery boycott—
People who haul maids harassed

MONTGOMERY, Ala., Oct. 17 — (AP) — White housewives who drive their Negro maids to and from work are being harassed by anonymous phone calls, The Montgomery Advertiser said today.

THE NEWSPAPER quoted persons who received calls as saying men had threatened physical violence and used profanity. Most of the post-midnight calls were limited to the question:

"Isn't it about time you went to get your nigger maid?"

Montgomery Negroes have been boycotting city buses since last December in protest to the arrest of a Negro woman for violation of a segregated seating law. A federal court decision that city bus segregation is unconstitutional is on appeal to the U. S. Supreme Court.

PENDING THE appeal, both enforcement of bus segregation and the boycott are continuing. An organization set up to coordinate the boycott operates a car pool that provides transportation for many Negroes.

The only phone call reported to him, Police Chief G. J. Ruppenthal said, was to a resident living outside the city. Postmaster Charles Moore said he had heard of no threatening letters but would investigate if any were reported.

Letters received in some South Montgomery areas said in full:

"Dear friend: Listed below are a few of the white people who are still hauling their Negro maids. This must be stopped. These people would appreciate a call from you, day or night. Let's let them know how we feel about them hauling Negroes."

The lists included a number of prominent Montgomery residents, The Advertiser said.

Negro calls tactics 'the forces of evil'

CORTLAND, N. Y., Oct. 17— (AP)—A leader of an antisegregation bus boycott in Alabama says such tactics are aimed at "the forces of evil," not at individuals.

The Rev. Dr. Martin Luther King of Montgomery, Ala., told the New York State Universalist Ministers Assn. last night that "tension" in his community was "not between white and Negro but . . . between justice and injustice."

Dr. King, a Negro, was found guilty in an Alabama court last March of leading what the prosecution termed an illegal boycott against the Montgomery City Bus Lines. He has appealed a sentence of a $500 fine and payment of $500 court costs.

The 29-year-old minister said a "crisis" in race relations had been precipitated by the Supreme Court decision outlawing segregation in public schools and by "a radical change in the Negro's evaluation of his nature and destiny."

DR. KING said that violent resistance created social problems, it did not solve them. He said that nonviolent resistance sought to win friendship and understanding, not to defeat and humiliate opponents.

The minister told the church group that "in Montgomery, we can walk and never get tired because we know there will be a great camp meeting in the promised land of freedom."

Is Confident That Progress Can Be Made

BY MARVIN L. ARROWSMITH

WASHINGTON (AP) — President Eisenhower today urged the nation not to regard the school integration issue as one which could separate Americans and create a nasty mess.

Eisenhower again, at a news conference, appealed for moderation. He said the problem of desegregation is one of deep emotion. But he said he is confident progress can be made.

For the second week in a row Eisenhower spoke with deep feeling of the controversy created by the Supreme Court's decisions striking down race segregation in public schools.

BOYCOTT MENTIONED

Discussing specifically the trial of a group of Negroes in Montgomery, Ala., in connection with the Negro boycott of that city's buses, Eisenhower said he understands there is an Alabama law covering that situation.

As for the situation generally in the South, Eisenhower said it is incumbent upon the people of that area to show some progress in good race relations.

That, he added, is what the Supreme Court asked for. The court, in implementing its segregation ban, called for progress with "all deliberate speed."

Eisenhower said we should not stagnate, and declared that again he wanted to plead for understanding between the races.

THE CHILDREN COMING ON . . .

GATHERING EVIDENCE

City Plans Legal Action Against Negro Car Pools

By AL McCONAGHA

The city of Montgomery is preparing legal action against Negro bus boycotters' car pools, the City Commission revealed yesterday.

The commission announced its plans after a group representing a trade union publication, The Alabama Labor News, asked for immediate action to halt the car-pool operation carried on by Negroes in a 10-month-old protest to racial segregation on city buses.

Jack D. Brock, editor of the labor publication, said he and others were ready to swear out citizens' warrants immediately if necessary to stop car-pool operations.

LEGAL MEANS

Brock's demand was made after Atty. John Kohn, representing the labor group, outlined "double barrel" legal means for halting the boycotters' station wagons and car-pool activity.

In a statement issued three hours after the special conference between city commission and the labor group, the city officials said:

"The city's latest activity in this connection (maintaining segregation) has been the assembling of evidence for action against the operations of so-called car pools.

INJUNCTION PLAN

"The commission is glad for individuals to take such action as they see fit in their own best interest; however, regardless of whether such action is taken or not, the city will follow its plans of bringing action for an injuction to stop all activities which the city considers illegal at this time."

In the morning session, Kohn declared the car pool a "sabotage of franchise transportation in this city" and an effort to do "by subterfuge what he commission had denied them the right to do."

Kohn referred to the commission's action several months ago in refusing to grant boycotters a franchise for operation of their own bus lines.

The Montgomery attorney added that the car-pool operation was an "emasculation" of city and state laws supported in part "by people who hate the South and don't understand it."

Kohn particularly cited a section of the state code which says "any firm, association, or corporation using the streets of any city" for the construction or operation of any public utility cannot do so without "first obtaining permission of the city commission," as evidence of legal authority for immediate action by the city commission. He asked for arrests and trials in recorder's court.

"What Tallahassee has done. Montgomery has the legal authority to do," Kohn said. He refered to Tallahassee city official's action against operations similar to those conducted here by bus boycotters.

Kohn presented the commission with a detailed legal memorandum outlining city authority in the situation and a proposed ordinance which he said would give the city legal opportunity to halt the station wagon and the car - pool operations.

The commission's statement said the visit of the labor news group was "appreciated" and added that the city's legal department had already offered them the benefit of studies made on the question and action the city hoped to take.

The statement said the city had advised the group "that the city planned to take certain action designed to stop these operations."

Adding that "we intend to maintain the way of life which has existed here in Montgomery since its origin, so far as we are legally able," the commission pointed to action already taken to resist racial integration here.

End Of Protest Awaits
Formal Notice Of Edict

By STEVE LESHER

The 11-month-old Montgomery bus boycott ended officially last night at the church in which it was born.

More than 4,000 cheering Negro men, women and children at the Negro Holt Street Baptist Church gave their approval to a recommendation made by the executive board of the Montgomery Improvement Assn. to call off the boycott and "return to the buses on a non-segregated basis."

The actual return of Negroes to riding city buses awaits delivery of a mandate from the U.S. Supreme Court to the U.S. District Court here declaring segregation on buses in Alabama unconstitutional.

EARLIER MEETING

Prior to the mass meeting at the Holt street church, another 4,000 Negroes at the Hutchinson Street Baptist Church approved the same recommendation read by the Rev. Martin Luther King, MIA president. Two meetings were held, King said, to accommodate the "great number of persons who wished to vote on this matter."

At both churches, the recommendation was approved unanimously.

PROCEDURAL MATTER

King, telling the cheering masses of Negroes about awaiting the mandate, said, "It is true that this is purely a procedural matter but it is a matter that might be used by reactionary elements to plunge us into needless harassment and meaningless litigation."

King said the "transportation system is no longer operating . . . the car pool is broken up." He said "we have assurance from authentic sources that this mandate will come to Montgomery in a mater of just a few days. For those three or four days we will continue to walk or share rides with friends."

King reiterated that Negroes should observe a policy of non-violence. "We must take this not as a victory over the white man but with dignity . . . Don't go back to the buses and push people around . . . We're just going to sit where there's a seat."

'INSULTS, FACTIONS'

King said later, "I wish I could say that when we go back to the buses on an integrated basis that no white person will insult you or that violent factions will not break out. But I can't say that because I don't know.

"If someone pushes you, don't

push him back. I know that is a hard thing not to do. Our Western philosophy teaches us that in the

(Continued From Page 1)

end there can only be violence. But we must refuse to hit back. We must have the courage to refuse to hit back."

When King entered the Hutchinson Street Baptist Church at 7:23 p.m. yesterday, the Negroes rose to a man and applauded him wildly. In their faces was confidence in the young, light-skinned Negro minister.

At least 21 newsmen and photographers saw the Rev. S. S. Seay break into tears when he said during the invocation: "Wherever the Klans may march; no matter what the White Citizens Councils may want to do, we are not afraid because God is on our side."

CONGREGATION WEPT

The congregation wept with him and several women screamed with what appeared to be a religious ecstasy.

Outside the Holt Street Baptist Church men and women lined the streets for five blocks in all directions. Loudspeakers outside the church told them of the business within. Negro men stood solemnly and Negro women wept and sang along with the choir in the church. They held small children in their arms as if not wanting babies to be absent from the momentous occasion.

The boycott began Dec. 5, 1955, after Rosa Parks, a Negro seamstress who refused to take a seat in the Negro section of a Montgomery City Lines bus, was fined $14 in police court.

At a mass meeting that night, Negro ministers and other Negro leaders urged the city's 42,000 Negroes not to ride the buses, in protest of the woman's conviction.

The Negroes complied at least 99 per cent, as shown later by bus company records, and they either walked or formed the now defunct car pools.

Boycott leaders at first did not demand an end to segregation but insisted that bus seating be on a first - come first served basis, starting with the back seats for Negroes and front ones for whites.

Company officials refused to drop a requirement that the 10 front seats be reserved for whites. The boycott leaders also demanded Negro drivers for Negro routes.

On Feb. 21, 115 Negroes were indicted by a Montgomery County grand jury (17 white men, one Negro) on charges of instigating the Negro mass boycott. The indictments were based on a 1921 state law, originally intended to curb violence in labor disputes, that outlawed organized boycotts that had no "just cause or legal excuse."

115 INDICTED

Of the 115 indicted, 90 Negro leaders, including 24 ministers, were arrested Feb. 22-24. All were released on $300 bond each. They were arraigned Feb. 24 and all pleaded not guilty.

The Rev. Dr. Martin Luther King, 27, pastor of the Negro Dexter Avenue Baptist Church and president of the Montgomery Improvement Assn., was found guilty by Circuit Judge Eugene W. Carter on March 22 of having conspired illegally to boycott the city's segregated buses.

King was fined $500 (or 140 days in jail) and assessed $500 in costs (or 246 days in jail). Sentence was suspended pending King's appeal to the Alabama Circuit Court of Appeals. None of the other Negroes indicted have stood trial.

Judge Carter upheld the state's contention that the MIA, under King's leadership, had conceived and directed the bus boycott and that once the boycott began King found he had "started a fire he couldn't stop." Cases of the 89 other Negroes were continued pending the outcome of King's appeal.

On June 5, a three-judge federal court here ruled by 2-1 that racial segregation on Montgomery city buses was in violation of the Federal Constitution. City and state officials appealed to the U.S. Supreme Court which upheld the lower court's decision Tues-

U.S. Court Order Asked by Negroes Against Injunction

End of Boycott Seen at Two Mass Meetings Tonight; Scores Walk

City authorities questioned the right of Montgomery Negroes to ask for a federal court order to continue their bus boycott car pool in face of a newly granted injunction in state court.

The Negroes asked U. S. District Judge Frank M. Johnson for an order to permit them to continue the motor pool operations even though the long boycott appeared near an end with city and state segregation laws knocked out by the U. S. Supreme Court.

They asked for the right to continue the car lift until the boycott is brought to an end, perhaps at mass meetings in Montgomery tonight.

City Atty. Walter Knabe asked Johnson to dismiss the Negroes' request primarily on the grounds that the Supreme Court decision has removed the need for the boycott and the car pool and also that it is purely a state matter outside the jurisdiction of federal court.

RULING WITHHELD

Knabe pointed out that the Negroes in their petition said they would ride City Lines buses again once they were desegregated.

Johnson withheld an immediate ruling on the city's objections and ordered the hearing to proceed with testimony from witnesses. He also refused a request from the Negroes to make Circuit Judge Eugene Carter a defendant. Carter issued an injunction yesterday against continued operation of the car pool.

The Rev. Martin Luther King Jr., one of the boycott leaders, testified that "there is no basic need" to continue the car pool in the face of the Supreme Court ruling. But he said the boycott has not formally been abandoned

MANY WALK TO WORK

Meanwhile, Negroes in uncounted numbers walked to work this morning because of the injunction against use of the motor pool.

A Negro leader, the Rev. Ralph D. Abernathy, said "on the whole" the Negroes "made the sacrifice and walked to work."

There were indications that the 11-month-old protest against segregated city buses—now ordered integrated by the Supreme Court—will

A scheduled mass meeting to announce the decision was broadened to two rallies tonight because, Abernathy explained, no Negro church is large enough to hold the expected crowd. One meeting will start at 7 p.m. (CST) and the second an hour later across town at another church.

STATE COURT INJUNCTION

The city won a temporary injunction in State Court late yesterday to halt the motor pool until further notice. Circuit Judge Eugene Carter granted the restraining order although the U.S. Supreme Court had outlawed bus segregation earlier in the day.

Negro lawyers challenged the state court's jurisdiction yesterday because the appeal to Johnson in Federal Court was already on file before the city got into court with its injunction request.

CLAIM RIGHTS VIOLATED

Both in their petition in U.S. Court and in arguments before Carter yesterday, the Negroes protested that any interference with their car pool operations—which they described as purely voluntary—would violate their civil and constitutional rights.

With or without help from the Federal Court, however, Carter's injunction destined to have little effect on the car pool system in view of a Negro leader's predic-

tion that the boycott itself would end tonight.

DECISION DUE TONIGHT

The Rev. Martin Luther King Jr., president of the boycott-supporting Montgomery Improvement Assn., told newsmen the decision will come at a mass meeting tonight at a Negro church.

The meetings are scheduled for Hutchinson St. Baptist Church at 7 p.m. Holt St. Baptist at 8 p.m.

While emphasizing that he couldn't speak for all the Negroes of his race, King said he felt certain the Negroes will vote to patronize Montgomery City Lines buses again now that the segregation laws have been knocked out.

CITY DECLINES COMMENT

The city commission at whose request Carter issued the injunction declined comment on the Supreme Court decision. All three commissioners are members of the pro-segregation White Citizens Council.

King hailed the ruling as "A glorious daybreak to end a long night of enforced segregation."

It came just shy of one year after the start of the boycott last Dec. 5, a protest which became the first mass use of economic force in the South since the Supreme Court ruled against public school segregation 30 months ago.

Negro attorneys sought to use the Supreme Court's decision in their argument before Carter yesterday, but he ruled it out. The judge held it was simply a question of whether the Negroes were operating a legal or illegal car lift and the ruling on segregation "has nothing to do with it."

The issue was primarily whether the car pool was a "private enterprise" operated without a license, as the city contended, or a voluntary share-the-ride plan provided as a service by Negro churches without profit or financial gain.

Along with private automobiles, the Negroes have used, in their own words, "some 17 or 18" church-owned station wagons to take bus boycotters to and from work.

"SERIOUS QUESTION"

City attorneys presented testimony whether the car pool operation is or isn't a private enterprise, but he said the city had presented enough evidence to "raise

a serious question."

That issue will be determined later on a ruling on the city's companion request for a permanent injunction, the judge said.

So will the matter of damages. The city asked for $6,000 on the grounds that the boycott has meant a loss of revenue. Two per cent of the gross receipts of the privately owned bus company goes to the city as a franchise tax.

TESTIMONY OFFERED

City attorneys presented testimony from Negro leaders themselves to show how the motor pool is financed by contributions from Negro churches, and how drivers and other employes are paid for their services.

But Negro lawyers insisted the boycotters have a right to use the car pool uninterrupted so long as the boycotters don't pay for their transportation.

Testimony showed the churches have received donations from Negroes both in Montgomery and throughout the nation to bear the costs of transportation, at one time estimated at $3,000 a week.

Week-Long Race Institute
Ended On Optimistic Note

Attendance Is Lower Than Anticipated; Coliseum Denied

MONTGOMERY, Dec. 9 (AP) — An enthusiastic crowd of about 3,000 Negroes today closed a week-long "institute on nonviolence and social change" that marked the first anniversary of the Montgomery bus boycott.

The Negroes packed into the Negro First Baptist Church to hear Dr. J. H. Jackson, of Chicago, president of the National Baptist Convention, a Negro group.

The Rev. Martin Luther King Jr., president of the Montgomery Improvement Assn. that has led the boycott and sponsored the southwide institute, told the group that "we have had a glorious week here together."

The week included seminars on the way Montgomery's estimated 50,000 Negroes have conducted the boycott that began Dec. 5, 1955. The passive resistance used in the protest against city bus segregation was described as an example to Negroes elsewhere in their battle against racial discrimination.

Jackson said that a man is not great on the outside; greatness is only on the inside. "When white supremacy (advocates) realize it, they won't care who touches the outside," Jackson said.

"Then we can sit together and talk together."

Montgomery Negroes have learned that "if only we stick together we will realize in our time first-class citizenship," the Rev. Ralph D. Abernathy told the applauding crowd. Abernathy is pastor of the church where today's meeting was held and is institute chairman.

'Tired Feet, Rested Souls'

He said Negroes will continue with "tired feet but rested souls" to conduct the boycott until they win.

The U.S. Supreme Court decided Nov. 13 that city bus segregation is unconstitutional and ordered it ended in Montgomery. A request for rehearing has been asked by the city and the state of Alabama.

Before the requests were made, a court official in Washington said the decision would probably reach Montgomery officials next week, but when it will go into effect is now uncertain.

Abernathy said "our heads are bruised from being beaten by the blackjacks of a prejudiced police department," but that Negroes were unbowed in their determination to fight segregation peacefully.

He estimated that about 3,000 persons were crowded into the main auditorium and basement of his church after he urged them to "sit neighborly" in order to get more in. About one hundred more persons heard the program broadcast outside the building in raw, wintry weather.

Attendance Off

Today's meeting had originally been announced as a statewide gathering of white and Negro religious and lay leaders, with 10,000 persons expected. Officials of the state Coliseum here told Negro leaders that a meeting there would have to be segregated, and the institute organizers decided to move elsewhere.

Only about a dozen white persons were in the audience today. During announcements of contributions to the boycott fund only a few out-of-town persons were in evidence.

Last night an institute banquet was held for drivers in the boycotters' car pool that provided transportation for Negroes until last Nov. 13. On that day a state court banned the system at the city's request and since then Negroes have walked and caught rides to work.

T. M. Alexander, an Atlanta insurance executive, told the drivers that the church-owned station wagons in the car pool were insured by Lloyd's of London "one day after white insurance companies (in the United States) had canceled their policies."

Alexander urged Montgomery Negroes to register as voters, saying "then we can put out of office such persons as the sheriff and the chief of police . . ."

AS LAWFUL BUS SEGREGATION ENDED

This was the scene at Court Square in Montgomery yesterday as city buses were making their final runs with white and Negro passengers segregated by state and city law. The era of racial separation on buses ended with the arrival of the U.S. Supreme Court's official decree. Last night Montgomery City Lines officials notified their drivers to cease enforcing segregated seating.—Staff Photo By Haywood Paravicini

PART FIVE

THE WHITE FOLKS

By Willy S. Leventhal

Excerpted From

"Drum Major For Justice . . .
Drum Major For Peace":
Recitals on the Unfinished Legacy
of Dr. Martin Luther King, Jr.

CHAPTER 1

"The unknown ground crew"

Prominently displayed in a glass enclosure within the third floor archives of the King Center in Atlanta is the handwritten draft of Dr. King's 1964 Nobel Peace Prize acceptance speech. On that yellow legal tablet, in his bold, deliberate cursive style, Dr. King noted that he was dedicating his prize to the courageous activists he termed "the unknown ground crew." He explained that these anonymous soldiers in the struggle for human rights made it possible for the well-known captains to chart and pilot the successful routes of the Civil Rights Movement.

This chapter illuminates the contributions of but a few of those involved in the Montgomery Bus Boycott who are part of that "unknown ground crew."

Many of the details and personalities of the struggle in Montgomery during the mid-1950s have been historically obscured, yet when closely examined shed new light on a variety of topics at the core of Dr. King's leadership and his later interactions with white associates, "black power" adversaries, politicians in the federal government, and, especially, the federal courts and the FBI.

There has evolved a "politically correct" view of Dr. King and the legacy of the 1950s and '60s. But what happened in Montgomery and the personal and political relationships the young King forged there were far more crucial to the later events in the Civil Rights Movement and to Dr. King's life than has been acknowledged.

Particularly at issue in any reexamination of the Montgomery Bus Boycott is the extent to which Dr. King and his followers interacted with whites of good will. To be sure, few whites publicly sided with the boycotters. Few stood against the "massive resistance" of Southern whites to the social activism and change that took root soon after World War II and burst into full bloom in the years immediately following the 1954 *Brown* decision.

Yet there were whites in the "Cradle of the Confederacy," as Montgomery is known, who did not go along with the segregationists. And some of those who stood against the tide were influential and politically well-connected. Their support was strategically and emotionally significant to Martin Luther King, Jr. In several instances the relationships that emerged helped to draw King more tightly into a web of surveillance and harassment by the FBI that would continue until his death.

One would assume that the legions of journalists and historians who have written thousands upon thousands of prize-winning pages about King would have thoroughly explored his formative relationships with white liberals. But they have largely missed or ignored the importance of this aspect of King's life. Even Martin Luther King, Jr., himself, in his autobiographical *Stride*

Toward Freedom: The Montgomery Story,[1] did not tell the complete story. As we shall see, he had his reasons.

ON THE EVENING of November 14, 1956, there were jubilant mass meetings at two Negro churches in Montgomery. Thousands had gathered to celebrate the ruling the previous day by the United States Supreme Court. This ruling affirmed, without comment, a June 5, 1956, lower court panel opinion[2] in which U.S. District Judge Frank M. Johnson, Jr., and U.S. Circuit Judge Richard T. Rives, both residents of Montgomery, had declared that the City of Montgomery statutes requiring segregated seating in public transit were unconstitutional.[3] (The third judge on the panel, Judge Seybourne Lynne of Birmingham, voted against Johnson and Rives.)[4]

Such decisions enacting and enforcing civil rights laws by the federal judiciary, though frequent in the 1950s and '60s, were opposed by most white Southerners. Both violence-prone terrorists and demagogic politicians (who masked racism with thinly veneered claims of "states rights") hated this activist intervention by federal judges.

In *Stride Toward Freedom,* Dr. King described the excited atmosphere at the celebratory mass meetings on that brisk fall evening in Montgomery:

> The eight thousand men and women who crowded in and around the two churches were in high spirits. At the first meeting it was clear that the news of the decision had spread fast, and the opening hymn had a special note of joy. Reading the Scripture that night was Bob Graetz, who had chosen Paul's famous letter to the Corinthians: "Though I have all faith, so that I could remove mountains, and have not love, I am nothing . . . Love suffereth long, and is kind . . ."
>
> When the slender blond minister came to the words: "When I was a child, I spoke as a child, I understood as a child, I thought as a child: but when I became a man, I put away childish things," the congregation burst into applause. Soon they were shouting and cheering and waving their handkerchiefs, as if to say that they knew that they had come of age, and won new dignity. When Bob Graetz concluded "And now abideth faith, hope, love, but the greatest of these is love," there was another spontaneous outburst. Only a people who had struggled to love in the midst of bitter conflict could have reacted in this fashion. I knew then that nonviolence, for all its difficulties, had won its way into their hearts.
>
> Later, Ralph Abernathy spoke. He told how a white newspaperman had reproached him for this outburst on the part of the congregation.
>
> "Isn't it a little peculiar," the journalist had asked, "for people to interrupt the Scripture in that way?"
>
> "Yes it is," Abernathy quoted himself in reply. "Just as it is peculiar for people to walk in the snow and rain when there are empty buses available; just as it is peculiar for people to pray for those who persecute them; just as it is for the southern Negro to stand up and look a white man in the face as an equal." At this his audience laughed and applauded.[5]

[1] See Chapter IX, page 163, *Stride Toward Freedom: The Montgomery Story*, by Dr. Martin Luther King, Jr., (paperback edition), 1986, Harper and Row (original hardback, copyright 1958, Harper and Brothers).

[2] See *Gayle v. Browder,* 352 U. S. 903 (Supreme Court); *Browder v. Gayle* 142 F. SUPP 707 (District Court, including facts and opinion).

[3] See *Owen v. Browder* 352 U. S. 903 (Supreme Court); *Browder v. Owen* 142 F. SUPP 707 (District Court, including facts and opinion). On the same day, by affirming the above ajoining case adjudicated by the same District Court panel, the Supreme Court had also ruled segregated seating throughout the entire state of Alabama similarly unconstitutional.

[4] Federal law required that only a three-judge District Court panel could grant "an interlocutory or permanent injunction restraining the enforcement, operation or execution of any State statute by restraining the action of any officer of such state"(28 United states Code Annotated at Section 2281). In this case, two District Judges — Johnson and Seybourn Lynne — and one Circuit Judge — Rives — from the U.S. Fifth Circuit Court of Appeals were so assigned.

[5] Pages 161-162, *Stride . . .*

[6] *Ibid*, see pages 158-161.

The 381 days of nonviolent protest, and the events culminating in the Supreme Court's intervention *were* peculiar. But the "peculiarities"—which involved the *leaders* (both white and black), as well as *the timing* of events that shaped the bus boycott—went far beyond those humorously noted at the pulpit by the Rev. Mr. Abernathy.

In *Stride Toward Freedom* Dr. King explained that on the very same day, November 13, 1956, that the Supreme Court issued *its* ruling, he and other local leaders had been gloomily sitting in a Montgomery courtroom where a municipal court judge[6] seemed ready to rule on a motion by attorneys for the City of Montgomery requesting that the bus boycott be declared illegal. King and other leaders of the African-American community were worried that if they lost in court that day, the courageous citizens who had given up public transportation for almost a year might not hold firm through a second winter of walking in the cold and rain.

The local court hearing was being held relative to an October 30, 1956, motion which, based on then-existing local and state statutes, requested that the car pool system developed by the Montgomery Improvement Association (MIA), be declared "a public nuisance," and shut down. Lawyers for the City government also asked the local court to fine the MIA—of which King was president—$15,000.

Obviously, such a decision by a Montgomery municipal judge would be a major setback to the boycott.

Meanwhile, the appeal to the U. S. Supreme Court by the City of Montgomery, in an effort to overturn the District Court panel, was but one of hundreds of cases the members of the nation's highest court were to consider in their new term which had just begun on October 8, 1956. It *was* surprising, too, that soon after the conclusion of their summer recess, the Supreme Court had moved with such haste to resolve this particular case ahead of so many others that had been under consideration for a longer period of time.

However, whether for reasons of coincidence, fate, or calculation, by issuing their decision on the exact day it would nullify any action by the local judge, the justices sent a simultaneous legal message: *defeat*, to the white Montgomery city officials; *victory*, to the black citizens of Montgomery and to their leaders in the MIA.

Implementation of the Supreme Court ruling effectively ended segregated seating: the buses were opened to Montgomery's African-American citizens without discrimination; the need for the car pool system was removed; and the legal basis for the city's motion was legally null and void.

The court battle, of course, was just a part of the struggle. The courageous perseverance of the people supporting the bus boycott had provided time for the promises of democracy to be fulfilled via the Supreme Court intervention. This historic victory led down freedom's road to more struggle in the continuing quest for the American ideal of equality.

CHAPTER 2

"That damn Hugo Black"

As Dr. King noted in *Stride Toward Freedom,* later on the night of November 14, 1956,

> the Ku Klux Klan rode [through the streets of] . . . Montgomery. The radio had announced their plan to demonstrate throughout the Negro community, and threats of violence and new bombings were in the air. My mail was warning that "if you allow the niggers to go back on the buses and sit in the front seats we're going to burn down fifty houses in one night, including yours." Another letter cursed the Supreme Court and threatened "that damn Hugo Black": "When he comes to Alabama we're going to hang you and him from the same tree."[7]

Dr. King did not explain why Hugo Black, one of nine Supreme Court Justices, should be singled out for personal threats. In part, it was because Black was a native son of the South who had twice been elected to the U.S. Senate from Alabama. In the 1920s, as an ambitious young lawyer, he had briefly been a member of the then politically powerful KKK. Thus, when Black voted with the other justices for Negro rights, the Klan and other segregationists considered him a traitor to the white race and they hated him even more than the Negro leaders whom they merely considered their enemies.

But there is even more to the story than is found in *Stride Toward Freedom* and all the subsequent King biographies. Within this omission lies an untold side of the Montgomery story, because Martin Luther King, Jr., had very personal reasons for not telling more about Hugo Black's connection to the unusual events in Montgomery. In part, King was trying to protect, as best as he could, whites of good will who had been supportive of him and of the emerging Civil Rights Movement.

Knowing how these white folks in Montgomery supported the freedom struggle of their black brethren is a key to understanding aspects of the entire Civil Rights Movement that are essentially ignored in the now historically authoritative view of the Movement. Knowing more about Dr. King's relationships with whites in Montgomery leads to a new understanding of such primary events in King's life as the mid-1950s' origin of his eventually dangerous conflict with J. Edgar Hoover, the nature of his disagreements with the mid-1960s' "Black Power" advocates, as well as his later decision to organize a "Poor People's Campaign" to protest economic injustices.

During the period of the bus boycott, King was acquainted with Justice Black's sister-in-law, Virginia Durr—and her attorney husband, Clifford, a former Roosevelt administration official, who lived in Montgomery. Dr. King

[7] *Ibid,* page 162.

[8] Page 252, *A Southern Rebel: The Life and Times of Aubrey Willis Williams, 1895–1965*, by John Salmond, 1983; University of North Carolina Press.

[9] Interview with E. D. Nixon by Willy Leventhal, December 4, 1975.

was also well aware that these relatives of a sitting Supreme Court justice were close friends of both E. D. Nixon and Rosa Parks, key characters in the Montgomery drama.

Nixon was born in the first year of the twentieth century and became a union organizer in his mid-twenties. By the 1930s he was the leader of the Montgomery affiliate of the Brotherhood of Sleeping Car Porters, the influential black labor union headed by A. Philip Randolph. Nixon was not only a protege and a great admirer of Randolph, but in the years before the boycott had earned the reputation as the most defiant and fearless black man in Montgomery. For twenty-five years, Nixon served as the president of the local branch of the NAACP and was twice elected to lead the state NAACP. In the late 1940s and early '50s he was often the person to whom Montgomery's black citizens would turn when they had a legal problem. In those troubled days before Montgomery had black attorneys, Nixon would often refer them to Clifford Durr.

Interestingly, given the segregated social culture of the times in Montgomery, Nixon was also a close friend of another white man, Aubrey Williams. Dr. King knew about the Nixon–Williams association, and he knew also that the Durr–Williams friendship stretched back to the early days of the Roosevelt administration and the New Deal.

Born in 1895, Aubrey Willis Williams grew up poor in Birmingham, Alabama. He became a successful businessman and played an important role in politics and government during the Roosevelt years. He was a leader in several important New Deal programs which helped the nation recover from the Great Depression. In 1946, with considerable financial resources at his disposal, he moved from Washington, D.C., to Montgomery. Thereafter, Williams and Nixon worked together on matters of mutual interest and Williams often provided financial support to Nixon's Montgomery branch of the NAACP. Williams also provided bail money for many black Montgomerians arrested during the boycott.

Years later, Nixon told Aubrey Williams's biographer: "You know, if it hadn't been for Aubrey Williams I don't believe we could have ever mustered up courage to do it. You don't know what it means to have a white man that Negroes can trust and we do trust Aubrey Williams. That man has so much self-respect that it rubs off on you."[8]

In my own interview with Mr. Nixon, he stressed that "there are hundreds of people who made a contribution . . . the Montgomery boycott was a big thing in a whole lotta' peoples' lives and it ought to be an honest-to-goodness true report . . . the children comin' on behind us ought to know the truth about this. The truth will set you free."[9]

Nixon, who was good at making close friends out of strong folks, had enlisted a local seamstress, Mrs. Rosa Parks, to be his secretary at the NAACP. Mrs. Parks also happened to be a close friend of the Durr and Williams families.

Virginia Durr—in her wonderfully entertaining memoir, *Outside The Magic Circle*—relates that before the bus boycott, she had told Mrs. Parks about a two-week scholarship that was available to the progressive Highlander

THE CHILDREN COMING ON . . .

Folk School. Organized during Roosevelt's New Deal administration, this institution in Monteagle, Tennessee, was committed to promoting civil rights, racial integration, and the American labor movement. Mrs. Parks wanted to attend the session at Highlander but had neither the funds for the travel expense, nor a suitcase nor a bathing suit to use at the Highlander pool. Mrs. Durr's daughters loaned the needed suitcase and swimsuit; Aubrey Williams provided her bus fare. As Mrs. Durr recalled,

> Rosa Parks is one of the proudest people I've ever known in my life. She hated to admit that she didn't have a suitcase or a bathing suit or money. It was painful for her. She was a very proud woman, so all of this had to be accomplished with a great deal of tact, which I am not noted for. But, Mrs. Parks was very fond of Aubrey Williams. By that time she'd gotten fond of me, too, and she really wanted to go . . . Our friend, Myles Horton, who ran the school, felt that Mrs. Parks's stay at Highlander encouraged her in the boycott . . . I think it gave her a great lift. She loved it.

Not long after her return from Highlander, Mrs. Parks refused to be mistreated on a Montgomery City Lines bus, and her arrest led to the boycott. She is now famous, and the story of her arrest is widely known. However, fewer people know about the phone call from E. D. Nixon to the Durr residence within an hour of Mrs. Parks's arrest on the evening of December 1, 1955.[10]

[10] See pages 278-280 in Virginia Durr's *Outside The Magic Circle,* 1989, The University of Alabama Press. See pages 37-44 in Howell Raines's *My Soul Is Rested: The Story of the Civil Rights Movement in the South,* Putnam, 1977. In these pages Mr. Nixon and Mrs. Parks relate the same story documenting the role of Clifford and Virginia Durr.

CHAPTER 3

"Mr. Durr, will you call the jail?"

Mrs. Durr, who had been a leader in the fight to outlaw the poll tax during the Roosevelt administration as well as a 1948 Progressive Party candidate for the U.S. Senate, continues her story:

> [E. D. Nixon said,] "Mr. Durr, will you call the jail and see why Mrs. Parks has been arrested?" The police recognized [Nixon's] voice as being that of a black man and they wouldn't tell him anything. They treated him with the utmost disdain. Cliff called the jail and said he was Clifford J. Durr and he was a lawyer. They knew who he was, I think. He asked why Mrs. Parks was in jail. They told him she'd been booked on the city segregation ordinance. So Cliff called Mr. Nixon back. Mr. Nixon asked if Cliff would go down with him to make bail. Cliff said, "Mr. Nixon, I don't have anything to make bail with." We didn't own any property at the time, and we only had three or four hundred dollars a month to live on. Mr. Nixon said, "That's all right. I can make bail, if you'll just go with me." He was afraid that they wouldn't let him make bail. I was determined to go, too, so I put on my coat and came running out.

Within a few days, Montgomery's black community, at E.D. Nixon's instigation, elected Martin Luther King, Jr., to lead the protest sparked by Mrs. Parks's arrest. On December 5, 1955, at the Holt Street Baptist Church, Dr. King gave his first speech as a civil rights leader. (This was the same church where Rev. Abernathy, a year later, described the conversation with the white journalist about the "peculiarities" of the bus boycott struggle.)

As Mrs. Durr recalls,

> There must have been ten or fifteen thousand black people crowding in and around the church. At that time I felt on very friendly terms with all the black community. I hadn't the slightest feeling of fear being the only white person, but I couldn't get into the church because of the crowd. King made a magnificent speech [amplified to the crowd outside the church] that electrified the black people. He became their undoubted leader that night.[11]

Virginia Durr didn't write about how her own, and Clifford Durr's, close relations with Hugo Black affected the federal court case resulting in the Supreme Court timely intervention into Montgomery's public transit dilemma.

However, in an interview many years later, Mrs. Durr acknowledged that her kinship with Hugo Black *was* an important issue in the case:

[11] See Virginia Durr, *Ibid*, page 281.

I never talked to him about it, but Hugo probably would know. The part about the busing case is that my husband, you see, helped Fred Gray—in the case that went to the Supreme Court. But, he was not a lawyer of record because he and Hugo were such good friends that [the MIA lawyers] were afraid that when the case went before the Supreme Court Hugo Black would recuse himself on account of Cliff, and wouldn't sit on the case. And, it was never known that my husband was an important part of it.

. . . The NAACP financed the [busing] case and Cliff never got paid any money for all his work because he couldn't be a lawyer of record. I suppose Hugo Black did know we were involved, but he would absolutely recuse himself from any case that Cliff was [officially involved] in[12]—and it was very hard on Cliff because he certainly worked very hard on the case, but won't go down in the history books.[13]

Jo Ann Robinson, in her book, *The Montgomery Bus Boycott and the Women Who Started It* (1987), did note Clifford Durr's legal assistance.[14] Rev. Solomon Seay, Sr., in his autobiography, *I Was There By The Grace Of God*, gave a great tribute to Clifford Durr's role; however, Seay's fine book has had little circulation outside Montgomery, Alabama, where it was published.[15] Neither book, however, nor any of the other boycott-related books, sheds light on whether the Durr-Black relationship impacted the timing of the Supreme Court decision on November 13, 1956.

Mrs. Durr explained to me, "The busing decision was absolutely thrilling because it did away with segregation in the theaters and the restaurants; before that Montgomery had just been completely segregated."

In our discussion, Mrs. Durr also clarified the feelings of her husband and Aubrey Williams, explaining, simply, that "they were not idealists: they just felt like this was *their* country, too, they had a stake in it; and they had deep feelings about that."

Clifford Durr, who died in 1976, had said:

I wasn't consciously bent on improving the lot of black people, although they were getting a bad deal. But I knew Rosa Parks well. She was a fine person. When she went to jail I found myself helping her instinctively. I never acted deliberatively; I'm not basically an ideological person. But you move instinctively when you see somebody kicked around.

Sometimes the Negroes would come around and tell me how much they appreciated what I was doing for them. I said, "Look here, I'm not a damn bit interested in your legal and constitutional rights as Negroes, but I am interested in your legal and constitutional rights as people because I happen to be people myself. I know from long experience that our legal and constitutional safeguards are not selective. They've got to protect everybody or in time they won't protect any of us. It's a matter of fighting for my own rights along with yours.[16]

[12] Roger K. Newman, in his definitive *Hugo Black: A Biography*, Pantheon Books, 1994, notes on page 336, "Black had disqualified himself on all cases in which the Federal Communications Commission was involved, however remotely, because Clifford Durr, his wife's brother-in-law, was a member." See also pages 431-443, for an in-depth discussion of Black's role in the *Brown* case.

[13] Interview with Virginia Durr, November 18, 1993, Atlanta, Georgia. In *Warrior at the Bar . . .*, a biography of Thurgood Marshall, by Michael G. Davis and Hunter R. Clark, 1992, Clifford Durr is depicted as an ". . . NAACP lawyer," even though he was never of record in the case, nor paid by the NAACP.

[14] Mrs. Robinson's account, which was edited by David Garrow, included a more thorough depiction of the bus boycott than Garrow's King biography, *Bearing The Cross*, 1986.

[15] Published by the S. S. Seay, Sr. Educational Foundation, Montgomery, 1990.

[16] Quoted in *Outside . . .*, page 306. Clifford Durr had resigned his position on the Federal Communications Commission in 1947 in protest of President Truman's "Loyalty Oath" program. Durr not only publicly opposed the implementation of the loyalty oath as an anti-democratic denial of due process, but defended federal government employees who were targeted by the FBI's web of accusations attributed to unidentified informants.

For perspective on how rare and courageous was Durr's stand, see *Loyalties, A Son's Memoir*, by Carl Bernstein, Simon and Shuster, 1989. Bernstein vividly explains the severe impact of the repressive loyalty oath policy upon employees who were involved with unions, civil rights and/or other politically progressive activities. Bernstein also points out how rare it was for any attorney in Washington, D.C., to defend those who came under the scrutiny of the loyalty oath dragnet. For background on Durr's work in Washington, D.C., during this period, see also Chapters Six and Seven in the Durr biography, *The Conscience of A Lawyer*, by John Salmond, University of Alabama Press, 1990.

[17] Mrs. Coretta Scott King confirmed, in January 1996, that she was "absolutely certain" and remembered discussions with her husband about the need to keep the names of the Durrs and other white supporters (particularly Aubrey Williams) out of his book to save them from being targeted for retaliation. See pages 43-52 in *Stride...* for Dr. King's account of Mrs. Parks's arrest. For another direct account of the danger to those who challenged the status quo, see a moving personal remembrance by New York Times newsman Harrison Salisbury (pages 42-63) in *A Time of Change: A Reporter's Tale of Our Time.*

[18] The Montgomery Human Relations Council was an affiliate of the Alabama Human Relations Council which was, in turn, one of an eleven-state network based in the old Confederacy states. The Human Relations Councils were organized by the Atlanta-based Southern Regional Council, whose origins date to 1919, being reorganized as the SRC in 1944. This interracial organization continues to promote quality education, voter registration, racial understanding, economic opportunity, and environmental justice, as well as other social reforms.

John Egerton's *Speak Now Against The Day*, Knopf, 1994 (paperback, UNC Press, 1996) describes the developments and bi-racial leaders that led to the formation of the SRC. Another recent book that explores the pre-bus boycott era of Southern and civil rights history is *Days of Hope: Race and Democracy in the New Deal Era* by Patricia Sullivan, University of North Carolina Press, 1996. Harry Ashmore, in both *Hearts and Minds: The Anatomy of Racism from Roosevelt to Reagan*, McGraw-Hill, 1982; and *Civil Rights and Wrongs: A Memoir of Race and Politics, 1944-1994*, Pantheon, 1994, covered some of this same ground. My in-progress King biography, *Drum Major For Peace, ...Drum Major For Justice* will deal with this until-recent blind spot in the scholarly analysis of the Civil Rights Movement.

King biographers and Movement historians have glossed over the close relationship between the Durrs and Hugo Black, as well as the circle of friendship among the Durrs, Aubrey Williams, E. D. Nixon, and Rosa Parks. Yet these interracial bonds of goodwill are significant. They are examples to be followed by all who today continue to work for the improvement of race relations and the fulfillment of the American democratic promise. And they help us understand both the personal character of Martin Luther King, Jr., as well as the strategic lessons he carried within himself about the leadership of the Civil Rights Movement.

The *first* reason there have not been adequate portrayals of the "peculiar" white Montgomerians who supported the bus boycott is revealed in Dr. King's narrative in *Stride Toward Freedom*.

When this first of his five books was written in 1957, Dr. King evidently believed that singling out the partnership of Aubrey Williams and the Durrs in the boycott would put them in greater danger than they already were. Courageous white Southerners who took the side of racial equality were subject to the reprisals threatened by the letterwriter who offered to hang King and "that damn Hugo Black" to the same tree.

Though Dr. King knew of the Durrs' role in arranging bail for Mrs. Parks, in *Stride Toward Freedom* he omitted specific reference, saying, "Only E.D. Nixon—the signer of Mrs. Parks's bond—and one or two other persons were aware of the arrest when it occurred early Thursday evening."[17]

Even before the boycott, the Durrs' and Williams's kinship to and friendship with Hugo Black, and their steadfast racial and political beliefs, had brought them economic reprisal and social ostracism in Montgomery.

By 1969, when Coretta Scott King wrote *My Life With Martin Luther King, Jr.,* she had no reticence about giving proper credit to the roles of Aubrey Williams and the Durrs, as well as of other courageous white allies in Montgomery. By that time, Aubrey Williams was already deceased, and the Durrs, though still in Montgomery, were no longer subject to reprisal. Mrs. King did not go into detail of individuals' specific involvement in Montgomery in the fifties, but she explained the intensity of the situation:

A few of our white friends in Montgomery stuck by us and paid dearly for it. There was the tragedy of Juliette Morgan, a white librarian who was a member of the Human Relations Council.[18] She had written a letter to the newspapers comparing our Movement to the Movement in India and praising it. From that moment on, the white community completely ostracized her. The pressure and isolation finally grew so intense that she committed suicide by taking an overdose of sleeping pills. It is hard to express how sad we felt. Then there was Aubrey Williams and his wife [Anita]—he had been head of the National Youth Administration under President Franklin D. Roosevelt—and Clifford and Virginia Durr. The Durrs suffered terribly for their support of the Movement and friendship with us. Mr. Durr's law practice suffered considerably, but they continued to attend the Human Relations Council meetings and she came to the mass meetings. Other white people like the Morelands and the

Smiths also continued to come to the Council meetings. Mr. Smith was an architect and his wife's family owned a laundry chain in Montgomery."[19]

As Mrs. Durr noted,

We were not the only ones by any means. Aubrey Williams had been working with Mr. Nixon even before we came back and he had paid for the telephone and the rent, I think, for the NAACP . . . he certainly had retribution because he was completely boycotted and he had very few friends.

. . . The Women's Society for Christian Service of the Methodist Church took action . . . Dr. Thrasher, who was the head of the Episcopal Church of the Ascension was the head of the Alabama Council on Human Relations at that time. And Mrs. Andrews . . . was head of Churchwomen United—then it was segregated and so she formed an integrated prayer group and a great many women came from all the churches. A lot of them are dead now but they were very active and very supportive.

. . . Lots of people supported us quietly and supported the blacks quietly. For instance, the Jewish community gave a good deal of money to the King movement [in Montgomery] but they always wanted it to be quiet.

Rev. Robert Graetz and his wife, Jeannie, who lived in the African-American communty and took an active role in the boycott as he pastored the all-black Trinity Lutheran Church, also recall courageous whites in Montgomery who were not afraid to show their support for the bus protest.

Mr. and Mrs. I.B. Rutledge, an older couple, were both members of established Southern families [and others] . . . willingly jeopardized their own safety to preserve our friendship . . . Mrs. Clara Rutledge, a proper Southern lady, rather mothered Jeannie . . . Through Mrs. Rutledge, Jeannie met Jane Katz, and we later became aquainted with her husband, Warren. About our age, the Katzes had young children, were very concerned about social issues, and shared many of our deeply held values. For Warren, a local businessman, even to admit that he knew us was an act of courage. But Warren and Jane not only knew us, they were among our best friends [who also included] Morrison and Vivian Williams . . . Morry's parents, Aubrey and Anita Williams, . . . Bob Hughes . . . Victor and Anne Kerns, another young Jewish couple, . . . and Virginia and Clifford Durr . . .

The Durrs experienced considerable tension in Montgomery even before the bus boycott because of Hugo Black's part in the May 17, 1954, Supreme Court school desegregation ruling, *Brown v. Board of Education*.

Years later, after Frank Johnson's school integration decisions (1964), as Mrs. Durr recalled, "The black children [who first integrated the schools]

[19] Mrs. King, writing more than a decade later, apparently separated Moreland Smith's name—assigning both first and last to different white allies. However, her characterization of the Smiths is correct. Due to the pressure over their support of the bus boycott and racial equality, his partners asked him to leave his architectural firm. Mr. and Mrs. Moreland Smith relocated in Atlanta. Mr. Smith has since died, but as of 1998 his widow still lived in Atlanta.

[20] Virginia Durr, *Ibid*, page 276; and excerpts from interview conducted as part of the Southern Regional Council Oral History Project. During the strife and tension of school integration in Montgomery in the 1960s, the bond of friendship between the Durrs and another community leader, Mrs. Johnnie Carr, was such that Mrs. Carr's son Arlam, Jr., would sometimes wait at the Durrs' home for his mother to pick him up after school. The Durrs then lived across the street from Montgomery's traditionally white public high school. Mrs. Carr had gone to school with Rosa Parks, was an NAACP and MIA activist, and has served since 1968 as MIA president.

[21] See *The Judge: The Life & Opinions of Alabama's Frank M. Johnson*, Jr., by Frank Sikora, Black Belt Press, 1992; and, *Taming The Storm*, Doubleday, 1993, and *Unlikely Heroes*, University of Alabama Press, 1981, by Jack Bass.

[22] *Ibid*.

were very brave. They were heroes in their own community . . . and they *were* heroes, because it was pretty tough . . . My children, Tilla and Lulah, were anything but heroes. They were pariahs and outcasts for being the nieces of Hugo Black and the daughters of Virginia and Clifford Durr . . . they really stopped going to school. So we had some friends in the north who got them scholarships and they went up to Massachusetts to school . . . These were friends we had from Washington days. That was a great help to us."[20]

In Montgomery—and throughout the South—the fifties and sixties were dangerous times. Black activists were most at risk, and dozens paid with their lives for their commitment to civil rights. Courageous whites were also at risk. When the "official" histories of the Movement ignore or downplay the contributions and sacrifices of white allies, a disservice is done to the movement that did exist, and today's much-needed ongoing movement is made more difficult.

Moreover, the families of Frank Johnson and Richard Rives were ostracized and harassed by racists after the judges' decision against segregated bus seating. For example, Judge Rives's son had died a few years earlier in a car crash. One night soon after Rives's bus boycott decision, his son's grave was desecrated. Interestingly, the younger Rives had told his father about his friendship with blacks while in the military in World War II, and of his feelings in support of racial integration. These conversations may have helped inspire Judge Rives to break with the segregated status quo.

Judge Johnson, who often clashed with Alabama Governor George Wallace and other Southern politicians, consistently opposed segregation and racial discrimination during four decades on the federal bench. During the bus boycott era Judge Johnson regularly received threatening phone calls and written death threats. On one occasion a decade later, night riders—no doubt thinking they were targeting Judge Johnson—bombed the home of his mother, Mrs. Frank M. Johnson, Sr. Judge Johnson has noted, ". . . there were many times that I felt alone. I don't care who you are, when something happens and the entire state rises up, through its politicians and its press, and lambasts you, and the Klan is making threats, you become apprehensive for your famiily, sometimes waiting for something to happen.[21]

Another white federal judge who issued many desegregation orders over the years was Elbert P. Tuttle of Atlanta. He and his family were also subjected to regular harassment and threats.[22]

During these dangerous days, Dr. King knew that including the names of his white friends and allies in *Stride Toward Freedom* would put them at risk of increased retaliation, and responded accordingly, with omission as the better part of discretion.

The second reason that the role of the Durrs and Aubrey Williams has been omitted in the King biographies, as well in most recent books on movement history is purely academic—having to do with David Levering Lewis's chronology in the initial narrative biography of Dr. King. A careful analysis of *King: A Critical Biography* (1970), shows that Mr. Lewis followed the same timeline and substance of events in Montgomery as did Dr. King in *Stride Toward Freedom*.

Therefore, since the roles of the Durrs, Williams, and other white supporters were not described in *Stride*, Lewis apparently saw no reason to research nor include information about the subject of interracial partnership in Montgomery.[23] Subsequently, the events in Montgomery in all King biographies have been largely derived from the incomplete Lewis chronology. In fact, three acclaimed King biographies of the eighties [*Let The Trumpet Sound*, by Stephen Oates (1982); *Bearing The Cross*, by David Garrow (1986); and *Parting The Waters*, by Taylor Branch (1988)], all follow a Montgomery timeline and general thematic format similar to Lewis. In addition, the latter books each follow prior accounts: Oates after Lewis; Garrow after Lewis and Oates; and Branch after Lewis, Oates and Garrow. Taylor Branch's work, though eloquent, is substantively derivative of Lewis, Oates, and Garrow.[24]

None of these four books reveals much about the interracial cooperation that was part of the Montgomery success and that was important to Dr. King.

Professor Garrow does include some detailed description and discussion relative to the participation by the Durrs, as well as that of Rev. Glenn Smiley, a white Fellowship of Reconciliation staff member who moved to Montgomery to help in the bus boycott. Unfortunately, Garrow doesn't place this information in a context that helps readers understand the personal lives of the "peculiarly" involved white folks, nor does he link the Durrs to their familial relations with Hugo Black; nor does he understand or explain its impact in King's later Movement leadership.

Taylor Branch provides an original and poignant description of King's predecessor at Dexter Avenue Baptist Church, the Rev. Dr. Vernon Johns. However, though much respect is due Rev. Johns (as Fred Gray points out), the pioneering leadership and contributions of E. D. Nixon were far more critical to the eventual success of the bus boycott. Nixon had local and national political connections, and moved within a powerful interracial network of friendships—with Rosa Parks, Jo Ann Robinson, Aubrey Williams, the Durrs, and others.

So, while Dr. King chose to protect the Durr and Williams families from further reprisal, Lewis and then Oates simply didn't recognize the importance of the Durrs and Aubrey Williams to the Montgomery movement. Subsequently, Garrow and Branch provided only fragmentary inclusion of their contributions.

These acclaimed historians may not have understood the reason for the peculiar omission in *Stride* . . . It may be that in their narrow view of Movement history, both before and after Montgomery, these authors could not fathom giving the central, predominant role to the black leaders *and simultaneously* giving credit to those whites who took risks for their belief in equality and freedom.

Such "authoritative" but incomplete histories of the movement by uninvolved writers and academicians have regrettably become the "politically correct" foundation for our national collective memory of the period. This revisionist history has diminished the value of the interracial partnerships that did exist and that can help white and black Americans today to move beyond bitterness and guilt to a higher common ground.

[23] David Levering Lewis noted in his preface that he had met Dr. King on two occasions, but was impressed neither with him in person, nor with his style of leadership. Mr. Lewis also makes it clear that he was annoyed that neither Mrs. King, nor Dr. King's SCLC associates would grant him interviews for his book. (Mrs. King was in the process of writing her own book and SCLC staff members were planning theirs. Therefore, Mr. Lewis got much of his thematic substance from others in the movement, including Dr. King's rivals in SNCC.)

[24] Neither the David Levering Lewis nor the Stephen Oates books make any mention of either the Durrs or Aubrey Williams. Even Taylor Branch inaccurately portrays both the Durrs and Aubrey Williams. Unfortunately, as Harris Wofford — who played a leading role in a variety of movement and political episodes of the fifties and sixties — has noted, the attempt by Branch to recreate Movement history with docudrama-type dialogue is often off the mark. Wofford told me in a 1989 interview, that in every case where Taylor Branch recreated the scenes in which he (Wofford) had firsthand knowledge, Branch missed the essence of the situation. In *Pillars of Fire*, Branch again looks backward toward Dr. King in post-World War II America rather than focusing on the global view and impact King had during the last five years of his life. Moreover, as in *Parting the Waters*, Branch, though again eloquent, provides very uneven description of those who served as the foot soldiers on Dr. King's staff. For example, in discussing the Savannah, Georgia, movement, led by the Rev. Hosea Williams, Branch ignores the role played by Benjamin Van Clark, the NAACP youth leader, Jimmie Wells, Judson Ford, and others who later were important members of the SCLC field staff. Savannah is an excellent example of how Dr. King and SCLC expanded their base so that they had the non-violent troops to take on a growing menu of local and national issues. In *An Easy Burden: The Civil Rights Movement and the Transformation of America* (Harper-Collins, 1996), Andrew Young felt it important to mention staff members Clark, Doug Swan, Leon Hall and others whose roles are ignored or glossed over in *Pillars of Fire*.

Martin Luther King, Jr., in his "Letter From A Birmingham Jail," the "I Have A Dream" speech, and elsewhere, recognized the courage and contributions of his white allies. Interestingly, by the time the King biographies of the eighties were published, an excellent volume of oral history, *My Soul Is Rested,* by journalist Howell Raines, already included personal accounts from E. D. Nixon and Rosa Parks describing the Durrs' roles in the boycott events.

In *Let The Trumpet Sound,* Oates referenced *My Soul Is Rested,* but ignored information about the Durrs, not mentioning them at all. Garrow and Branch drew on Raines's account and mentioned the Durrs and Williams, but only in passing.

The Civil Rights Movement has fared little better in Hollywood—the films can be counted on the fingers of one hand. Compared with the many Vietnam-era films, we've neither remembered much as a nation nor provided the generations yet unborn with adequate information about this critically important period of American history. One notable exception is *Long Walk Home,* a movie about the Montgomery Bus Boycott written by Montgomerian John Cork and starring Whoopi Goldberg and Sissy Spacek.

There *have* been some distinguished documentaries on the movement—the most widely seen being the PBS series, *Eyes on the Prize.* Unfortunately, in the *Eyes* segment on Montgomery, any mention of the Durrs was edited from E. D. Nixon's filmed recollection of Rosa Parks's arrest. (Mr. Nixon had specifically noted the Durrs in *My Soul Is Rested,* as well as in his many oral history interviews.)

In any event, by the late 1980s, by the time of the Garrow and the Branch books and the *Eyes on the Prize* PBS series, it had become politically correct to tell the Montgomery story without much interest in the white folks who had joined in partnership with their black friends in Montgomery.

Another unfortunate aspect to this now politically correct view of the sixties is that much attention is paid to the reasons "black power" advocates felt the need to exclude the white co-workers from the Student Nonviolent Coordinating Committee—without much interest in why Dr. King and his staff at SCLC worked even harder to keep white activists involved in the freedom struggle.

Very recently, John Lewis in *Walking With the Wind,* David Halberstam in *The Children,* and Arnold Ramperstad in *Jackie Robinson* have challenged the politically correct orthodoxy by documenting the role of white activists in the black-led civil rights movement of the fifties and sixties.

CHAPTER 4

J. Edgar Hoover's "Revenge"

Beyond the value as examples of the Durrs and Aubrey Williams in Montgomery, however, there are other historical issues in the intersections of their lives with E. D. Nixon, Mrs. Parks, and Martin and Coretta Scott King, as well as others in the Montgomery struggle. One especially interesting area involves the origins and timing of the FBI's interest in Dr. King's career.

Knowledge about the lives of the Durrs and the Williamses helps explain when and why J. Edgar Hoover's FBI *first* decided that Martin Luther King, Jr., was involved with troublemakers—if he was not one himself—and had to be watched closely. Even without the benefit of some destroyed or otherwise unavailable Bureau documents, my analysis shows that the FBI interest in Dr. King was a full five years earlier than indicated in the King biographies by Garrow and Branch.

This is admittedly an esoteric area, but it is important for two reasons: first, if the historical record relating to the King/FBI scenario has been skewed or spiked, it deserves to be corrected so that the foundation of movement history and Dr. King's contributions are not thereby distorted; and second, the episode sheds light on the political and cultural forces at work during the first half of the twentieth century, which set the stage for the civil rights movement. We are thus dealing with historical and political accuracy in regard to fundamental principles of democracy and of governmental process in a crucial period of legal and societal changes in race relations — which continue to impact our nation and peoples. A clear comprehension and complete perspective of this period in our recent past can help us address future challenges in race relations in our continued development as a nation.

Charting the journey of Clifford and Virginia Durr and Aubrey and Anita Williams, therefore, sets the historical record straight—not only about their personal involvement, but also by illuminating details in the web of intrigue surrounding Dr. King, Hoover, and the FBI.

One of President Lyndon B. Johnson's biographers described these four Alabama natives as members of a relatively small circle of influential Washington insiders who had access to President Franklin and Eleanor Roosevelt in the late 1930s and '40s during the height of the New Deal. In *Path To Power*, by Robert A. Caro, both Clifford Durr[25] and Aubrey Williams are depicted as having performed extraordinarily well in a variety of top government jobs. Moreover, with Virginia Durr and Anita Williams, they were part of the social/political network in Washington, D.C., that has always been a prominent part of high-level policy making. Virginia Durr was an active player on the Washingtonian scene in part because her sister was married to Hugo Black. At that time, then-Senator Black was one of Roosevelt's closest associates, often

[25] See Newman, *Ibid*, pages 381-382 and n. 684, for an illustration of Hugo Black's poignant respect for Clifford Durr.

[26] Hoover, of course, not only surveiled those in the general public, but was also bugging and wiretapping many upper-level members of government, including Hugo Black and other members of the Supreme Court. See Newman, *Ibid*, pages 422-424 for Black's anger about Hoover's tapping of his phone lines.

[27] Newman, *Ibid*, pages 381-82, describes Hugo Black's role, instigated by President Truman, in trying to get Clifford Durr to accept Truman's request that he continue to serve on the FCC. These pages include excerpts of Black's letter of respect for Durr to the *Nation* in 1966 which described the incident, as well as his private thoughts expressed to Durr at the same time. Black conveyed similar feelings to a law clerk in 1961, but noted that Durr "frequently makes fights that are not completely necessary and thereby impairs his influence in matters of more importance." Ironically, Durr's rejection on principle of a presidential appointment put him and Virginia Durr in position to help launch the Montgomery Bus Boycott, and with it the career of Martin Luther King, Jr.

[28] In the late fifties, the Durrs were selected by the State Department to be the official hosts in Montgomery for visitors and dignitaries from around the world who wanted to learn about King and the boycott. Their selection shows how well their participation in the boycott was known in Washington, D.C., not only by Hoover, but by former New Deal associates. See pages 110-119 and 135-143 in *Conscience of A Lawyer*, by Salmond.

[29] Salmond, *A Southern Rebel*, see page 21.

mentioned as a potential vice presidential running mate. Mrs. Durr, a close friend of Eleanor Roosevelt, was also a force in her own right because of her feisty charm and strongly held political views.

During their stay in the nation's capital both Aubrey Williams and Clifford Durr confronted institutional racism head on. These Southerners challenged not only political conservatives opposed to New Deal policies but also the powerful bureaucrats who maintained the Washington infrastructure. This brought both, particularly Durr, into direct conflict with J. Edgar Hoover.[26]

Clifford Durr was one of the few who took on Hoover directly. In 1947, Durr, as a member of the Federal Communications Commission, had a very public fight with Hoover over the FBI's recommendation against the issuance of a broadcast license to some Californians. The Bureau considered these businessmen to be linked to "Communists." According to Mrs. Durr, "Hoover tried to get Clifford to give him the power to decide all the bids on channels and Cliff . . . wouldn't let that happen." Durr challenged the quality of the Bureau's investigation and conclusions. Hoover responded with public criticism of Durr, and a number of nationally syndicated columns recorded the rancorous allegations and counter-allegations by Durr and Hoover.

In fact, Hoover was so incensed by Durr that he made the former Rhodes Scholar singularly notorious within FBI procedures for security clearance interviews. As Mrs. Durr recalled recently, "So what Hoover did to revenge himself on Cliff, when [anyone] would get a good job in Washington, Hoover had to investigate them. And, he had a little paper, 'Did you belong to this, are you a member of this, are you a member of that? [and so on] . . . and he added one sentence: Do you know one Clifford J. Durr? Imagine what that did to Clifford's law business. I thought the kind of things Hoover did were absolutely awful . . . People were just scared to death [of Hoover]."

The Durrs left Washington in 1948—following Clifford's public refusal to go along with the loyalty program instituted by President Harry Truman.[27] However, as Durr's biographer details, Durr's criticism of the FBI—while he was on the FCC; in 1949 in radio and television debates; and in 1950 while serving for a year as the president of the National Lawyers Guild—led to "continuous Bureau surveillance for more than a decade (and the compiling of a large file at Hoover's headquarters)."[28]

Aubrey Williams had an unusual journey to the halls of power in Washington during a dramatic and eventful life. Williams joined the French Foreign Legion to fight for freedom in World War I, serving with distinction even before the United States formally entered the war. When the U.S. First Division reached France he enlisted immediately and survived a brutal combat tour. Later he was sent to officer candidate school, commissioned as a second lieutenant, and made the acquaintance of another young American officer, Harry Truman. Williams's biography, *A Southern Rebel*, recounts that after the armistice, Lt. Williams decided to take advantage of the "offer from a grateful French government to those who had fought for the legion and remain in France and study at a French university."[29]

His educational background, particularly without any foreign language training, had poorly prepared Williams for the "rigorous and elitist" demands of French higher education. Still, he won a diploma after presenting the required philosophical thesis in French, English, and Greek and orally defending it in French before a faculty panel. During this period, he also had the opportunity to "meet trade union leaders from all over the continent and sit in on their discussions".[30]

From these experiences, Williams returned home with a broad interest in political ideology and labor issues. After marriage to Anita, a union that later produced four sons, he studied social work at the University of Cincinnati. Soon after, his energy, experience and skills helped him get the position of executive director of the Wisconsin State Human Welfare Conference where his effectiveness landed him, first, consultant jobs with the federal government's new job training programs; and then opportunities to implement such programs as they expanded during the New Deal. Williams kept an exhausting schedule, traveling the nation helping to provide relief to those who had been economically displaced and were without work during "The Depression." Particularly, in his work with African-Americans while directing the National Youth Authority (NYA), he was recognized as an exceptional advocate. As the *Chicago Sunday Bee*, a black newspaper noted:

> No federal agencies have been fairer to colored Americans than the NYA, none as tolerant. It is the NYA that has distinguished itself by placing Negroes in policy-making positions. The NYA is ahead of all federal agencies in working toward the full integration of colored people in the defense program and in American democracy. Aubrey Williams has been to the NYA what the Prince of Denmark has been to Shakespeare's Hamlet—he gave it life, substance and direction.[31]

He assigned Mary McLeod Bethune to administer the NYA Negro Division, and enjoyed her regular visits at his home. Williams also developed a friendship with NAACP Director Walter White and they often lunched together at a restaurant near the White House, despite the fact that in the late 1930s Washington, D.C., was a rigidly segregated town.

Williams occasionally joined forces with Virginia Durr and Eleanor Roosevelt to defy local segregation ordinances at various meetings of integrated organizations. One such defiance occurred in Birmingham, in the late 1930s, at the first meeting of the Southern Conference for Human Welfare (SCHW)—an organization that promoted effective social welfare programs and labor issues, fought racism, and pushed legislation to abolish the poll tax.

The extent of his travel throughout the U.S. was such that Nat Welch, his friend and colleague during his later years as the publisher of the *Southern Farmer* in Montgomery, recalled, "Aubrey could throw his hat out of a plane anywhere in the United States, and whatever town in which it would land would be a place where he had friends."[32]

As Williams's biographer notes: "From time to time, recognizing the special regard that African-Americans had for Williams, President Roosevelt used him as a troubleshooter with the black community. In the winter of

[30] *Ibid.*
[31] *Ibid,* page 171.
[32] Interview with Nat Welch, January, 1994.

[33] Salmond, *A Southern Rebel*, page 171.

[34] *Ibid.*

1939, for example, sharecroppers in southeast Missouri staged a roadside demonstration under the auspices of the Southern Tenant Farmers Union (STFU)" and Williams traveled to their side offering what assistance he could.[33]

During the New Deal era, U.S. communists and socialists were often involved with or associated with the same programs supported by liberal and progressive Democrats such as Mrs. Roosevelt, Mrs. Durr, and Aubrey Williams. Williams and Virginia Durr came into contact with these individuals and groups, and such contact was noted not only by conservative opponents of the New Deal, but also by the FBI.

Moreover, Williams was very frank in his public views on race and politics. His outspokenness provided ammunition for virulent racists such as Theodore Bilbo of Mississippi and Kenneth McKellar of Tennessee, who successfully opposed Williams's 1944 nomination by President Roosevelt to the directorship of the Rural Electrification Administration. The nomination was bitterly fought in the newspapers around the nation as well as magazines such as *The New Republic*.

To Senator Bilbo's attack upon a column Williams had written which had called for an end to "white supremacy" politics, Williams was unequivocal:

> "I'm a Southerner," he replied, his drawl self-evident. "I was born in the South and have been proud of the fact that I was born in the South, but I have been saddened that the South has not progressed . . . One of the reasons for that is due to the fact that in its economic life it has allowed a condition to continue wherein the working people of the South had to compete against the Negroes of the South . . . I hold that the sole basis of giving or refusing employment should be whether a man is able to do the work which he is hired to do."[34]

To the charge that the Presbyterian Church had paid his tuition to attend a religious college before he entered the service and that had he had then turned his back on the Church by deciding not to go into the ministry, Williams replied:

> The matter of my not going into the ministry was a question of my own conscience. I frankly do not feel that is any concern of this committee. That is a matter between myself and my God, and I am happy to say that the Constitution of the United States definitely prohibits . . . any religious test being made . . . and I do not want to be a party to it by even condoning it to the point of discussing it."

President Roosevelt refused to withdraw the nomination. Williams received the backing of a liberal coalition led by various pressure groups including organized labor and the NAACP, and a timely, strongly worded personal endorsement from Vice President Truman. In the end, however, the nomination was defeated—his views about racial equality costing him the decisive "no" votes cast by moderate Southern senators.

Beyond the race issue, however, Senator McKellar introduced a government "report," using FBI sources, among others, in which Williams was alleged to have been "a member of either four or five of the Communist-front organizations."

Williams's support was still considerable in Washington, and another powerful friend, Senator Allan Ellender, countered with an FBI affidavit that had "given him an entirely clean bill of health." Williams himself was typically outspoken on the issue, challenging "anybody to produce one single iota of evidence that I ever had one single thing to do with anything committed to the Communist Party, that I have ever been connected with it or even favorable regarding it. I was anathema to the communist element from the very beginning of my stay in Washington for the simple reason that apparently they didn't like the way I thought or the way I spoke."

Illinois Democratic Senator Scott Lucas remarked, " . . . it has been apparent that a smear is the chief weapon being used against Mr. Williams, and some opposed to him seek to convict him of communism."[35]

After the defeat, his friends held a dinner in his honor early in 1945 that was attended by Mrs. Roosevelt, his friend Lyndon Johnson, three Senators, former vice president Henry Wallace, and others in his Washington, D.C., social circle. By that time Williams had received an offer too good to refuse from Marshall Field, a politically liberal millionaire from Chicago. Field offered to support whatever endeavor Williams might take on. Field and Williams decided to invigorate a then-small farm monthly called the *Southern Farmer* with a half million dollar bankroll. Through the magazine, based in Montgomery, Alabama, they hoped to infuse grassroots opinion in the South with the spirit of the New Deal.[36]

[35] *Ibid.*
[36] *Ibid,* page 186.

CHAPTER 5

"Born into a racist society"

With these peculiar events in the aftermath of World War II, the Durrs and the Williamses were among the first patriotic Americans whose lives were disrupted by the politically charged climate in the nation's capital. As usual, they were ahead of their times. In a few years the "McCarthy era" allegations of communists in government were to be a matter of great national controversy.

This repressive era began just after the end of World War II, helping to launch Richard Nixon and other opportunists into public office. The years of damaging accusations continued until Senator Joe McCarthy was censured by the Senate in the mid-fifties. By then, virulent fears of Communism, along with allegations of communist sympathizing, had infected politics and were not far below the surface of American life. And, the files of the FBI were bloated with information on tens of thousands of law abiding Americans, including elected officials and Supreme Court Justices.[37]

Leaving powerful friends behind in Washington, by 1951 the Durr and Williams families were reunited in Montgomery. Mrs. Durr recalled,

> Soon after we moved back South [in 1950], we met E. D. Nixon who was head of the NAACP, and it was soon after that he began bringing my husband clients all the time. There was no black lawyer at the time—Fred Gray came in [a few years after] that time, but he was just out of law school. So Mr. Nixon brought these cases to Cliff . . . mostly cases where black people had been beaten by the police. It was hard to get a conviction because the juries were all white, but Cliff would try the case and get publicity on it and the police who had done the beating would have to get a lawyer. We had a friend, Ray Jenkins, on the *Montgomery Advertiser*, and he'd write it up; so the police did slow down on that . . . but we would never get paid. Aubrey did give him the legal work for his newspaper, the *Southern Farmer*, but what saved us was that Cliff's brother gave him all the business for the Durr Drug Company."

The ideological conflicts that led the Durrs and the Williamses away from Washington, D.C., were seemingly behind them—but they had been public and political in a manner such that J. Edgar Hoover had not forgotten.

It defies logic that the partnership in the bus boycott between Dr. King and the Durrs and Aubrey Williams in 1955–56 could have gone unnoticed by J. Edgar Hoover's FBI. Yet that is the impression given by most King biographies and other histories of the Movement. The timelines in all prior biographies and histories argue that Hoover had no serious interest in Martin Luther

[37] See *Cloak and Gavel: FBI Wiretaps, Bugs, Informers, and the Supreme Court*, by Alexander Charns, University of Illinois Press, 1992, for an excellent study of the data. One significant finding is that from 1941 through the mid-1960s, the FBI eavesdropped without legal warrants on more than 10,000 individuals (more than ten of whom were Supreme Court Justices).

Such information puts in proper perspective the attempt by Hoover and his associates, during the mid-1970s congressional investigations, to put the blame on Robert Kennedy for the surveillance of Dr. King. This dubious Hoover-era FBI scenario was also disseminated in two books by David Garrow (*Martin Luther King Jr. and the FBI* and *Bearing the Cross.*)

This information also casts doubt about the alleged "national security" basis used to deny requests for information about FBI domestic counterintelligence activity. Moreover, John Egerton, in *Shades of Gray*, LSU Press, 1991, quotes an FBI agent in the Atlanta office on the illegal and unethical actions that the Hoover clique and some of their operatives employed against Dr. King. This information corresponds to the depictions provided in the mid-1970s congressional hearings on the King assassination.

King, Jr., before 1961, and that during much of the bus boycott the FBI files had him confused with his father, Martin Luther King, Sr.[38]

By 1954, both of the former New Dealers were well settled in Montgomery, and had become friends with Mr. Nixon, Mrs. Parks and others in Montgomery's black community. The Kings had not yet arrived to take over pastoral duties at the Dexter Avenue Baptist Church. Virginia Durr explained the societal situation just before Coretta and Martin King arrived in Montgomery:

> By early 1954 we knew the Supreme Court would soon decide the *Brown v. Board of Education* [desegregation case]. Nobody knew when, but it was already a topic of conversation. Jim Eastland was running for reelection to the Senate from Mississippi on the platform that if the Supreme Court voted to desegregate the public schools, it would show that the court was clearly an arm of the communist conspiracy. Eastland was on the Senate Judiciary Committee and head of what was called the Internal Security Subcommittee [which corresponded to the House Un-American Activities Committee].[39]

Little more than a year before the boycott, conspicuous events provided the Durrs and Aubrey Williams unwanted nationwide notoriety—along with further entries into Hoover's FBI files.

In anticipation of the *Brown* decision, Senator Eastland brought a McCarthy-era roadshow to the South. On March 6, 1954, Aubrey Williams was subpoenaed to appear at an Eastland-chaired Internal Security Subcommittee hearing in New Orleans on March 18. Within a few days, Virginia Durr received her subpoena.

Also subpoenaed were two other white friends who had been leaders in the Southern Conference on Human Welfare (SCHW): James Dombroski and Highlander Folk School founder Myles Horton. It is important to recall that such prominent Americans as Hugo Black and Eleanor Roosevelt were also active in SCHW.[40]

In a 1993 conversation, Mrs. Durr recalled that Eastland "was trying to use us to taint my brother-in-law, Hugo Black, with communism because I had been active in the SCHW in which there was one person who was a Marxist. I don't know if he was a member of the Communist Party, but he was a Marxist . . . Aubrey Williams was about as far from a communist [laughs], you know, as the man in the moon."

Whatever scenario Eastland had in mind for the New Orleans hearings did not come off as planned.

First, after Mrs. Durr made a calls to old friends in Washington, Eastland was unable to get either the Democratic or Republican members of the subcommittee to accompany him to New Orleans. In the outrage that she shared with her husband and Aubrey Williams, Virginia Durr first got her friend Senator Lyndon Johnson out of bed with a late-night call to the nation's capital. Johnson was then the Senate Majority Leader, but Aubrey Williams had given Johnson his first job in the New Deal when he hired the ambitious 26-

[38] David Garrow, who is cited by Taylor Branch as having explained the King-FBI relationship, notes that Dr. King had become a national figure early in the bus boycott. Despite this fact, Garrow still gives credence to documents provided by the FBI which purport that during and after this period Hoover, and the Bureau, confused MLK Jr. with his father, MLK Sr. (see *The FBI and Martin Luther King, Jr,* Note 2, Chapter 1, page 234). Moreover, Garrow builds his theory about all the subsequent FBI activities against King on his analysis that during this period (prior to 1961), "The FBI had yet to develop any curiosity about King . . ." (see *Bearing The Cross,* pages 651-52, note 34; see also, ". . . despite this notoriety, until May 1961, the Federal Bureau of Investigation had not taken much notice of King."—*The FBI and Martin Luther King, Jr.*, page 22, note 2, page 233; see pages 21-25 and 27-60, "Notes": pages 233-247). Such authoritative comments aside, Garrow draws upon some of the events in Lawrence Reddick's initial King biography, *Crusader Without Violence* (1958), enumerating when Dr. King was the subject of national attention, including: a *TIME* cover (1957); periodic updates on radio and TV networks after Dr. King was stabbed in Harlem while promoting his book on Montgomery (1957); addresses to the Democratic and Republican National Conventions (1956); participation in youth rallies in Washington, D.C., and meetings with both Vice President Nixon and President Eisenhower (1957–58); a highly publicized trip to India and Israel (1958); etc.; etc. In the "Notes" cited above, Garrow apparently doesn't believe such incidents raised the interest of the FBI; and, though he also points out a myriad of substantive reliability and accuracy problems in FBI documentation (both in files released under the Freedom of Information Act [FOIA] as well as other "missing" or destroyed files), Garrow still sees no problem in using FBI data to build his mosaic portrait of Dr. King, personally, and of historic events relative to the Civil Rights Movement, in general. Some of the above was included in the information I discussed in 1987 on "Tony Brown's Journal" (PBS) in my more extensive critique of *Bearing The Cross*.

(Ironically, though Taylor Branch repeatedly references Garrow and gives him credit for the "pioneering" analysis about the FBI attacks upon King, Branch's own research at the Dwight D. Eisenhower

Presidential Library provided documents showing that in early 1956 J. Edgar Hoover gave a White House briefing on the bus boycott and other race relations matters. This information is another reason that it seems beyond belief that Hoover and his top aides had scant interest or knowledge about Martin Luther King, Jr., until 1961; see *Parting The Waters*, page 181 and pertinent footnote re: March 9, 1956, Hoover briefing on page 942.)

Rev. Robert Graetz, both in his book, *A White Preacher's Memoir: The Montgomery Bus Boycott* (Black Belt Press, 1998), and in our interview during the 40th anniversary boycott commemoration in 1995, related that the local FBI agents had day-to-day knowledge and made an official investigation of the bus boycott. These local agents were interested in the activities of Dr. King as well as with the other boycott leaders during 1955-56. Graetz felt (then and now) that his FBI contact was sympathetic and helpful, and noted that this agent was always concerned about involvement in the boycott by individuals with "communist" affiliations.

[39] Virginia Durr, *Ibid*, page 254.

[40] See Newman, *Ibid*, page 333: "The Southern Conference for Human Welfare once again presented him (Hugo Black) its Thomas Jefferson Award. Senate Majority Leader Alben Barkley presided, reading a letter from President Roosevelt. . . . Mrs. Roosevelt attended, along with much of political and official Washington . . . ." By 1954, the SCHW had given way to its subsidiary organization, the Southern Conference Educational Fund (SCEF; also called "The Southern Conference"). SCEF's current activities, in which Williams, Durr, and the others targeted continued to have leading roles, were the alleged justification for the Eastland Hearings.

[41] See Anthony Sommers, *Official and Confidential*, 1993, for references citing Bender's close association with J. Edgar Hoover from the early 1940s through the time of the Eastland Hearings.

year-old to direct the National Youth Administration programs in Texas.

In her oral history autobiography, Mrs. Durr provides a colorful account of the conversation:

> "Lyndon, what are you doing sending these bloodhounds down here after Aubrey and me?"
>
> "Why, honey, I don't know anything about it."
>
> "Here you are the Majority Leader of the Senate and you don't even know that we're going to be hauled up before the Senate Internal Security Subcommittee?
>
> "Why, baby, I don't know a thing about it. That's terrible. What can I do for you?"
>
> "Can you stop it?" I asked.
>
> "I'm afraid I can't stop it now," he said.
>
> "Well, if you can just see that no other Democrats come, that will help a lot."
>
> "Well," he said, "I can't promise anything, but I'll do the best I can."

And Johnson kept his word, because no Democrats went with Eastland on his "red-baiting," guilt-by-association trip to Louisiana.

However, Mrs. Durr was far from finished with her response to the Eastland machinations. By the weekend before the hearing, she had also contacted her friend, Republican Senator George Bender[41] of Ohio, with whom she had worked in the anti-poll tax fight. Bender, as she recounted, "let the poll tax committee (of the SCHW) use his mimeograph machine and his [congressional postage frank]. We'd send out things all over his district and put his name on it. It really did him a lot of good [because he was trying to get the black vote]."

Continuing her dramatic recital, Mrs. Durr recalled:

> I called up George in a little place called Chagrin Falls [Ohio]. I said, "George, this is Virginia Durr."
>
> "Sweetheart," he said, "are you as beautiful as ever? What can I do for you?" He was the biggest flatterer you ever knew.
>
> "George, I've been called up before the Internal Security Subcommittee down in New Orleans and I just think it's terrible."
>
> "Oh, honey," he said, "you don't have to worry. You never did anything wrong. A sweet girl like you. All you have to do is tell the truth."
>
> "Yes, George, that's exactly what I'm going to do, but they're investigating the Southern Conference, which started the fight on the poll tax. If I'm going to tell the truth, I'm going to have to tell how we used your frank and your mimeograph."
>
> "Now, Virginia," he said hastily, "there's a provision of the Constitution that you don't have to tell everything you know."
>
> "Oh, no, George, there's no Fifth Amendment for me. I'm not a Communist, never have been a Communist. I'm not going to invoke the Fifth."
>
> "Well, Virginia, what can I do for you?"

THE CHILDREN COMING ON . . .

"George, if you'll just see that no Republicans come to New Orleans with Jim Eastland, that will help a lot."[42]

[42] Durr, *Ibid*, pages 256-257.
[43] Durr, *Ibid*, page 258.

When Eastland got to New Orleans and began questioning Mrs. Durr, he was by himself, except for, as Mrs. Durr relates, "a horrible character named Richard Arens, who was the lawyer for the subcommittee."

Eastland's *second* problem was that a retinue of journalists had come from all over to report the proceedings. The extent of the press coverage was *not* surprising to Aubrey Williams, since he had written a telegram of protest to Senator Williams E. Jenner of Indiana, an ardent admirer of Sen. McCarthy—and then released it to fifty newspapers all over the nation.

Eastland's *third* problem was with his paid government witness, former communist Paul Crouch, who eventually set in motion Sen. McCarthy's conflict with the U.S. Army. McCarthy used Crouch's written accusations in his allegations of communist influence during the "Army-McCarthy Hearings" which finally brought the Wisconsin Senator into national disgrace.

Crouch had already been paid to testify in a number of sedition trials after serving three years in Alcatraz on federal charges of trying to organize for the Communist Party while a private in U.S. Army. He had accepted an early release from prison to go on Uncle Sam's payroll as an informer.

"He said that the Russian Navy was going to land at Miami Beach because there were so many Jews there, recalled Clifford Durr."[43] Thereafter, Crouch described two Jewish men from Miami as communists. They refused to cooperate and took the Fifth Amendment. The men explained that they had received help from SCHF during [an outbreak of anti-Semitic vandalism]. With this, the hearings rapidly became a stage for theatrics by all involved.

Next, Crouch claimed that he had knowledge that the sole function of SCHW "was to promote Communism" in the South. At first, the press was not very interested in Crouch's initial specific allegation that Dombrowski was a communist, nor with Dombrowski's subsequent sworn denial.

However, the newsmen couldn't easily ignore Virginia Durr.

When she was called to testify, she simply read a statement that she was the wife of Clifford Durr, was not and never had been a Communist, would not invoke the First or Fifth Amendment, and then concluded by saying "I stand in utter and complete contempt of this committee." Eastland immediately threatened that he would hold *her* in legal contempt due to her refusal to answer any further questions, but Mrs. Durr's response delighted the news photographers and the TV cameramen: she remained silent and powdered her nose.

While Mrs. Durr was still powdering her nose, Crouch was recalled to the stand and wove a tale that was indeed peculiar:

"Claiming to have known the Durrs during his Communist Party days, he charged that Virginia Durr had used her kinship with Justice Black and her friendship with Mrs. Roosevelt to introduce top Communists into the White House circles during the days of the New Deal," thereby making the Roosevelts "unwitting accomplices to Soviet espionage activity." [Furthermore, he charged]

[44] John Salmond, *A Southern Rebel*, page 236.

[45] Salmond, *Ibid*, page 236.

[46] Salmond *Ibid*, page 237. Neither Garrow in *Bearing the Cross* nor Branch in *Parting the Waters* provided details of this background material on Williams or Mrs. Durr — or its link to Hoover's interest in the Montgomery Bus Boycott. In *Pillars of Fire,* pages 188-189, Branch includes a glimpse of the courageous political commitment Williams had always pledged in Democratic politics. Unfortunately, this scant account dismisses Williams as a "casualty of the race issue"—just a footnote in the struggle. The life and death of Aubrey Williams in the eyes of E. D. Nixon, Martin and Coretta King, and their compatriots in Montgomery, was much more.

[47] Durr, *Ibid*, pages 261-263.

"she went beyond that; she plotted with the Communist leaders to exploit her relationship as a sister-in-law of a Justice on the Supreme Court in the interests of the World Communist conspiracy and interest in overthrowing our Government."[44]

As Aubrey Williams's biographer related, through all of this Mrs. Durr continued to powder her nose, "to the delight of [the] reporters [who] were still digesting the startling statement that Hugo Black's sister-in-law had been instrumental in enabling Soviet agents to penetrate the White House social scene."[45]

Aubrey Williams got his turn next. Williams's run-in with Crouch and another paid government witness soon became volatile. Crouch and the other paid government witness alleged that they had been informed by officials of the Communist Party that Williams was a "secret member." Williams, "furious with rage, interrupted the testimony, 'I feel it a personal privilege to say that I challenge this man to go out into the hall and make that statement in the presence of newspapermen,' he roared. 'I'll sue him the minute he does.'" Crouch chose not to give up the legal protection of the Eastland subcommittee.[46]

Eastland then made the mistake of letting Clifford Durr crossexamine Crouch. As Clifford Durr, who was not under subpoena but was involved as Williams's counsel, recalled,

> These were the yarns that Crouch would spin . . . he'd had one year in the Army as a private and the Russians had him lecturing at their military college which was the equivalent of our West Point. And they let him in on their plans against the Panama Canal . . . he said he spent five thousand hours telling the FBI what he knew about Communist activities and he wasn't through yet.
>
> [Finally] I said, "Mr. Crouch, are you still a Communist?" All I got was a speech. Then I said, "Can you prove you're not a Communist?" At that point, Arens, the counsel, leaned over and said, "Mr. Crouch, is Mr. Durr a Communist?" Crouch said, "I don't know if he still is, but I saw him at meetings of the top Communist echelons in New York."
>
> Eastland got a little uneasy then and said, "Let's have another witness." But I said, "Let's get all this on the record." Crouch then alleged that "between 1939 and 1941" he had seen Clifford Durr at Communist Party meetings with the Party's hierarchy, but couldn't remember many particulars including where even one of the meetings was held . . .
>
> At that point, I asked Mr. Eastland to put me under oath, and I was sworn in. I said, "Now, Senator, every word that he has said about my attending those meetings of the top Communist echelon is an absolute and complete lie. I've never been to a Communist Party meeting. I've never been a member of the Party. I've never even thought about being a member of the Party. Now, both of us are under oath, and it's your responsibility as chairman of this committee to see that one or the other of us is indicted for perjury." Well, of course, nothing was ever done about it.[47]

THE CHILDREN COMING ON . . .

[48] See Salmond, *A Southern Rebel*, pages 239-240; and Durr, *Ibid*, 263-264.
[49] Salmond, *Ibid*, page 241.

Clifford Durr's testimony concluded the second day of the hearing, but with the bizarre testimony, especially about Virginia Durr taking Communists into the White House, the proceedings were featured in major newspapers all over the nation, usually with a photograph of Mrs. Durr powdering her nose.

The third day of the hearing began with Myles Horton denying that he was a communist. Horton also explained the goals of the Highlander Folk School: "Its principal aim was to educate southern 'rural and industrial leaders for democratic living and activity.'" Crouch then returned and briefly named the Communist leaders that Virginia Durr had allegedly taken into the White House. With that, and a brief statement by Eastland that his investigation of "the Communist Party, of Communist Front organizations" would soon "convene again in the city of Birmingham" the hearing was adjourned.

> As the committee room cleared, Crouch and Clifford Durr found themselves face to face. The frail, normally mild-mannered lawyer lost control. The accounts of the exact wording of Mr. Durr's outburst vary, but the gist was: "You dirty son of a bitch, I'll kill you for lying about my wife." Clifford Durr, who had a weak heart, then blacked out and had to stay in the hospital for tests and recuperation.[48]

Given the politics of the times, with McCarthy still riding tall, the Southern and national press were surprisingly supportive of the Durrs, Aubrey Williams and their friends. An editorial in the *Montgomery Advertiser* commented: "There is a matter of Southern honor involved here. A Southern gentleman and lady have been publicly branded with the most opprobious term of the hour. They have denied it under oath . . . This is a type of character lynching which Southern Senators should deeply resent." Eastland was further denounced outside the South. In one memorable editorial in Colorado, the Durrs, Dombrowski, and Williams were described as "liberals fighting for a new day in the South . . . Is it necessary for Eastland to break the spirit and backs of outstanding citizens who have devoted their lives to their country? Does the Senator realize that it is the liberals who have given the common man a new life and made him reject communism?"

In her syndicated column, Eleanor Roosevelt, defending her old friends Aubrey Williams and Virginia Durr, wrote: "We had better understand what communism really is . . . Those who hold liberal views which may go a little further than their most conservative neighbors are still not communists."[49]

Eastland canceled the Birmingham hearing and never followed through on his threat to issue contempt citations against Virginia Durr or the witnesses. Unfortunately, though Williams wrote to his friends in Washington, D.C., he was unsuccessful in getting Congressional redress.

Contradictions in Crouch's testimony were later exposed in nationally syndicated columns, and he was discredited as an obvious, perhaps sociopathic, liar. By then, though, the damage was done to the lives of Aubrey Williams, Virginia Durr, Clifford Durr, and others. During this sorry chapter in Ameri-

⁵⁰ Salmond, in *Conscience Of A Lawyer*, explains on pages 138-39 that even after 1959 "periodic investigations [of Clifford Durr by the FBI] continued until 1965." See Salmond, in *Conscience Of A Lawyer*, page 121, on Senator McCarthy's support of Durr in the 1947 FCC matter.

can history, a simple unsupported charge of communism could be devastating. The American Legion wrote to every one of the advertisers in the *Southern Farmer* and urged them to stop supporting Williams and the paper. Before long, Williams had to shut it down.

As Durr's biographer documents,

> immediately after the New Orleans hearing, his [Durr's] FBI surveillance was increased, and this was not modified until May 1959. With this background, it is hardly surprising that the FBI would be concerned about "communists" in Montgomery during the boycott and the issue would resurface many times over the ensuing years. From the late 1940s up until 1959, ". . . [Durr's] speeches and other public utterances were collected and analyzed; his movements were closely monitored, even to details concerning the transfer of his furniture from Denver to Montgomery in 1951; and his correspondence and that of his family was intercepted and read; and some even being filched from his desk. Various professional informers . . . routinely testified that Durr had been 'under Communist discipline' in the 1930s and '40s . . . Ironically, one of the first to declare in his favor [for reappointment to a second seven-year term on the FCC in 1947] was the junior senator from Wisconsin, Joseph R. McCarthy, who had written as early as May 1947, praising his stand on various issues and offering to help in any way he could . . . but this was before McCarthy had discovered the potentialities for political advancement in the issues Durr had begun to oppose so vehemently.[50]

If J. Edgar Hoover had forgotten the Williams-Rural Electrification Hearings, or the embarrassment caused to the Bureau by Clifford Durr in 1947 over the FCC license denial or by Durr's report on the anti-democratic nature of the FBI's domestic espionage as the president of the National Lawyers Guild in 1950s, the FBI director's interest was surely focused upon the conspicuous events of the Eastland Hearings during the spring of 1954.

The following year, Mrs. Rosa Parks, recently returned from her visit to the Highlander Folk School, took her history-making action on a Montgomery city bus. Virginia Durr, Clifford Durr, Aubrey Williams, and a few other whites gave strong support to the bus boycott. As the boycott went on, Clifford Durr gave much of his time to the litigation. Williams was having health problems, in part due to the stress of the continued loss of business brought on by the Eastland Hearing allegations of "Communism." He was, however, always ready to help.

Of all the written and documentary history on Dr. King and the Movement, only in *Parting The Waters* is there much attention to the Eastland Hearing. But, even this brief reference omits the significant history and distorts many facts. Branch erroneously claims Durr challenged *Senator Eastland* to fight and that this outburst (rather than the "communist" allegations) damaged Durr's reputation and law practice.

This depiction of the Durrs' and Williamses' life in Washington and Montgomery before the Bus Boycott is tangential to Dr. King's subsequent leadership in the Civil Rights Movement. However, the Durr/Williams background with J. Edgar Hoover and Sen. Eastland is relevant to the FBI's later behavior toward Dr. King. The King–FBI relationship has been widely if not always accurately discussed by journalists and historians. Much of that part of Dr. King's life is outside the scope of this book's focus on the Montgomery Bus Boycott. However, to probe beyond the FBI paper trails that have been used by some historians, it must be considered that the Durr/Williams involvement in the bus boycott case was well-known in Washington—from the chambers of Justice Hugo Black to Hoover's "Personal and Confidential" files in the director's office at FBI headquarters. As Martin Luther King, Jr., began his public career in Montgomery, the backgrounds, as well as the local relationships, of these two Southern white families were intertwined with powerful political forces operating on the national level. The role of the Durrs, Aubrey Williams, and other white supporters during those early days had a profound impact upon Dr. King. From the very beginning of the bus boycott King, and the black people of Montgomery, had found their few white supporters to be reliable, courageous, and valuable allies.

Nat Welch, Aubrey Williams's colleague on the *Southern Farmer* and later executive director of the Atlanta Human Relations Commission, remembers his friend as "a magnetic personality, a vibrant intellect. Aubrey was a positive person who believed in the ultimate good in people and in the human spirit."

Welch also noted, "Clifford Durr, because of his work on the Federal Communications Commission, is considered the 'Father of Public Television.' In the mid 1940s, Cliff insisted on reserving some of the airwaves for public and educational material."

During his time on the FCC, Clifford Durr not only single-handedly kept 90 FM stations open for those returning from overseas service in WW II, but also used his influence and skill to benefit the public interest in other matters. Durr was concerned that "broadcasting is becoming primarily an advertising medium rather than a medium of public service supported by advertising. Durr spoke out against the notion ". . . that advertising agencies should hand us our culture, all ready made to their pattern."[51]

In our interview in 1993 when she was 91, Mrs. Durr summarized her feelings about her husband and Aubrey Williams:

> Clifford Durr and Aubrey Williams were brave men. I don't think that I was as brave as they were because I was always supported financially, I didn't have to make a living myself. Clifford was absolutely outraged about what was happening in Washington after the War with the loyalty oaths. Clifford resigned a good job in the government and wouldn't take re-appointment to the FCC because he opposed the loyalty oath . . . The first case Cliff had after he left the FCC was with a young man who had won honors for bravery for his military service in WW II, and he lost his government job because he liked to go to a book store where they sold Marxist books. It was outrageous.
>
> Aubrey Williams, you see, had very strong feelings about integration.

[51] Salmond, *Conscience Of A Lawyer*, pages 83-84.

That's one of the reasons he came back South, because he wanted to integrate the Farmer's Union, and he succeeded in doing that, but it didn't last; but in any case, he preached integration through the *Southern Farmer*.

. . . Clifford and Aubrey were very, very Southern men. Very devoted to the South . . . I mean they wanted to live in the South, felt they were part of the South, felt they were a part of the state of Alabama. And the people who were against them felt they were pretty bad, but they understood because they had been racists themselves. See. And I was too. If you were born in the South around the turn of the century, you were born into a racist society and it takes you quite a while to get out of it.

AFTERWORD

Revisionist History, Cultural Authority, and Collective Memory

This retrospective is about the Montgomery Bus Boycott and attempts to show how courageous Southerners of both races won the first major post-Reconstruction victory against legalized segregation. However, because the Montgomery events also launched the modern civil rights movement and the career of Martin Luther King, Jr., it has been necessary to show a larger context. In particular, four aspects of the Civil Rights Movement and the career of Dr. King—following directly from the Montgomery Bus Boycott—have been distorted in acclaimed King biographies and should be addressed.

First, as Fred Gray, E. D. Nixon, and others (including Harris Wofford and Bayard Rustin, in the EPILOGUE that follows) have explained, the popular wisdom that Dr. King was a "reluctant leader" in the bus boycott is a gross oversimplification.

Secondly, the collective voices show why it is wrong to give only a historical footnote to the roles played by the Durrs and Aubrey Williams in the Montgomery movement.

A *third* issue concerns revisionist history of the role the federal government played in the Movement, particularly that of the Justice Department and the federal courts. Chapter Four illuminates the career of Frank Johnson—both in the bus boycott decision and in later events, including the Selma March. As Judge Johnson points out, President Kennedy, in his inaugural address, put the nation on notice that a generational change would impact American life, including relations between the races.

Fourth, there has been a revisionist reconstruction of Movement events (and Dr. King's life) based on faulty FBI documentation.

In retrospect, the legacy of the fifties and especially the sixties still casts a shadow on American race relations. Great leaders were lost. However, as the full story of the Montgomery Bus Boycott reminds us, there were also victories and progress. The idealism, the courage, and the sacrifices need to be remembered—it is, in its broad, unrevised depiction, an empowering history in which all Americans can take pride and inspiration.

MONTGOMERY VOICES

V

THE FORERUNNERS

Solomon S. Seay, Sr.:

EDITOR'S NOTE: This passage is excerpted with permission from Seay's 1990 autobiography, I Was There By The Grace Of God. *Seay was born and raised in the rural area outside Montgomery, but he rose from humble beginnings to become one of the great African-American preachers of his day. He was active both locally and in state and national affairs of his denomination, the African Methodist Episcopal Zion Church. A fearless advocate in his own right against injustice and discrimination, he was older than the two young ministers, Martin Luther King, Jr., and Ralph Abernathy, who became the principal spokesmen for the Montgomery Bus Boycott and later went on to lead the civil rights movement nationally. Numerous interviews and articles indicate that King and other younger ministers had a special relationship with Seay, and valued both his counsel and his long years of service and experience as bridges to the Montgomery community, both black and white. After King and Abernathy had both left Montgomery, Seay himself served as president of the Montgomery Improvement Association. His autobiography is an amazing book. It was largely dictated by Seay into a tape recorder and transcribed by family members after the great preacher's health had declined in his final years. The echoes of his powerful oratory can be heard in the phrasing and organization of his memoir.*

Most of the forerunners of the Bus Boycott were at this meeting that was called (after Mrs. Park's arrest) by the Interdenominational Ministerial Alliance. A need had arisen for organization and for leadership. More than forty leaders of the black community attended this meeting that was held at the Dexter Avenue Baptist Church. Most of them were ministers. I was out of town on church matters.

Out of this first meeting of concerned citizens, the Montgomery Improvement Association was born and was named by Dr. Ralph Abernathy. Dr. Martin Luther King, Jr., was elected president; Rev. L. Roy Bennett, vice-president, and Mr. E. D. Nixon, treasurer. I was later added to the Negotiating Committee, still later became the executive secretary, and finally, in 1962, became president after both Dr. King and Dr. Abernathy had left Montgomery.

The First Mass Meeting and One Day of Protest were scheduled for the following Monday, Dec. 5. On that Monday, the buses were empty, and on that Monday night Dr. King delivered his soul to the people at the Holt Street Baptist Church:

"But there comes a time that people get tired. We are here this evening to say to those who have mistreated us so long that we are tired — tired of being segregated and humiliated; tired of being kicked about by the brutal feet of oppression . . ."

These words were like the shots fired at Fort Sumter that were heard around the world. The effect of this speech set the tone for a movement which gained international importance.

A statement that should never be forgotten was made by Ed Nixon: *"We'd better decide now if we are going to be fearless men or scared boys."* How great was Ed Nixon's faith in God? That I have never been able to determine. All I know is that he had the kind of human compassion and dedication that were in line with the cause before Montgomery and with the will of God in 1955. So had Abraham Lincoln, Citizen Tom Paine and others.

Ed Nixon was not a preacher. He never pretended to be an intellectual. He had an entwined combination of courage and wisdom. He was well qualified to be standing at the threshold of a change in the course of history. His offering was a Divine acceptance.

The unexpected turn of events prohibited any meaningful or effective power struggle. At this time, spontaneity counted. There were jealousies and greed for leadership acclaim, but the tide was too strong and too sudden to be successfully resisted.

The transportation of persons who depended upon the buses was facilitated by organized car pools, taxis and vans. A paneled truck that I owned was one of the first vehicles volunteered for the cause. Thousands walked.

As the Protest progressed, the Mass Meetings became the refueling events. Again the ministers were the needed persons to fit a central purpose. Some of the strongest pulpiteers filled the pulpits at that time on each Monday night, men who could move masses. The ministers poured their souls out to capacity crowds who supported the Protest both spiritually and financially.

The central nature of the Protest was spiritual. The *spiritual approach* was a common ground upon which everyone could stand. A common cause existed that the average person could feel and understand. How this came about, and how this resulted in a Movement that was witnessed all around the world can best be explained as the work and purpose of God being fulfilled at the historical moment in American history.

Those persons poised for the historic adventure which later became a movement were men and women of mortal flesh and blood. There were no saints. Each had and struggled with an infirmity, however characterized. And whenever we felt safe and far enough ahead of the enemy, we would gather in groups and engage in telling jokes and other trivial parlance. We would speak our minds in a teasing fashion, to each other, about one another. At such times, we never thought the FBI was among us. We thought the group was esoteric; however, we learned later that there were some vultures around, or even among us, who were picking up whatever weaknesses that were in evidence about the group, especially about Dr. King. While in this group of ministers, we discussed everybody and everything. We spoke of Dr. King as plain "Martin." This man was young, dapper, and the hero. Women chased him. How many, if any, caught up with him, perhaps they, whose assignment it was to find out, did know. But we who struggled with him know that whatever happened in such private encounters he never took his eyes off the ball. He had a "*rendezvous with destiny*". And we who are left on the stage of action go on heart throbbing: "*The dreamer dies; his dreams never die.*"

The One Day Protest extended into days, and gained momentum as all efforts to successfully negotiate with the Bus Company and the City Commissioners failed. Such attempts involved the Council on Human Relations, the Men of Montgomery, the City Commissioners, the Bus Company, and the Montgomery Improvement Association. Violence erupted among the opposition. King's home was bombed. Dynamite was thrown on the lawn of Ed Nixon's home, KKK signs appeared everywhere. At some point during this time *a pellet* fired from a pellet gun by a group of young white males, *entered my wrist as I stepped out on my front porch*. But for the Protestors, non-violence was the order of the day. This *non-violence was never intended to be passive, but rather* was *dynamic, aggressive resistance*.

On February 21, 1956, the Grand Jury of Montgomery County declared boycotting illegal. Following the session of the Grand Jury of Montgomery County, a meeting was held in the Baptist Center on Dorsey Street. Dr. King appeared very apprehensive. From that day forward, I would always read his feeling whenever I saw him. As he sat in a state of apprehension, I was feeling as he was, except that my compassion was reaching out to him. *Many of us knew that efforts had been mounting to isolate him as the leader of the Boycott. Almost involuntarily, I said to the group: "Let us all go to jail."* One minister leaped to his feet and went out of the door while asking, "How are we going to do that?" My response was: "I don't know, but let us consult the lawyers, for Martin is not the sole blame for whatever is happening here." I will never know the legal intricacies. I only know that *on February 22, 1956, some 91 persons voluntarily went down to be arrested.* Twenty-seven of those persons were ministers. Momentum had been building up around Dr. King as the leader. Efforts were being made to have him bear the blame for the boycott. *Those poised for this important event in history did not allow him to bear the blame alone.* We all decided to go to jail rather than wait for the arrests. *Responses to our cause began to pour in from around the country and from around the world.* Contributions and letters of encouragement poured in the Montgomery Improvement Association's office. Reporters came from all parts of the country. On March 19,1956, the day that had been set aside for the trial, more than five hundred Negroes from Montgomery, along with reporters and representatives of many groups from all over the world, crowded into the tiny courthouse in Montgomery. Badges were worn by many of those in attendance saying, "Father, forgive them." These badges were printed in our home by our son, Cameron, upon the request of his father, S. S. Seay, Sr.

The story of the conviction of King, the first person tried for the instigation of the Boycott, the appeal, and the eventual ruling of the U.S. Supreme Court declaring unconstitutional the Alabama state and local laws of segregation on buses are well documented elsewhere. The Protest, itself, was organized and operated almost entirely by black citizens of Montgomery, Alabama. Beyond the Protest, the Movement took an interfaith and interracial complex. Standing at the close of the Protest loomed a galaxy of legal minds. First I'd like to mention a few of the outstanding black lawyers who were involved in the legal aspects of the struggle: *Fred Gray, Peter Hall, Orzell Billingsley, Arthur Shores, and Oscar Adams II.* There were also other lawyers who participated who came into Montgomery from other states.

When we looked at *Fred Gray*, we looked at a person who had to have some kind of faith beyond that of an ordinary person. He traveled a road that was rough, and came through college and through law school, and now, in Montgomery, he had not even made his imprint as a brilliant lawyer. He looked and somewhat sounded like a mediocre person, sort of a lawyer that might not have the spine and the courage and the daring to do what finally, as things turned out, he had to —and did do. I repeat, black people everywhere should thank God for the coincidence, or whatever you might call it, that Fred Gray was here at that time as our *only black lawyer*. But Fred Gray did have deep religious faith and convictions, and the kind of dedication that we did not know he had until the day when he had to stand before the courts here in Alabama and thunder away at juries and judges, and rebut some of the most brilliant lawyers Alabama could throw at him—standing many days before the court, reading sharp and cutting questions from his notes . . . My heart was leaping for joy and tears were running from my eyes. No one could explain what was going on inside me but myself. I had come over a long road, knowing what was needed to be done; no lawyers around. Preachers during that time were busy carrying folk to heaven and forgetting that they had to eat and wear clothes here. While sitting in those courts, my prayers and forebodings of years of toil in the South began to bear down upon me. And I thank God I sit in a court now listening to the voice of a black lawyer; something I never foresaw; something I had dreamed and prayed for, but never quite had faith that I would live to see. And the man is fighting for his people and the people for whom I had been making my feeble efforts over a long period of years. To think about it even now brings tears to my eyes. There Fred Gray stands . . . But there is something about this you ought to know—something that is not generally known.

There's a white man . . . His shadow is not seen there. His image is not there beside Fred Gray. He's hidden in the dim secrets of an office somewhere. I want to mention that man's name, because, apparently, we have been a little bit timid about mentioning the fact. I want to pen it down before my hands become feeble and I cease to be able to remember. That lawyer is attorney Clifford Durr — in the dimness of his years — one of the most brilliant lawyers who ever came through Alabama. He had been beaten and battered and bruised — living in the shadow and shades of his years.

Attorney Clifford Durr handed out to Fred Gray what knowledge he had — what brilliance he brought with him — what guidelines he could give. Fred admits himself that Clifford Durr actually taught him law after he came here to Montgomery. When Fred Gray was standing up there as a black man, the dim shadow of a white man, Clifford Durr, was somewhere hovering around him. I wouldn't write this book unless I penned his name in it. Then, while I am writing his name, I have to include the name of Mrs. Virginia Durr, his wife, who traveled the complete road with us, from the time that I came to Montgomery until — even now — some black intellectuals sort of discouraged her and drove her out by arguing about who was liberal and who wasn't. She stood out in the vanguard for what she believed to be just for all men.

. . . Younger generations who may happen to read this book should have some appreciation for those lawyers whom I have always considered to be outside of and beyond the color line when it comes to criminal justice. These men are the ones who had to do with the glorious conclusion of the Bus Protest:

Judge Richard T. Rives . . . condemned racial segregation, predicting that it would "rub a moral cancer on the white man." One of his final political battles was waged against the "Boswell Amendment," a piece of Jim Crow legislation designed to further disenfranchise black voters. He was born in Montgomery, Alabama, in 1891. Judge Rives was characterized by Judge Johnson as "the real hero of the South."

Judge Frank M. Johnson, Jr., was twenty-five years younger than Judge Rives. He and Judge Rives ruled together against bus segregation in Montgomery in June of 1956. Their ruling became known as the "Rives-Johnson Ruling" in the Montgomery Bus Boycott Case. This was the first of a series of landmark civil rights rulings to be made by Judge Johnson. During the next two years, Judge Johnson ordered the desegregation of Montgomery's public libraries and museum systems, as well as the public facilities at the city Greyhound Bus Depot, and at the Montgomery airport, Dannelly Field.

THE FORERUNNERS OF THE MOVEMENT: . . . A number of other persons of Montgomery had been working faithfully and continuously in the area of civil rights for many years, and had been helping to create the groundswell of unrest upon which the Civil Rights Movement began. To name just two:

RUFUS LEWIS was a graduate of Fisk University. He served for some time as the football coach of Alabama State College. He married a Miss Jewel Clayton, whose parents were in the funeral business. Lewis learned the intricacies of dealing with the power structure. The business with which he was identified was the largest black funeral business in Montgomery at that time. His business experience was useful to the organization that overnight became a big business as well as a protest. Lewis was never an articulate, aggressive person, but he was a meticulous plodder. His assignments with the new adventure were wise and properly executed. He served as chairman of the all-important Transportation Committee of the MIA during the Boycott. For years, Rufus Lewis was active with labor unions and voter registration. He was head of the Citizens Committee through which he conducted his voter registration drives.

MRS. A. W. WEST, a native of Perry County, Alabama, was born in 1892. Her mother and father were members of the first graduating class of Alabama State Normal (now Alabama State University). Mrs. West was a graduate of Alabama State Normal, and attended Tuskegee and Hampton Institutes. She was married to Dr. A. W. West, who was a dentist in Montgomery for many years. Mrs. West was a fearless woman who was involved in every movement that had as its goal the freedom of her race. She was instrumental in bringing [UN Ambassador and Nobel Peace Prize laureate] Ralph Bunche to Montgomery during the Bus Boycott. He spoke at the Alabama State College gymnasium one year after the inception of the Bus Boycott. Mrs. West was a member of the NAACP, Council on Human Relations, the Urban League, Women's League for Peace and Freedom, Church Women United, Royal Grand State Treasurer of the Eastern Star, and had numerous affiliations with other civic organizations For her outstanding community services she received numerous awards and citations.

[Rev. Seay also pays his respects to the following "forerunners," many of whom he also profiles in his book, but for which space limitations allow only a list of honor:]

J.T. Alexander, Dr. James E. Pierce, Frank A. Bray, Dr. Ruby Jackson Gainer, Oscar W. Adams, E.D. Nixon, W.C. Patton, Emory O. Jackson, John LeFlore, Dr. R.T. Adair, Dr. Marshall Cleophus Cleveland, Sr., Arthur Alexander Madison, Arthur C. Shores, Bayard Rustin, Mrs. Rosa Parks, Mahala Ashley Dickerson, Miss Georgia Washington, Eli Madison, Charles Bronson, Charles Brassell, Carrie Madison Motley, General P. Madison, Dr. Vernon Johns, Dr. Moses Jones, Robert D. Nesbitt, Attorney Charles Langford, Mrs. Jo Ann Robinson, Dr. Mary Fair Burks, Rev. Ralph D. Abernathy, Rev. L. Roy Bennett, Rev. A.W. Wilson, Rev. E.N. French, Rev. William Vaughn, Rev. Felix James, Rev. H.H. Hubbard, Rev. A.J. Knight, Rev. H.H. Johnson, Rev. W.P. Alford, Rev. J.W. Hayes, Bishop James Claire Taylor, Mr. Tom Campbell, Rev. William Bascom, George Whylie Clinton, Mrs. Larshley Bell Miller, [the following teachers]: Dr. Spurgeon Bryant, I.C. Reese, Maude Leake, John Porter, Jeanetta Huff, Ruth Peterson, Anna Ricks, Miss A.A. Taylor, Mamie Henry, Thelma Woods, Mary Jane Hall, Mary White Ovington, William English Walling, and W.E.B. DuBois.

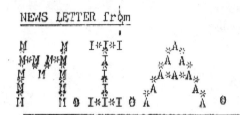

NEWS LETTER from

Vol. 1, No. 6

THE MONTGOMERY IMPROVEMENT ASSOCIATION

530 South Union Street
M. L. King, Jr., President   March 8, 1957   Montgomery, Alabama
                                                                       Telephone AM-53354

RECENT HAPPENINGS

On Tuesday, November 13, 1956, the U. S. Supreme Court affirmed the ruling of a three-judge federal district court, which was made some time ago, that segregation on public transportation in Montgomery and Alabama was unconstitutional. When this affirmation was promulgated, Negroes who had boycotted city busses for eleven months,

An MIA Newsletter Edited by Jo Ann Robinson

The March 8, 1957, newsletter partially reproduced above is from the files of the Montgomery Improvement Association, which still operates under the guidance of President Johnnie R. Carr. The full text of the newsletter follows:

Recent Happenings

On Tuesday, November 13, 1956, the U.S. Supreme Court affirmed the ruling of a three-judge federal district court, which was made some time ago, that segregation on public transportation in Montgomery and Alabama was unconstitutional. When this affirmation was promulgated, Negroes who had boycotted city busses for eleven months, voted to ride public transportation carriers again, this time on a non-segregated basis. The thirteenth month of the boycott was well-underway before actual integration on busses took place, because the Court gave the contesting groups —the city and state—time to file petitions requesting "reconsideration of the ruling."

Such petitions were filed by both city and state officials, but the Court refused to act upon the petitions. When the mandate was received by the federal district court on Thursday, December 21, and filed, segregation laws affecting public transportation were officially dead and Negroes boarded city carriers on Friday, December 22, for the first time in thirteen months.

For a few days integration worked smoothly without incident. Both races appeared indifferent and seemingly accepted the inevitable. Bus drivers, who had been "furloughed without pay" for months, were noticeably happy.

City Authorities Speak:

Then the city officials spoke. They announced publicly that they had no alternative but to "bow to the court's decision," however, they pledged to continue their fight for segregation on busses. They warned Negroes that there would be bloodshed if they attempted to integrate and advised them to "conduct themselves in such a way that would not embarrass the race and lead to bloodshed."

Negroes requested the authorities to use precautionary measures for the first few days by putting a police escort on certain busses after dark, as had been done when the boycott started thirteen months earlier. To this request the city officials refused.

There was repeated prediction from officials that trouble would start. The prediction, along with public announcement that "busses were not protected," seemed to invite violence, for after a few days of operation, December 26, two busses were fired upon. Two days later a bus was fired upon twice in the same evening. By December 29, five city busses had been hit by gun pellets, coming either from passing motorists or from a deserted park, or some obscure place.

As a result of the shootings, the City Commission imposed a 5:00 [p.m.] bus curfew, ordering city buses to halt their service after five o'clock, in order "to curb violence stemming from racial integration." However, numerous requests from both races were acknowledged by city officials asking that "buses be put back into operation during the rush hours until down-town stores closed."

Service was restored, but two days later another shooting occurred, this time striking one person—a Negro expectant mother—in both legs. City officials imposed the five o'clock curfew again and extended it from eight to eleven days. When the curfew was lifted the city officials made a public announcement (*Advertiser*, January 9, 1957) that "no extraordinary measures were being taken to prevent a repetition of violence." People complained that the announcement was an invitation to more violence. That same night another bus was shot into. The Commission promptly halted *all* bus services for the night.

Homes and Churches Bombed:

On early Thursday morning, January 10, "bombs fell on Alabama" when four Negro churches and the homes of two ministers of Negro congregations were bombed, almost within minutes of each other. One of the churches—Mount Olive Baptist, a newly-built, brick structure, was totally without insurance and was completely demolished. Only parts of the walls still stand. A new building must replace the bombed one. Another church badly damaged and condemned as being "unsafe for use," is the Bell Street Baptist Church. It had only a small amount of insurance, insufficient to rebuild.

The services for the Mount Olive Church are being held out-of-doors by the pastor, Reverend E.D. Bell. The Bell Street Baptist, of which Reverend Uriah J. Fields is pastor, holds its services in the basement of another church.

Reverend Fields accused the City of being responsible for the bombings, because it "failed to provide proper police protection to prevent the attacks." He requested the city to "pay for the damage to his church." He also accused "some of those in responsible positions of contributing to violence by advocating opposition to integration." The city refused to assume financial responsibility for the bombed property. The other churches bombed were covered by insurance and are being repaired.

The homes of Reverend Robert Graetz and Reverend Ralph D. Abernathy were also badly damaged. Repairs and rebuilding of the bombed property will extend into the thousands of dollars. Solicitations are being made for funds to rebuild that property that was uninsured.

Second Bombing Attacks:

In addition to the bombings of the church and ministers' homes, a Negro cab company and an adjoining filling station and home of a Negro laborer were bombed the following Saturday night, causing considerable damage. On this same night twelve sticks of smoldering dynamite were found on the porch of Reverend M.L. King Jr.,'s home in time to prevent the second bombing on the MIA president.

On this same night highway patrol men guarded the homes and churches of boycott leaders all over the city to prevent repetition of the numerous attacks.

Two Men Arrested:

The Negro men were arrested at the scene of the filling-station-bombing for "freely expressing open opinion" that the police force was not making earnest effort to apprehend the guilty. When they were warned by the investigating police to cease their loud accusations, to which the men failed to comply, they were arrested and fined. One, a soldier, was fined fifty dollars and costs; the other was fined $100 and costs and given sixty days at hard labor.

Bus Service Halted:

The bombings influenced the city authorities to halt <u>all</u> bus service in Montgomery and both whites and Negroes suffered the consequences. They walked, rode taxis, or "thumbed" rides.

City Refuses Outside Help:

Following the first bombings of he homes and churches, the city authorities refused outside help in apprehending the guilty persons. They felt that they could handle the situation.

But when the second onslaught of bombs started, the Department of Public Safety and the highway patrol joined forces with city police to investigate. Governor Folsom, who deplored the violence, labeled the acts "anarchical" and told citizens of Montgomery that "no one was safe as long as men who would stoop low enough to bomb churches were around." He offered a $2,000 reward for "information leading to the arrest and convictions of the hoodlums." After the second bombing attack, the city also posted a $2,000 reward.

Seven White Men Arrested:

Following the second series of bombing attacks, seven white men were arrested in the case. Three of them were charged with misdemeanors for having thrown the bombs that failed to ignite. Four were charged with felonies for having bombed occupied homes and churches, and one for shooting into the busses.

These men were turned over to the County Grand Jury for investigation. That body, lashing out at "the cowardly stealth and violence under cover of darkness," but at the same time reaffirming the "determination of the people of Montgomery to preserve their segregated institutions openly and honestly," indicted the four men charged with felonies, and their cases have been set for a May hearing. The three charged with misdemeanors have been set free.

Since the arrests there has been no further violence. Four hundred whites, alleged members of WC and KKK organizations, have been conducting a "water-bucket, street campaign" to solicit $60,000 for the men's legal defense.

Bus Service Restored:

The City of Montgomery of approximately 130,000 people went without bus service for a solid week before city officials consented to reinstate partial daylight service, this time with police escort on the last twilight run. On Tuesday, February nineteenth, the curfew was lifted completely and city busses now run their regular schedules. Police escort was also removed. The busses have since been operating normally on an integrated basis and both Negro and white passengers are riding now without trouble.

Few Incidents Recorded:

There were a few incidents at first on the busses when integration first began. A Negro woman was slapped by a white man as she alighted from the bus. A Negro man was "roughed-up" by two white men as he descended from the carrier. A white woman, evidently a plant, slapped a Negro man as he sat down behind her, accusing him of "winking at her." When she discovered the man's wife was behind him, she got of the bus and got into one of the parked cars that were waiting at the bus-stop.

In each of the flare-ups the Negroes refused to fight back. The doctrine of non-violence and passive resistance was religiously adhered to. Negroes just refused to strike back.

"All White" Bus Service Planned:

In the meantime two city attorneys and a third lawyer conferred with U.S. District Judge Frank M. Johnson, Jr., on the possibility of operating a now all-white bus system. According to published reports, the system would be operated by a club plan and only "white members" would be permitted to ride.

The City Commission petitioned Federal District Court to learn if a "club" bus-line could operate legally there. The officials asked for "an advisory position" on three legal points: Can the city hold a hearing on an application of the Rebel Club for a franchise? 2. Can the city logically issue a franchise? 3. Will the city have to enforce racial integration on this new line? The Federal Court requested written arguments on the proposed system. Negro attorneys and bus company attorneys have filed briefs protesting the move.

It will be remembered that during the peak of the boycott Negroes asked the City for a franchise to operate a similar service for Negroes and were refused the franchise on the grounds hat "sufficient and adequate bus service was already provided." What the whites' chances are for securing such a franchise and operating on a segregated "club" plan, the people can only speculate.

Off to Africa:

Upon receipt of an invitation to Dr. King from government officials of Ghana, Gold Coast, in Africa, he and Mrs. M.L. King, Jr., were sent by the Dexter Avenue Baptist Church where he pastors, as special representatives from Montgomery to witness the independence celebration of that nation from Great Britain. They left the country by plane on Saturday, March 2. The coronation is March 6. They, along with other American representatives, will visit Nigeria, Switzerland, France, Italy, England, and other countries before returning to this country a month hence.

The *Time* magazine Tribute

Did you read the very fine tribute paid to Dr. M.L. King, Jr., and to Montgomery, Alabama, in the February 18, 1957, issue of *Time* magazine? Dr. King's picture decorated the front page and was a tribute to the race. Don't miss reading it.

Edited by Jo Ann Robinson

R. D. Nesbitt, Sr.:

I was born November 22, 1908, in Montgomery, Alabama, and have lived here all my life.

We thought nothing about it [segregation] . . . we were awakened to the situation that we were equal, just like the white. We first had to encounter a whole lot of difficulties. We were segregated from top to bottom. We were told that we had a place and that is your place and was the place . . . we had to associate ourselves with . . .

But to begin with, and I want to be very frank about it, it made no difference to us because we were somewhat conditioned to it. But when we began to mature we cold see that there was something missing . . . something needed to have been done about it.

I can recall the first thing that struck me was what the NAACP did here in the city of Montgomery. I think they opened our eyes to a whole lot of things, particularly . . . lynching was a big issue in this state. Records were being kept of lynchings in the state of Alabama . . . the NAACP came in and was successful in getting that outlawed.

Then the matter of segregation of teachers and their salaries. That, I believe, was the thing that made me conscious of the fact that there is a dual system, and something needs to be done about it.

I had two sisters that were teaching. I could talk with them. They would talk with us and, comparatively speaking—salaries. We knew they were not getting paid for the services they were rendering.

Compared to the public school systems now, I think we got a good education. Because, even though the teachers were not paid properly, they were dedicated and they were teachers. But, behind all of it you had a family. You didn't romp the streets all night long. You came in there and put yourself in front of that fireplace and studied your lessons. And, if you did not make good marks, something happened to you.

I think the educational conditions then were far better than they are today. I'm not talking about segregation. I'm talking about the educational process, itself. The teachers now are not dedicated, and they're not dedicated because the children are not disciplined.

The Dexter Avenue Church, that was the name of it at that time, the church was without a pastor at that time. I was clerk of the church; I served as clerk for a period of thirty-five years. I was appointed chairman of the Pulpit Committee.

I was working as auditor for the Pilgrim Health and Life Insurance Company. I was under the Atlanta District; the largest district at that time and I knew the manager. We were going over to see him at the Atlanta office. I had been there several times previously and I knew his connections. He had very good connections—rapport with people in the city of Atlanta.

Being in the office in Atlanta, Georgia, I asked the manager, W.C. Peadon was his name. I said "Pete, my church is again without a minister. I'd like to know if you could recommend anybody to me . . . Atlanta has a whole lot of ministers. You know them all around here. You've been in school with them."

He popped his finger . . . and said, "Yeah, I've got the man for you. Martin Luther King is available."

"Luther King isn't thinking about leaving Ebenezer?"

He said, "I'm talking about his son."

I didn't know Dr. King at that time. I said, "Well, where is he?"

He said, "He's probably at home. Let's call him."

So, I called him and introduced myself to him over the phone and told him what I wanted and told him I'd like to talk with him before leaving and going back to Montgomery. He said, "OK."

I said, "Well, when can I see you?"

He said, "About Friday at two o'clock?"

I said, "That's beautiful. I'll be out there."

[Mr. Nesbitt convinced Dr. King to come and preach a trial sermon at Dexter, and then a second, and finally, Dr. King answered the call to come to Montgomery. The rest *is* history.]

. . . if you think about history, you find there has been changes in history over the years. I guess the only thing that we could have looked forward to was that history was going to bring about another change. Then, when I think about the situation, I look at it this away, that God had a man and that man was Martin Luther King, and this is the writing of new history, that he's going to change the course of history in America and in the world.

That's during his lifetime and lifetime beginning here in Montgomery. Because see, things begin to change, not only in Montgomery but throughout the country. Blacks begin . . . to know they were human beings, and they were somebody, and have to have the respect that any other human being that was created on this earth had.

Once he sold us on the idea, that was it and you just expected change. But, I said to start with, young people don't realize that.

To be frank about it, I don't think the white has actually changed on his own. Now, you've got some good white people. We had some good white people that worked with us on the bus boycott. The change has come about because he was forced to because of legislation.

The position the black takes, and I think the white man misses it . . . I don't want to sit down and socialize with him, but in the event that I want to, I'm not prohibited from doing so. I think that's the black man's philosophy. Whether or not I belong to the Kiwanis, Rotary, or Civitan, that's immaterial. But, the only thing I'm concerned about is—can I be? Am I permitted to be? Am I permitted to hold this job or hold this job, the same as the white man. Now, that's my philosophy. If I'm qualified, capable, able, and willing, don't deny me because I'm black.

EPILOGUE

Reflections on Dr. Martin Luther King, Jr.

Harris Wofford:

(CEO of the Corporation for Natural Service and former U.S. Senator from Pennsylvania from 1990-94, and, earlier, a close friend of Dr. King as well as President Kennedy's advisor on civil rights and Associate Director of the Peace Corps. Author, Of Kennedys and Kings: Making Sense of the Sixties.*)*

In 1952 I did a law school study on the status of Negroes in Dallas County, Alabama. And also another paper on how the whites hold onto railway labor unions which was broken by some lawyers and law students. In both cases, I got to know E.D. Nixon, who was the NAACP leader in Montgomery, Alabama, and a Pullman Porter Brotherhood man—and a very courageous man—.

I had a wonderful time interviewing him. I told him, "You're sort of a Gandhi with a gun." At one time he carried guns with him to register blacks—Negroes, back then. Yes, he was very Gandhian in other ways. I kept in touch with him during those years and sent him a paper on why Gandhi should be applied to the civil rights problem in the South.

In the fall of 1955, I used the same paper as the basis for a speech at Hampton Institute in Virginia. I sent E. D. Nixon a copy of the speech, and he sent it around to a number of people. One of those he said he had given it to was Martin Luther King, Jr.

I'd heard about King from Nixon, and when the boycott began, I wrote to Dr. King. So I had written him early in the boycott, and he replied that he had read the paper of mine, and we started corresponding. Then I went down to give a seminar on nonviolence and social change for the Montgomery Improvement Association at the end of the boycott . . . a celebration at the end of the boycott.

Meanwhile, I'd met him during the boycott in Washington, D.C. He was speaking in Baltimore; and at his suggestion, my wife and I met him and Coretta at the airport in Baltimore and drove them from the airport to Washington, D.C. That drive was one of my most vivid memories from those early days. We talked about the danger.

Coretta told my wife about how she had a regular nightmare about her husband being killed which came out of her own experience in Marion, Alabama, and her father's house being burned down. In any case, Coretta King told my wife about this recurrent dream that she had that Martin was going to be killed. He was in the car, and we (Martin and I), of course, could hear what Coretta was saying. His reaction to most things like that was, 'Yes, yes.' He was very calm and slow, and, in a sense, thoughtful.

Earlier that night, he had given a great speech to a black fraternity in which he accosted them for spending more and more on alcohol on the weekends—more money than the NAACP's total budget was in a year. It was a very passionate, relatively successful speech . . ."

Lerone Bennett :

(Editor of Ebony *and author of numerous books, including* What Manner Of Man? *and* Before The Mayflower.*)*

I had personally seen King as a student at Morehouse College. He was a year ahead of me, he finished in 1948, and I finished in 1949. I didn't know him all that well, but he was a person on the campus that I knew and a brilliant young man who was more deeply involved in (Atlanta) politics, primarily because he lived in the city—and there's a wholly different texture between cats who lived in the dormitory and those who lived in the city. He was obviously very brilliant. Later when I came to do research on it, I found out a number of things that other people have said about the fact that he was going through a great struggle at that time about what he wanted to do with his life.

Then I worked at the *World* in Atlanta and saw him summers and from time to time when he would come back to school. I went to Chicago and then the boycott started, and I went to Montgomery in the first couple of months of the Movement to do a story on Mrs. King and then saw him from time to time.

[As time went on] he was obviously more focused. He knew what he wanted to do. He found a kind of inner peace that obviously made a difference. He had developed, by the time I saw him in Montgomery [in 1956]—not as much as he had in the March on Washington [in 1963]—an eloquence and a tremendous rapport with people from a platform. He had this—and even later—no matter how much it might have cost him personally—this ability to swing with people in the streets. People that he'd never seen. They'd say, "Hey, Reverend," and you know, he could deal with them. . . . From my standpoint, Morehouse is a college for men with tremendous traditions of producing leaders. But, Morehouse wasn't a [social] class [-oriented] school. Many—most of the students were poor. So even—sure, he came from a prominent minister's family, but there again, you have a minister's Baptist church intimately, directly connected with the masses of black people of the town, never able to get away from it. Morehouse was not a

class school.

I was a poor boy—hundreds of poor boys from Mississippi, Alabama, Georgia, Cleveland, Harlem. It would have been laughable if anyone would have pulled a great class rank thing—it just didn't exist. Not in my knowledge did it exist. An additional factor, and I stressed this in my book, and I have stressed it repeatedly since then: Benjamin Mays was president [of Morehouse], at the top of his form, and he was intimately, deeply involved in the NAACP and social action, in efforts to reform the church and for four years, at least once a week, preached this to us: "I don't care if you're a doctor or a lawyer, a preacher—you have the responsibility to get involved in social action, a responsibility to be a man, a responsibility to relate to the masses of people." I mean for four years.

So it's part of the air there, so I don't find it all incredible that any number of people from Morehouse—Maynard Jackson, Julian Bond—you can just start naming them—had the same general orientation toward black people. There's always some sort of action; well, the truth of it was, at Morehouse you were supposed to be involved in some sort of action to free yourself and free black people.

It's not happening as much now—in those days it was almost a missionary kind of spirit going on there between the black teachers and the black students. [Now] the world has changed—television and all sorts of electronic revolution—that you can't replicate the situation, but you can just try to hold on to as much of that as possible and I think some schools are holding on to a great deal

of that, but that was a great genre.

Dr. Harold Deats :

(Professor Deats was a faculty member at the Boston University School of Theology while Dr. King was a student there in the early 1950s.)

I knew King in student days—and he was not well-known on campus. He was in theology in Boston University, but studying philosophy at Harvard, and it was in the same building that the Sociology Department was. He attracted almost no attention here during his student days. I met him, not here [at Harvard] where he was studying philosophy while I was doing sociology over there.

I'm afraid he didn't make much of an impression on me. He was a nice guy, he was bright, he was handsome, but we were all busy studying as hard as we could . . . this would have been in '52, '53.

I only saw him very irregularly back then. Amongst his colleagues, I'm not sure that many knew him. There was not then and is not now a very cohesive community of graduate students. We're all scattered out and many of us, particularly in the division of theological and religious studies, had some Church responsibilities when we were students, and so we were off in different places and saw each other only in class. There was not any indication in his student days that he was going to be a civil rights leader.

. . . [At B.U.] we were all pleasantly surprised by his emergence in Montgomery. We just didn't know that that would be something that he would do.

I think, in all fairness, there

have been a lot of people who will trace out how the natural history of Martin's life led him to the bus boycott, and he would say he spent a lot of time getting ready but he didn't know what he was getting ready for. Let me read you one thing that came from his application to the graduate school in 1950:

"For a number of years I have been desirous of teaching in a college or school of religion. Realizing the necessity for scholastic attainment in the teaching profession I feel that graduate work would give me a better grasp of my field. At present I have a general knowledge but I have not done the adequate research to meet the scholarly issues with which I will be confronted. The teaching of theology should be as scientific, as thorough and as realistic as any other discipline. In a word, scholarship is my goal."

And he went on then to compare the conceptions of God in the thinking of Paul Tillich and Henry Nelson Wieman in his dissertation. It was a very scholarly dissertation.

None of us knew anything about his oratorical ability. You wouldn't have noticed this in a seminar—just sitting around a table. [He wasn't] standing in front of the Lincoln Memorial giving a speech. We were not surprised that he could rise to the occasion. I think he had no idea when he went to Montgomery that he was going to be the leader . . . Rosa Parks planned that more than he did.

It's important to say that one of the reasons he came to the Religious Emphasis Week at Fisk [in the early days of the boycott] at which we were both present, was that he needed to get away. He was very well

protected.

There were reporters there the whole time, and he would get long-distance calls. They put us in a small dormitory and would not give out information and this was the first of many times later on where he just had to get away from the Civil Rights Movement and get to where he could think things through. This was a recurring pattern.

. . . He found that first month [of the boycott] so hectic that he needed some time. He was good enough that he could preach, and he could speak to the students without a lot of preparation—so he was using the time to get off by himself.

The students greeted him with great warmth and affection. I think certainly in the black community and most certainly in the black student community, he was the hero of the occasion. In the university community [the boycott was big news nationally and internationally], we were aware of it . . . It's one of the reasons I was delighted to go to Fisk to get to be with him.

I remember (that) my impression of Martin was that he was still struggling with the leadership of the Movement. How do you bring the very disparate forces together? How do you lead it without it becoming a personality cult? And, how does it fit in with this whole understanding of the role of the Church?

A lot of the Movement was criticized because there was little attention to organizational details. Letters would not get answered, appointments would not be kept. There was some question about budget raised in that period. I am not sure he was giving his attention so much to organizational details as to

his role—and of how to relate to the Church, how they could take the people along. There were already emerging leadership struggles.

During that week at Fisk, very few people were interested in pushing him on any issues other than what was happening in Montgomery. What did these events mean for the struggles of the black community? You remember that this was just 18 or 19 or 20 months after the *Brown* decision and we were in the first throes of school desegregation which we [saw repeated] again in Boston, Louisville and in other places. What was on people's minds was how the bus boycott related to the desegregation of schools. For the first time, it looked as if the segregation barriers might come down.

I don't think his personal questioning was in terms of what if you win this, what next? He was sure that the bus boycott was not an isolated thing. He was sure that the struggle of the black community to achieve justice and freedom was going to be a long struggle. But, I don't think he at this point was trying to connect this item, and this item and this item—or this Movement and this Movement in an overall strategy. He was still, at this point, a reflective person, feeling his way in knowing what his dream was. I think he could have articulated well the dream that there would be no real barriers in American society. But, the steps between 1955 and 1963 or 1968—I don't think he had started thinking those through. Strategically—but that's not a put-down. Anybody who tells you what he's going to do . . . without knowing what it is he's responding to is foolish.

I may be wrong. Of course,

there are a lot of people that have had a lot more contact with him. I don't think he ever was, or ever became, gregarious. He was never a hail-fellow-well-met. He could have a good time with a group of people. He could shout 'hello' and slap people on the back and this kind of thing; but, I think he stayed reflective, withdrawn.

Bayard Rustin:

(The late Bayard Rustin was a close associate of A. Philip Randolph and served for many years as the Executive Director of the A. Philip Randolph Institute. Mr. Rustin was the organizer of the 1963 March on Washington. At the time of the Bus Boycott he was a staff member for the Fellowship of Reconciliation (FOR), and along with a white FOR staff member, Rev. Glenn Smiley, was sent to Montgomery to help in the boycott.)

I had predicted some of the changes that occurred in the '50s and '60s because, you see, I had been going all over the South for years. I took a journey of reconciliation (for the Fellowship of Reconciliation) in '47. I wrote an essay for the NAACP after that experience and said that the most important thing they had to do was to get a decision which would fortify blacks because until the Supreme Court made it perfectly clear that blacks were indeed citizens and had all rights of citizens, my thesis was that there could be no breakthrough. Not that it was inevitable. Had not the Supreme Court made the *Brown* decision, in my view, there could not have been a Montgomery movement . . .

The Supreme Court does not make decisions on the basis of psy-

chological or historical factors. The Supreme Court is like a ballet dancer balancing two hands, one concerned with justice and the other one with justice to the degree that society can handle it without disruption. Now there were many things which led to that decision that are never talked about. The Montgomery protest could never have occurred unless three additional things had occurred in the South. One: the urbanization of the South. Two: the industrialization of the South. And, Three: the unionization of the South. The Supreme Court could now take a chance without total disruption. The Supreme Court is very sensitive to what will and will not be socially possible. So that at one minute, they say take *Dred Scott* back and another minute they say we can't take it back."

Harris Wofford:

The reaction against Bayard Rustin then—who I respect on a lot of things—or against his role, was that he was blatantly talking about King as . . . a fortunate vehicle for something Bayard was doing and believing in for years.

And during that period, I heard Bayard talking about King, with King and with other people and reacted very much against the sense that King was a symbol that we were all manipulating. I may not have reacted verbally, but I certainly remember feeling it. And, I may have myself been doing it. I mean, I rushed down there to Montgomery to see this new black leader . . . I still have this lingering reaction from that period and a lingering reaction against Bayard and his role back then.

In the early days, everyone was viewing King in a certain way to do things that we wanted to be done—but by 1960, King was his own character on the national stage and everyone knew it and was now trying to figure out how to get his support . . .

I have a theory that he had a fairly strong case of Messianism which he handled very well. I don't want to make it too strong a proposition because so many people thought of him that way. "Messianic complex" may be too strong a characterization. There was a quality about him that he successfully made fun of himself. I didn't have the sense that he wasn't healthy about it. I think he felt very early, very early that he had been called.

Jack Nelson;

(Jack Nelson, the long time Washington Bureau Chief for the Los Angeles Times, covered Dr. King and the Movement for many years for both the Times and the Atlanta Journal-Constitution.)

People sort of stood back, almost in awe, when he came around, and that's literally true; I thought that overall the press treated him with great reverence too. Reporters from the networks and from newspapers, generally. But, I'll say for Dr. King, he tried to put people at ease, he tried to be friendly with you, but he also had a certain bearing about him . . . He was a civil rights leader, but he seemed more than that. He was not easy to get to. The best way to get to him was to run up to him when he was on a platform and talk to him. It was not that he was standoffish, but he was pro-

THE CHILDREN COMING ON . . .

tected, sometimes to almost too great an extent, with all of the aides that surrounded him.

. . . and, then, there were times that I saw him with the people. ..he really had an extraordinary effect. I can remember one occasion — down in a little place in Alabama called Gee's Bend. And, I'd really have been sorry to have covered the whole movement and missed this occasion.

It was winter time, and we had to get there over muddy, dirt roads. And, really, the whole story of the movement and Dr. King was kind of on display right there. It was cold, and he was speaking in a little country church with just a bare light bulb hanging from the ceiling. Dr. King was preaching, and he was impassioned, his eyes were moist: "I'm here to tell you that you are all children of God—that you're 'Somebody.' You're just as good as the best white man or the best white woman in this county." And the old people there in the church would nod their heads up and down and say, "Ain't it the truth, ain't it the truth." He could reach folks in ways that no one else could. He really could make them believe they WERE somebody.

Harris Wofford:

I've tried to imagine my sense of what the timing of the change that was coming to the South after my trips down to Alabama when I was a student a Howard Law School in the early 1950s. In a way, it was the same. I think in a way you keep repeating your life—because recently in South Africa, I had conversations very close to the ones I had in the early '50s in Alabama. I said on both occasions, 'Time is not on your side,

you'd better change.' But as to just how fast it would come, I can't remember what I thought back in Alabama in the early '50s. My line with my white friends was that, "The world is moving in on you, you better change . . ."

In the early '50s, though, whites in the South were really very confident that they had everything under control—and so they took it all in stride. It wasn't until the Montgomery Bus Boycott began, and I went back, that my very close white friends let me know, "You're either for us or against us." Some of my best friends felt that way. After many months of the boycott, they were not enjoying it—and it's only been in the last five or six years that it's been worked out. Y-e-a-h, it took quite a while . . . .

I tend to think that before Montgomery, whites in the South did see blacks as people. The line [by many whites] in the South had some truth. It went something like this:

"Down here we love the blacks as individuals, but don't like them collectively. Up North, you love them collectively, but you don't want anything to do with them individually." [W. J. Cash made a similar observation in *The Mind of the South*.]

There's some truth to that. In the South, my recollection is that there was not an equal relationship, but that there was a certain warmth that was lacking in the North. There was a certain positive relationship. There was not very much of it, but there was some.

Originally, the reaction of my white friends in Alabama was benign when I went to Howard Law School and even when I brought (the Indi-

an-Gandhian-Socialist) Lohia to speak in the black belt of Alabama. They were benign even when Lohia spoke about hearing a speech in Paris by Josephine Baker where she said that, "Someday all the world will be mulatto." And he gave this account to a large gathering of white farmers that assembled in a little rural community where I had been a lot.

But, his main speech was about how—and the reason they liked him was that he gave a speech about how—on the world stage, the Jeffersonians had always lost to the Hamiltonians and that the time had come for the village people and the farm people—the people who knew the sunrises and the sunsets—to rise up and to see that for once, the Jeffersonians won over the Hamiltonians; and that people close to nature prevailed. He gave a really beautiful Gandhian speech in that regard, but it had very strong racial stuff in it, including a statement that the blacks—Negroes—needed to learn about jail-going.

The leader of that white community stayed up till four in the morning talking to him about Gandhi, and the farmers were full of typical Southern responses to the proposition that blacks were capable of this kind of action.

Lohia asked to meet some "Negro leaders," and his host said, "There aren't any Nigra leaders, they're just Nigras!" And Lohia spoke about jail-going by blacks to change the civil rights situation, and whites said, "You just come down and try it, and we'll shoot you."

The whites didn't think that anything was going to come. And neither did E. D. Nixon. He said he could count on the fingers of his hands the Negroes in Montgomery who would really be willing to stand up and fight. That talk I gave about learning from Gandhi and applying it to civil rights issues had a big response from some local Negro leaders, including E. D. Nixon. The response was, "This isn't the time."

And this was in the fall of 1955, and they all said, "This isn't in us, and there isn't any Gandhi here to make this work." . . . Mr. Nelson, Dean Nelson of Howard University, who had actually lived with Gandhi and was a Quaker pacifist, wrote me [that] we in America had no hope through nonviolence—that there was just no Gandhi in us . . . that we were consumed with the American concept of success. The ethic of success in America and middle-class Americans was persuasive and there was just no chance of success. He said, "There's just none of this in us, we'll just never do anything like this." Everybody I talked to said that.

And two months later, the Montgomery Bus Boycott began. After it began, they were very excited. E. D. Nixon was elated. I think really it was "dry tinder and spark." It was a hallelujah mood . . . that, "It's happened. We've taken these whites by surprise!!" So Nixon and many others were pleased.

. . . However, Fred Gray, the young black attorney who handled the litigation [during the boycott] was another story. He never appreciated civil disobedience and the nonviolence side of King. Gray was a lawyer; I mean, he was trying to be a good lawyer. He was either the first or second black lawyer . . . one of the very first black lawyers in Alabama. There had been Arthur Shores in Birmingham and some older ones.

But he was bothered by the jail-going. He didn't mind the protests, but his job as a lawyer was to keep King out of jail.

And it's a high legal doctrine . . . and judicial restraint . . . on the one hand, and really all legal theory states that it's a lawyer's duty to keep all issues from going to very high controversial constitutional issues when you can resolve them at a low level; and, therefore, any technical reasons to keep somebody from putting you in jail—you should use them.

And it was a very clear professional duty from Gray's side to keep King out of jail if there were good legal reasons available—if the police had broken the law, etc. And King, on occasion, was ready for jail—was wanting to go to jail. Wanted to suffer, sort of itching to get his Gandhism into orbit, to achieve a Gandhian solution. And Fred Gray was, in a sense, resisting. That's why [Martin Luther King, Jr.] used to tease me, saying that I was the only lawyer that was willing to help him get into jail—the others were trying to keep him out of jail.

Bayard Rustin:

Well, a few days after the boycott began, I heard about it because Mr. Randolph of the Brotherhood of Sleeping Car porters had told me that E.D. Nixon, his man down there was involved in things and he was trying to get together with Dr. Martin Luther King. That's the first time I heard the name King, when Randolph had told him the ideal man to take it over was King. And, of course, you know Martin was very reluctant to take it over.

There's no contradiction, the fact that Martin was reluctant and did want and had to be urged to take on the boycott—the leadership for very good reasons. He felt, number one, that he was young and that older people could do it better; number two, that he had just come to town and that he had to make church work first, and, number three, felt that he was just beginning to have a child and raise a family and didn't know if he could carry those burdens. Purely a part of Martin's basic humility and Martin's basic carefulness.

Now if you want to get the story as Nixon told it to me and I helped him write an article for it, you'll find that in *Liberation* magazine; they can give you the exact details . . . Well, the boycott began in December '55 and ended in December '56. So it would have to be in that year. Now the second occurrence . . .

After we talked to Nixon, frankly, I was involved and didn't do a great deal of thinking about it. What made me really think about it was a telegram I got from Lillian Smith, who said, 'Bayard, you've had a lot of experience with these things, and I think you ought to go down to Montgomery and see what you can do to help King.' This was about two weeks after things had begun. I think King had become president of the MIA about a week before. I went to see Mr. Randolph and made some financial arrangements to leave the work I was doing and went down. I went to King's house. He wasn't at home, and I went to Abernathy's. I waited at Abernathy's overnight and met King the next day.

I knew absolutely nothing

about him. I had never heard the name Martin Luther King before the boycott started. I had not known his father. His father had never been active in the kinds of protests that I had been interested in up until that time.

. . . Well, after a year, I think if it had not been for that Supreme Court decision that the NAACP pressed for, there would have been a wind-down, that's a pretty long time for people to be walking. And people were becoming a little edgy. But that does not in any sense mean that had that decision not come down I think the people could have held out for a considerable period of time, but not merely because of what they were but because they now believed the entire nation was watching and that was his ace in the hole.

And from every state in the union, financial contributions poured into these mass meetings. Night after night there was somebody there from out of town whose support could be introduced, to say, "We're with you, what can we do for you?"

Curiously enough, when the decision was handed down, [and] it was now quite clear that we were going to win, I was surprised that Martin showed practically no emotional response to that in my presence whatever. His attitude essentially was, "Well, now we've got to get on to something else."

SCLC was actually formed before the victory. It was called for, it had something to do with transportational busing. I remember that because I had the original papers. So, the SCLC actually grew out of a conversation which I had with Martin in a low point in which I remember

quite clearly saying to Martin, "The Montgomery Improvement Association cannot win the fight unless there are similar protests all over the South, and they cannot win unless SCLC wins. Therefore, you must take the responsibility of becoming the leader and stimulating these protests everywhere." And King and Reverend Shuttlesworth [from Birmingham] and Reverend C.K. Steele [from Tallahassee] and the rest of those guys have got now to come in with you, or all of us are going to lose.

He was enthusiastic and willing to take the leadership of the entire Southern part of it. He had no choice. He had no choice mostly because these guys had already begun to run to him and ask him to come in.

There was a sense in which Martin was just picked up by the times. The times propelled him. It's an interesting thing. I watched Martin over that year, and you could almost measure by a ruler his speaking ability. But it was not merely his speaking ability which certainly greatly improved; almost to say, he became a perfect speaker. But it was almost that he was evolving new and exciting ideas constantly, which made him a fresh speaker.

Hosea Williams:

(Hosea Williams served as the SCLC Director of Voter Registration and Political Education from 1963–68, and has since had a lengthy career in politics and working with the poor of Atlanta, Georgia.)

One of the most beautiful things about Dr. King was his ability to choose a talent for a given job—and he surrounded himself

with able men—strong willed, bright, young men. All [of us were] leaders in our own right. He was the leader of leaders, kind of like being the king of kings. And we were all good at a particular thing. Like, my job was to arouse the town and get the movement going. Andy's was to soothe it down and get whites and blacks together. Jim Bevel led the young people and talked to them in language they could relate to and understand.

. . . He had a good sense of humor—just a few minutes before he died, he played a joke on Andy. He had sent Andy out to do something and Andy had been gone all day. Andy had not called in and when he finally got back, Dr. King began a pillow fight. And he pushed him on the bed and hit him with the pillow and they were tussling and he was hitting Andy with the pillow and saying, "I'll show you who's boss."

. . . We used to get a lot of exercise on staff retreats. Dr. King was a great believer in physical fitness. He was a good athlete and enjoyed softball, table tennis, volleyball, swimming and even though he was not tall, he was good at basketball.

Dr. King was a great believer in healthy living. He used to go up to the White House Hotel and have a buffet for lunch—salads and healthy food. Dr. King believed in a good diet, though he liked soul food, like pig's feet and barbecued chicken, too, he generally tried to eat a balanced meal. He would also fast sometimes and take days of silence and just read and think—much like Gandhi did..

. . . Any place I went in the world [during an around-the-world SCLC ambassador/people-to-people tour in 1971], they didn't believe I knew him—that I ate with him, talked with him and slept in the same room with him. Once they believed that, the red carpet was always laid out. I became a celebrity instantly—became a guest of the government and was able to wine and dine in palaces with kings and queens because I was close to Dr. King. That's all they wanted to talk about.

It's amazing how much influence it had. I would expect that in Israel; but you wouldn't expect it in China. Israel is a religious country, but China, there's few westerners that those people would bow to.

There are problems of racism in every part of America, but we made some real progress in the South. We always said that if a white man didn't like you in the South, he'd tell you so. In the North, he wasn't up front about it and so you never really confronted the racism directly. Northerners and Westerners haven't really been touched by the movement in the same way that the South has.

. . . We need to remember what Malcolm X taught us. We don't need to move into white areas to get good schools and good houses. We can stay in our own neighborhoods and fix them up and make it a better place to live—we can participate in the schools in a way that will make them places where our children get quality education. We don't have to sit next to a white child in a white school or live in a white neighborhood to have a god life. It's not easy to make a neighborhood place to live, it takes hard work and time, but we must use time constructively, not destructively.

Tom Offenburger:

(Tom Offenburger, a native of Shenndoah, Iowa, gave up a job as U.S. News and World Report's Chicago Bureau Chief to work for SCLC. He interviewed Dr. King about SCLC's work in the inner city of Chicago, and after the interview asked about working for Dr. King and later became the SCLC public relations chief and eventually, after Dr. King's death, the press secretary for former SCLC executive, Andrew Young—in Congress, at the UN, and in the Atlanta Mayor's office. Like many of Dr. King's aides who lived with years of stress, Tom Offenburger died at a relatively young age in 1986 of heart failure during an open heart surgery.)

SCLC seemed like a family. And there was, I think, a genuine friendship among SCLC's staff and that was—I think that was instilled in people, if they didn't have it before they came there. It was instilled in them because SCLC was serious about non-violence and they were serious about blacks and whites working together. And never abandoned that. I came to SCLC in September of '66—soon after the Meredith March [in Mississippi]. [For] about two months—I was Deputy Assistant to the press person at SCLC—Junius Griffin. Junius Griffin left about two months later and then I became the—I was called the Director of the Office of Public Relations. . . . [It was the] press job at the SCLC.

. . . One thing that Dr. King always insisted on in that period, was that blacks should not permit their leadership and their organization to be divided because differences were played up in the media. The news

media in those days, was always saying there was a tremendous split between say, SCLC and SNCC. But they would never report that members of the groups continued to maintain communications all the time. . . . I think the split was greatly exaggerated.

In terms of policy, I think that Dr. King in that period deliberately, for example, asked for some white members on the board of directors. One was Stanley Levison. Dr. King thought that he had to make a show that he and SCLC continued to want to work with whites and included whites in the organization. Now there was a bit—there was significant change though in terms of the role of whites. It was becoming increasingly apparent that blacks could organize in the black community and whites were not as good at that. And, I think that whites in the Movement that I knew recognized that too. So many of them moved on from SNCC, or what have you, or SCLC, or whatever, into other things.

. . . But, SCLC still felt there was a role that whites could play. One of them was what you might call a kind of role people play with some kind of technical or professional experience that could be useful—I probably fell into that category. I was never an organizer—to this day I never organized anything, but I had some experience with the news media and writing and research, and so I could hopefully make a contribution in that area.

And a little later down the line, whites became important with movements like the "Poor Peoples Campaign" where we established contact with low-income whites,

American Indians, Chicanos, and Puerto Ricans—in fact, we took some of those groups on to the staff.

. . . What made the movement tick? That is an interesting question. Well, first of all it hung together in a great measure because of one man, who was Dr. King. I mean—he did have charisma and he could rally people—very strong willed people. In fact, I've always maintained that you had to be fairly strong willed and even to have a fairly healthy ego to even get on to the SCLC staff . . . because of things like potential dangers and because it was almost—I maintain also, that it was revolutionary, what was going on.

. . . Well, I think the people that knew Dr. King best, really, literally, have not had the time to write about it. That's been an eternal problem for people who were there and who really know what happened and who can really offer an authentic analysis of what happened.

Willie Bolden:

(Willie Bolden, a native of Savannah, worked with Hosea Williams and the Chatam County Crusade For Voters in the early '60s and when Hosea Williams took the position as Director of Voter Registration and Political Education for Dr. King, Bolden, like Judson Ford, Jimmie Wells, Ben Clark, and many others from the Savannah civil rights movement followed Rev. Williams to Atlanta and took a job working for him on the SCLC Field Staff.)

I didn't pay a lot of attention, to be quite honest with you, about the boycott going on in Montgomery. I read about it, I heard about it—I suspect subconsciously I was highly—maybe not highly—but I

was concerned about it. But—you know, I didn't sit down—it was not part of everyday discussion with me about the Montgomery Bus Boycott. And, I don't think so—I don't think it was because I didn't understand exactly what was going on at that time.

Well—my mother was in Savannah—I was in the service at Parris Island and I saw her maybe once or twice a year—Oh yeah, we talked about the boycott when I came home.

To the best of my recollection—that's been many, many, many, many years ago—I think what she talked about at that time was about Dr. King—I think she was more fascinated about his oratory ability. She would always talk about that too—about how great a speaker he was—how he was able to—it was obvious that he was highly educated, but he could speak and everybody would understand what he was talking about. And—the fact that the bus boycott lasted for so long—she felt that for the first time in history of black folks—black folks were coming together.

It didn't mean much to me personally at first. But, you know, I'd listen to her and I'd say, 'Damn, you know that's great'—and I think after that I began to listen to Dr. King whenever I would see something on TV or heard on the radio or something . . .

As far as the people I knew, from the streets in New York in the late '50s . . . It was basically house parties on the weekend or club parties. It wasn't, you know—the people that I hung around with then had absolutely no concept what Martin Luther King was all about. And, for

me to even have tried to discuss that issue (with them) at that time—me not yet being committed—would have been a waste of time . . .

I never thought that I would ever—if anybody told me back in the '50s that I would be able to sit with Dr. King . . . say, be with this man . . . sit with this man or eat with this man . . . or sit next to him—I would have said, "You've got to be out of your mind"—I mean that was the furthest thing from my mind.

Harry Ashmore:

(The late Harry Ashmore was the editor of the Arkansas Gazette *in Little Rock, Arkansas, for many years, including the time period in 1957 of the school integration crisis which resulted in President Eisenhower sending in the United States Army so that nine black children could attend the previously all-white Central High School. He was the author of numerous books on race relations in America.)*

I grew up in South Carolina and started into the newspaper trade there before World War II, and when I came back from service in Europe in the War, I wound up in Charlotte, North Carolina. I was there for a couple of years, and then I went on out to Little Rock, where I was executive editor of the *Arkansas Gazette.* We had a crisis of our own around the battle for school integration at Central High School [which] became the focal point.

But before that, I had become aware, and I was really just starting out in South Carolina before World War II, and there was, at that time, no racial crisis and no concerted attack on the issue of the institution of segregation per se. There were court cases on individual issues and actions on voting rights and so on, but there was no head-on attack on what was a truly segregated society.

They war accelerated and changed a lot of that in Charlotte. The NAACP was becoming more active about treatment in the courts, and a series of lawsuits began which finally led to the *Brown* decision. Public accommodations was not so much of an issue, but there were attempts to equalize the schools. Blacks, or Negroes, as we called them at that time, accepted segregated schools but demanded that the 'separate but equal' doctrine become a reality. All this is now ancient history.

In any event, I became involved fairly early in all of this. Not so much, I think, because of any abstract personal or moral concern, and couldn't say that I really separated out the question of race as a special issue of concern to me, but it was just that if you're going to be the editor of a newspaper in the South, it was so intertwined in everything that was happening that it was practically unavoidable. And also, the South itself, in general terms, was beginning to change very rapidly. (In the 1940s) there was a generational transition taking place before the one (in the '60s).

I didn't hear of Martin until the demonstrations began in Montgomery, and I didn't really meet him until he had moved back to Atlanta. By the time of the Montgomery Bus Boycott, I was in Little Rock, as I've explained. The newspaper that I worked for was liberal—liberal on the issue of race, as Southern newspapers go, and among the best newspapers in the South and one of the most concerned. And, as I say, we

were all beginning to think about it and realized that this issue was going to come up and become acute. I didn't know King, but I think that anyone who was sensitive about what was happening in any Southern community could sense that there was a difference in what was passing, in at least a surface sense, for acceptance of segregation—and that it was beginning to go in the black communities.

What was happening was that I, in the meantime, was becoming a national figure, and I had appeared on a number of national newscasts—and this must have been in 1948. That far back, television was just beginning and The Old Town Hall of the Air took place in New York. They had a session on the segregation issue, principally the school issue, which was beginning to come up.

I remember that Hodding Carter, Jr., who was an old friend of mine, and I were on the program along with Walter White, who had been the head of the NAACP and somebody else, a newspaper man from Ohio, we were the panel. And when we were preparing for the show, we had dinner together. It was the first time I had ever really talked to Walter White. He was in the desegregation litigation in the beginning, and Walter was an extraordinary fellow. He was tall, and he was so fair-skinned that he could pass for white, which was one of his great utilities since he could go into the South. He was almost pink and his hair by then was almost white.

We were talking in a most friendly kind of way, and I was taking a relatively modern position that we could really change things, and

this was the goal. But there was no way to lick this segregated society head-on. But it was gonna have to be done through the courts and it's going to have to be done pretty quick, and it's going to have to be done stage by stage.

I remember Walter White saying to me, "What the hell are you afraid of?" And I said, "I don't think that I'm afraid of anything." "Well," he said, "for Christ's sake, look at you. You're the editor of the biggest newspaper in Arkansas. You've got blue eyes. You grew up in the South. You're white. You're six feet tall. What the hell can anybody do to you?" Well, I hadn't even thought of it in those terms. He said, "Why don't you say what you really think? You know, if you really think this system's unjust, why the hell do you keep saying that it can't be changed? If it's unjust, it can be changed." And I was impressed by that, and I've always remembered it and it shook me up some and I suppose it sharpened my views generally.

Roy Campanella

(Roy Campanella was one of the first black players in the National League after a distinguished career in the Black Professional Leagues. He was a teammate of Jackie Robinson and was Most Valuable Player in the National League three times.)

We talked about the Civil Rights Movement from the time of the Montgomery Bus Boycott on, and we raised money for civil rights, but the Dodgers finally felt that the politics of it were a little out of line for us as ballplayers. We were not able to participate in the marches or demonstrations, but we went around and did public speaking."

Well, we couldn't just say that we knew what Jackie and myself and others breaking the color line in professional baseball was going to lead to, but we had to take it into consideration and we had to prove ourselves on the field and off of the field as well. This proved to be quite a challenge, but thank God we went through that challenge and were successful, and it carried on from there.

Pee Wee Reese played quite a part, being the captain of the Dodgers and playing beside Jackie in a shortstop/second base combination. He contributed so much to making it work out. This was more so than a lot of things that happened on the Dodgers—the important thing was that the fellows that played alongside us accepted us. No one else wanted to. For them to accept us and to play with us and wind up with a championship team—this changed a lot of peoples' heads.

The Dodgers would schedule games in places like New Orleans, Birmingham, Atlanta, Nashville, Memphis, so that we could play in the Deep South in front of both blacks and whites. The Dodgers contributed so much to this movement in the theory that when we would play in these cities, blacks were allowed to pay their way into the ballpark like anyone else. These were times when blacks were not allowed to sit in the bleachers, but this changed when the Brooklyn Dodgers would play in those places.

On one occasion, we went to Atlanta to play a game with the old Atlanta Crackers. And this is how Jackie and I met Dr. Martin Luther King. The Ku Klux Klans had told the Dodgers not to bring Jackie and I to play in Atlanta. But Dr. King

got in touch with the Dodgers and Mr. [Branch] Rickey and asked him to be sure to bring Campanella and Robinson to Atlanta that weekend, and the Dodgers took us to Atlanta regardless of the Ku Klux Klan's threats and everything. Dr. King, after the game, took Jackie and I over to his home, and we had dinner there, and this was our first meeting with Dr. King.

The Dodgers had gotten all these threats from the Klan, and the FBI was there to protect us and all the black organizations in Atlanta had asked Mr. Rickey to be sure to bring Campanella and Robinson to play. And that was how Dr. King got involved. He said not to worry about a hotel or about a place to eat because he said, "You can stay at my home and eat at my house," and he took care of everything we needed that weekend in Atlanta.

Daniel Ellsberg

(Dr. Daniel Ellsberg was a consultant at the Rand Corporation in Santa Monica, California, where he released some classified government data on the Vietnam War which came to be popularly known and published in a book known as The Pentagon Papers.*)*

As someone who took no part in the early Civil Rights Movement at all and yet in fact the connection in the peace movement [to me] was very direct. In March of '68 at a meeting . . . I met an Indian woman who caught my attention by commenting at the table. "For me, an enemy doesn't exist," I sort of heard her. She spoke in an impressive way, was exotic-looking, and I sort of listened to the sentence in a way I

might not have and I thought about it—what did she mean by that? She explained the notion that one could hate the acts but not the person. Look at the possibility of change and so forth and recognize the humanity of everyone.

Now, I lived my life—The Rand Corporation, the Defense Department, the Marine Corps earlier—entirely organized around the concept of enemies, so this was a very exotic notion. And we began to talk about—she told me about Gandhi—she was a follower of Gandhi's but also of Martin Luther King. Now he was a name to me, of course, like everybody. But I didn't know particularly what he stood for in the way of ideas, and we spent a large part of that week discussing that. Sort of moved away from the Conference and talked about it a lot. At the end of which, we were together when the announcement of King's death occurred, saw it on the evening news.

It was a shattering moment. I literally spent the first week of my life thinking about Martin Luther King. But later that year, after, you know, a terribly, fantastically discouraging summer—I got hold of King's book, *Stride Toward Freedom*, there were a lot of things in that that spoke to me. It's really worth reading. And it gives the particular account of the Montgomery Bus Boycott and the story of Rosa Parks. And you know he talks about being moved by two things. First, he heard a lecture on Gandhi, read about Gandhi, and read *Gandhi and Notions*. Second, he was confronted, face to face, with a personal example, with Mrs. Rosa Parks.

And it took the combination—Dr. King said he realized that Rosa Parks was confronting him with the situation that Gandhi was writing about. That to acquiesce was to be part of it, to be responsible for it and to be an accomplice. Had it not been for the theory which he read, and which I came to read later, and for the personal example, he wouldn't have moved at the way he did at that moment in his life.

Well, years later, I was in New Orleans with the SCLC. Oh, I should say this was a week after I was indicted [by the Nixon administration for releasing the Pentagon papers]. I was called on a Saturday afternoon in Cambridge and they said, 'We're having a conference tonight and could you come?' I left my bags to be sent on to Los Angeles with somebody else and I literally just—without even a toothbrush—got on a plane to get out to New Orleans. Because like other people, moved by specific examples, I wanted to tell people how they affected my life. It was a movement I had no part of.

So I arrived and got to the airport, and went right to this football field where they were holding the thing; out in the wet, dark, damp, hot night—on the platform—and I wanted to be able to say to these people, 'If it weren't for you, your late leader, Martin Luther King, I wouldn't be where I am today—on my way to arraignment for having found a way to influence an evil war.'

On that platform was Rosa Parks. I was very thrilled by this. I had the chance to ask her because I was now interested in this—I had a similar experience—and I wanted to ask her, "What went through your mind, sort of, at the moment, and how did it come about at that mo-

ment that you didn't get up." I asked her, and she said, "No, I didn't get up." I assumed, by the way, that as a Southern black woman that she had been faced with the situation a hundred times—

"What happened this time?" She said, "Well, I had never been in the position before. I had been asked to give up my seat by women before and I had, but it had never happened that a white man had asked me to give up my seat." And she said, "I had often asked myself what I would do if that happened." And I said, "What was the answer to yourself?" She said, "I didn't know. And when this white man stood in front of me . . . ."

By the way, the story that is often told that Rosa Parks was especially tired that day, it wasn't like that. It was an existential situation—she didn't know what she was going to do, but she had thought about it and she said no not because she was tired but when the situation confronted her, she said, "No." And I realized later as I talked about Rosa Parks to my Indian friend—you know my heroes didn't used to be women; they didn't used to be black women.

One of the people who recruited me into the Marine Corps was John Wayne from *The Sands of Iwo Jima*. I used to have the same heroes as most people—mostly white males, you know, and I suddenly discovered that my heroes had been changed. Changed by this American southern movement, which had been influenced by the Gandhi movement and that now to me the way of acting effectively and morally in the world was posed by a black Southern woman who said, No, this is wrong, I'm not going to

do it. So, the effect on my life was very direct. And with a lag.

Dr. Kenneth B. Clark

(Dr. Kenneth B. Clark is a renowned psychologist who, in the late 1940s and early 1950s did the research on the negative impact of segregated education on African-American children that was presented to the U.S. Supreme Court in the Brown *case.)*

In the South in the early '50s and early '60s there was hate, but also respect for Dr. King. That's a fact. That's hard for me to say because on the one hand you think that there are changes taking place and on the other hand you're confronted with things being pretty much the same. I will concede that it would seem to be very difficult for one other than a sick person, white or black, not to be in some way influenced by the consistency, the dignity, the humanity of Martin Luther King, Jr. These positive characteristics being personified by a black could arouse backlash, hostilities in whites who were ordinarily considered sane.

Certainly Martin didn't have any easier time as the years progressed. In fact, he seemed to me to be much more revered and accepted after his assassination than he was in the last two years by the general public. I suppose there were many people who raised their eyes to the fact that he was given the Nobel Prize. He deserved it, but at the same time there was—jealousy, hate, hostility, etc., but I don't see how that really mattered because I don't think you can judge the effect of this man on American history.

I don't think you can judge the importance and the significance of

Martin Luther King in terms of any observable change in American system or maturity or democracy any more than you can judge the effect of Jesus Christ on the immediate effect of his times. The only explanation I guess would be Gandhi, who seemed to have an immediate, direct effect, but I'm not even sure of that.

I think it's very well put to say that he was for a long time the nation's psychiatrist. He provided an avenue of catharsis.

Dr. Harold DeWolfe

(Dr. Harold DeWolfe was Dr. King's professor, friend, and primary advisory during King's academic career at Boston University. They stayed in regular contact throughout the remainder of DeWolfe's life. This excerpt is taken from his testimony on the bill to make Dr. King's birthday a national holiday.)

. . . We need to recall that Dr. King persuaded thousands of embittered, angry people to renounce violence and work for change within the system. He was a patriotic American. In speech after speech, he recalled passages from Thomas Jefferson, Abraham Lincoln, the Declaration of Independence, and the Constitution.

The people that knew him best understood well his love of country despite all its injustice . . . Tell all future generations that the power of the dream will live so long as men and women of faith and sacrifice [are present] to make the dream come true.

SELECTED BIBLIOGRAPHY

BY OR ABOUT BUS BOYCOTT PARTICIPANTS:

Baldwin, Lewis V., & Woodson, Aprille V. *Freedom Is Never Free:A Biographical Portrait Of E. D. Nixon,* (A Joint Venture of Tennessee State University, Nashville & Alabama State University, Montgomery/funded by United Parcel Service), 1992.

Baldwin, Lewis V. *There Is A Balm In Gilead*, Fortress Press, 1986.

_____ *To Make The Spirit Whole*, Fortress Press.1992

Bass, Jack. *Unlikely Heroes*, Simon and Schuster, 1981.

_____ *Taming The Storm, Doubleday*, 1993.

Carr, Johnnie R., as told to Randall Williams, *Johnnie: The Life of Johnnie Rebecca Carr*, Black Belt Press, 1995.

Clayton, Edward T. *Martin Luther King, Jr.: The Peaceful Warrior*, Prentice Hall, 1964.

Daniels, Pearl Gray. *Portrait of Fred Gray*, Vantage, 1975.

Durr, Virginia Foster (Barnard, Hollinger F., ed.), *Outside The Magic Circle*, University of Alabama Press, 1985.

Garrow, David. editor, *The Walking City*, Carlson, Brooklyn, 1989.

Graetz, Robert E. *A White Preacher's Memoir: the Montgomery Bus Boycott*, Black Belt Press, 1998.

Gray, Fred. *Bus Ride To Justice,* Black Belt Press, 1995.

King, Coretta Scott. *My Life With Martin Luther King, Jr.*, Holt Rinehart and Winston, 1969.

King, Martin Luther, Jr. *Stride Toward Freedom*, Harper & Brothers, 1958.

Parks, Rosa L., with Gregory J. Reed. *Quiet Strength*, Zondervan, 1994.

Reddick, Lawrence D. *Crusader Without Violence: A Biography of Martin Luther King, Jr.*, Harper and Brothers, 1959.

Robinson, Jo Ann. *The Montgomery Bus Boycott And The Women Who Started It*, University of Tennesse Press, 1989.

Rustin, Bayard. *Down The Line*, Quadrangle Books, 1971.

Salmond, John. *A Southern Rebel, The Life and Times of Aubrey Willis Williams, 1895-1965*, The University of North Carolina Press, 1983.

_____. *The Conscience of a Lawyer: Clifford J. Durr and American Civil Liberties, 1899-1975*, The University of Alabama Press,1990.

Seay, Solomon S., Sr.*I Was There By The Grace Of God*, S.S. Seay Educational Foundation, 1990.

Sikora, Frank. *The Judge: The Life and Opinions of Alabama's Frank M. Johnson, Jr.*, Black Belt Press, 1992.

Thornton, J. Mills and Caver, Joseph. *Touched by History: A Civil Rights Tour Guide to Montgomery, Alabama*, Black Belt Press, 1990.

PHOTO STUDIES ON DR. KING, MONTGOMERY, AND THE MOVEMENT

Schulke, *Flip. Martin Luther King, Jr.: A Documentary . . . Montgomery To Memphis*, Norton, 1976.

_____. *King Remembered*, (with Penelope McPhee) Norton, 1986.

_____. *He Had A Dream: Martin Luther King, Jr. and the Civil Rights Movement*, Norton, 1995.

BIBLIOGRAPHIC STUDIES

For comprehensive Montgomery Bus Boycott / Martin Luther King, Jr. bibliographies, see those developed by the Walter P. Reuther Center for Labor Studies at Wayne State University, or by the Martin Luther King, Jr., Center for Non-Violent Social Change Papers Project.

ORAL HISTORY

Levine, Ellen. *Freedom's Children*, Putnam, 1993.

Raines, Howell. *My Soul Is Rested*, G.P. Putnam, 1977.

Stein, Jean, with Plimpton, George. *An American Journey: The Times of Robert F. Kennedy*, Harcourt, Brace & Jovanovich, 1970.

Terkel, Studs. *Hard Times*, Pantheon, 1970.

Viorst, Milton. *Fire In the Streets*, Simon and Schuster, 1979.

Warren, Robert Penn. *Who Speaks For The Negro?*, Random House, 1965.

OTHER SELECTED STUDIES

Egerton, John. *Speak Now Against The Day*, Knopf, 1994/ UNC Press, 1996.

Erenrich, Susie, ed. *Freedom Is a Constant Struggle*, Black Belt Press, 1998.

Halberstam, David. *The Children*, Random House, 1998.

Lewis, John. *Walking With the Wind: A Memoir of the Movement*, Simon & Shuster, 1998.

Morris, Aldon. *The Origins of the Civil Rights Movement*,The Free Press, 1984.

Ramperstad, Arnold. *Jackie Robinson, A Biography*, Knopf, 1997.

Salisbury, Harrison. *A Time of Change: A Reporters Tale of Our Time*, Harper & Row, 1988.

Young, Andrew. *An Easy Burden: The Civil Rights Movement and the Transformation of America*, Harper-Collins, 1996.

_____. *A Way Out of No Way: The Spiritual Memoirs of Andrew Young*, Thomas Nelson, 1994.

INDEX